RECIPES FO~ ~
HEALTHY HEART

More easy and healthy recipes from the author
of the bestselling *Light-Hearted*
and *Everyday Light-Hearted* Cookbooks

Anne Lindsay

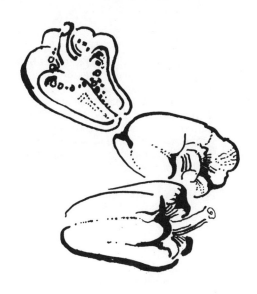

GRUB STREET · LONDON

Published by Grub Street, The Basement,
10 Chivalry Road, London SW11 1HT

First UK impression 1996

British Library Cataloguing in Publication Data
Lindsay, Anne
Recipes for a healthy heart
   1. Low-fat diet – recipes   2. Heart – Diseases – Diet therapy
   I. Title   II. Family Heart Association
   641.5′638

ISBN 1 898697 42 6

Cover photograph: Tim Imrie
Food Photography: Doug Bradshaw/Bradshaw Photography Inc.
Illustrations: Madeleine David
Food Styling: Olga Truchan
Prop Coordination: Janet Walkenshaw
Nutrient Analysis: by Info Access (1988) Inc., using the
nutritional accounting component of the CBORD Menu Management
System. The nutrient database was the 1991 Canadian Nutrient
File supplemented when necessary with documented data from
reliable sources.

Typeset by Pearl Graphics, Hemel Hempstead
Printed and bound by Biddles Ltd, Guildford and King's Lynn

This book is dedicated to my husband,
Bob Lindsay, with love.

It is also to the memory of
Wendy Buda and Sarah Martin.

Acknowledgements

I was very fortunate to work with a wonderful team to produce this book. I appreciate and thank all the people who were involved, and give special thanks to: Shannon Graham, dietitian, friend and co-worker, for helping with recipe testing for all four of my cookbooks. Nancy Williams, my sister-in-law, for her help with the book. Denise Schon, at Macmillan for the many extra hours she has put into all aspects of this book and to Bob Dees, Kirsten Hanson and everyone else at Macmillan for their patience and enthusiasm for this book. Bev Renahan for her expert editing of the recipes. Barbara Selley and Sharon Joliat for the nutritional analysis, their advice and extra work. Elizabeth Baird, food director, and Daphna Rabinovitch, test kitchen manager at *Canadian Living*. Many recipes first appeared in articles I wrote for the magazine. I'm very fortunate to have had Olga Truchan do the food styling for this and my *Light-Hearted* cookbooks. Thanks also to Doug Bradshaw, photographer, and Janet Walkenshaw, props coordinator, for the great photographs and enjoyable week spent in the studio. Kerry Dean and Lynn Roblin for their help with the introductory material. Andrew Smith for his great design. Linda Alexander Leonard for reviewing the entire book.

Contents

GENERAL
INTRODUCTION

Acknowledgements   iv

Foreword by the Family Heart Association   6

Introduction   8

Healthy Eating, Delicious Food   8

Guidelines for Healthy Eating   10

Vegetarian Meals   14

All About Cholesterol and Fat   16

Getting Enough Fibre Foods   21

The Latest News on Vitamins   22

Dieting – Who Needs It!   24

Shopping and Eating Out   25

Where to Go for Help   26

Menus   27

Information on Ingredients   32

RECIPES

Appetizers, Snacks and Beverages   33

Soups   57

Salads   71

Poultry   89

Fish and Seafood   109

Meat   121

Vegetables   133

Pasta   145

Grains, Legumes and Meatless Main Dishes   165

Breads, Cookies, Cakes and Squares   187

Desserts   207

Index   233

Foreword

Heart health is determined by many features including your genetic make-up, your age and gender, but also the way you eat and live.

The first and most essential task is to keep the cholesterol in your blood at a level that is right for you. That means getting your dietary fats sorted, both the balance of different types of fat, and the total amount.

Healthy eating can be fun. It need not be expensive or time consuming. And there are *many* different ways to construct a healthy eating plan taking account of your personal food preferences. Dip into the recipe book and see what you fancy.

It is worth noting that cholesterol is not a villain, indeed it is essential for life. The body therefore does not rely on a dietary souce but makes its own, mainly in the liver. Problems arise when there is too much cholesterol in the body.

Some people, about 100,000 in Britain, inherit a very high cholesterol. They have Familial Hypercholesterolaemia, known as FH. For them strict diet and drug therapy are necessary. Millions of others have an inherited predisposition to a high cholesterol. Faced with the way of eating and living that we have come to regard as 'normal' their blood cholesterol rises to unhealthy high levels. Usually this problem can be dealt with by careful management of eating and living but *everyone*, not only those with an obvious inherited problem, can benefit from adopting a cholesterol lowering diet and lifestyle; there is no harm, only benefit from doing so.

There has been a great deal of controversy about cholesterol during the past fifty years, but it is now sorted out. Scientific evidence has proved that prolonged elevation of blood cholesterol is the major factor causing atherosclerosis (hardening of the arteries) increasing the risk of angina and heart attack. And, importantly, it has been shown in clinical trials that reducing blood cholesterol is beneficial, whether you have coronary heart disease or not. Doing so substantially reduces the risk of a future heart attack.

There are, of course, other factors as well as excess cholesterol which increase heart attack risk, including smoking, physical inactivity, high blood pressure, insulin resistance or diabetic tendencies. Being overweight or drinking to excess do not help either. But an excess of cholesterol in the body as well as causing problems by itself plays its part by increasing, it seems, the body's sensitivity to the harmful effects of these other 'risk factors'. That is why adopting a cholesterol-lowering eating habit is so important.

To get the balance of dietary fats right usually means less saturates with more of the monounsaturated and polyunsaturated fats, not too much more. *Balance is all*, do not go 'over-the-top'. Most people will benefit from going easy on fatty foods which, apart from anything else, will help with body weight management.

It is all very well for dietitians and journalists to go on and on about different types of fat and how much of each is suitable. *But it is not your job to become a nutrition expert*, it is our job as the Family Heart Association to find ways of presenting information that makes it easy for you to eat the foods you enjoy but still find your way to an *overall* food intake that is suitable in the amount and type of fat, proteins, carboyhydrates, dietary fibre, vitamins and minerals. One way we do that is with our 'Guide to Healthy Eating' which helps you with your food choices (free with an s.a.e. to FHA, PO Box 303, Maidenhead, SL6 9UX) or through recipe suggestions such as in this excellent book.

You will find healthy recipes every bit as tasty as unhealthy ones.

ENJOY YOUR FOOD

Dr Michael Turner
Chief Executive of the Family Heart Association

Introduction

HEALTHY EATING, DELICIOUS FOOD

Most people don't think about healthy eating until their doctor tells them they have to. Oh, no! cry household cooks, fearing they'll have to change their way of cooking, and that no one's going to like it. This negative perception of healthy eating is very common. After all, 'healthy' cookbooks in the past had their faults. The good ones could be forbiddingly earnest, for instance. And vegetarian cookbooks often defeated their own purposes by balancing the virtuous brown rice with high-fat cheeses, nuts and oils. Health-resort cookbooks offered picture-pretty dishes that enslaved you in the kitchen for hours. Cookbooks on the fringes of good sense took sparse regimens to dangerous extremes. Well, that was then. Now, we know more.

We know that variety, not self-denial, is the key to healthy eating. We know that moderation works better than fad diets. Most of all, we know that just because people want to eat healthily doesn't mean they want to enjoy their food any less.

My philosophy of healthy eating is that food should appeal to the senses: it should taste delicious and look fabulous. Healthy eating, in my view, is not just for when the doctor says so – it's for all times, and for all ages.

It's even, believe it or not, for when guests are coming. For some reason, people have always thought they had to throw good sense out the window when they entertained. The healthy cookbooks stayed on the shelf, and out came the special-occasion volumes calling for masses of double cream and rich oils. But all this is changing. I know Britons are already interested in reforming their eating habits because of the way they have embraced the recipes in my previous healthy-eating cookbooks, and are still asking for more. They have especially requested entertaining menus that aren't overloaded with fat and calories.

For this book, I have responded by working out whole menus (see pages 27 to 31) – many of which I have served to friends – as well as individual recipes, following the recommendations of the Department of Health and the Family Heart Association and my own creed that everything must taste and look good. (I just get there by different routes from the butter-and-oil brigade.)

In the 1990s, creating good taste the healthy way is easier than ever. In decades past, when produce wasn't great at all times of the year, the temptation was to cover things up with creamy sauces. But now all sorts of great new food products are available.

- Herbs and spices are my trademark, and happily, thanks to growing awareness and demand, a wider-than-ever variety is available. I like to use lots of fresh garlic and ginger, of course, and lemon and mustard; beyond these, fresh coriander, sun-dried tomatoes, hot chilli peppers (fresh, bottled and dried) and rice vinegar – all things that can make food taste great without fat.

- When I wrote my first cookbook, *Smart Cooking*, in 1984, light versions of high-fat foods such as mayonnaise, sour cream and cheeses were almost unheard of. Today's light versions have cut the fat in half, and with yogurts we have a huge range of low fat and virtually-fat free products. In 1984, only a couple of low-fat cheeses existed, and they were about as tasty as rubber balls. Now, a good delicatessen might stock half a dozen cheeses at less than 15% fat, and virtually fat free fromage frais – and, yes, many of them taste great. Add to this a truly low-fat version of ice cream at less than 1% fat. New products are coming on the market all the time. Brand-new extra-thick but reduced fat Greek-style yogurts are just reaching supermarket shelves, and I can hardly wait to start experimenting with them as low-fat alternatives in creamy dips, salad dressings and desserts.

- Meats are getting leaner, even since my 1994 cookbook, *Everyday Light-Hearted Cookbook*.

New feed and grading systems for pork and beef have resulted in much leaner cuts – which in turn require new cooking methods.

- A good variety of quality frozen fish is now available across the country.

- Improved transportation and storage techniques make good-quality produce – those fruits and vegetables we keep being reminded to eat more of – plentiful year-round.

All these great new developments are reflected in these pages, as is the way our cooking habits have changed for the better. Where the cook in the '50s fried in bacon drippings, and the cook in the '70s fried in butter or oil, the cook in the '90s is not frying, period.

When creating recipes, I've also kept the busy person in mind. Recipes are fast and easy to prepare, and use only ingredients I believe to be widely available. If an ingredient seemed unnecessary, I deleted it; if a recipe could be made as easily in one bowl as in two, I made it in one. And you have my busy sister-in-law, Linda Elliott, to thank for the make-ahead information that accompanies each recipe. She pointed out that my books were no good to her without it.

Who needs to eat healthily? Every single member of the family!

Young children need the right kinds and amounts of foods to help them grow and develop properly. Healthy foods help them establish positive eating habits that may reduce their chances of nutrition-related diseases later in life.

Healthy eating during adolescence can be challenging. Male teens are okay – they usually satisfy their nutrient needs by eating lots of everything. But the more complex eating habits of a teenage girl often result in a lack of basic nutrients in her diet. Her social life may involve hanging out at the local burger joint eating fries; at the same time she desperately wants to stay pencil-slim.

Women who hope to become pregnant or who are pregnant or breast feeding require an increase in specific nutrients. Women in general have to be careful to choose balanced, nutrient-packed meals.

Finally, healthy eating is important for all adults concerned about nutrition-related illnesses such as heart disease and cancer. Since almost 70% of adults in this country have higher than desirable levels of blood cholesterol and more than half face potential health risks because of their weight, preventive eating habits are a must.

I know from experience that many of these different dietary needs and concerns can easily reside in a single household. But that doesn't mean you have to prepare a lot of separate menus every day. Look at my family: my husband has elevated blood cholesterol; my university-age sons eat mountains of food; my teenage daughter has a good appetite yet worries about her weight; I am constantly trying to exercise away the results of the business I'm in – and we all love to eat. So I make the main courses of our dinners low in fat for my husband. This also suits my daughter and me because they're lower in calories. My sons make up the difference in snacks and other meals. In the fridge, we keep low-fat and regular choices in certain foods: semi-skimmed and skimmed milk; standard Cheddar and skimmed milk cheeses; dairy full-cream ice cream and the reduced-fat option.

Healthy eating reduces everyone's risk for all disease. It helps you feel better, perform your best, handle stress and maintain a healthy weight. No single miracle food or pill can do this for you. This book will provide you with valuable nutrition information and wonderful recipes and menus to help you and your family continue on the road to healthy and happy eating.

Anne Lindsay

GUIDELINES FOR HEALTHY EATING

For the average healthy person, healthy eating means making food choices that will contribute to your nutritional health and help you feel great. That means choosing a variety of foods from each basic food group of grains, vegetables and fruit, dairy products and meat and alternatives. Healthy eating also involves eating less fat and including more carbohydrates and fibre in your diet. Healthy eating doesn't mean avoiding your favourite foods. It means enjoying your food, but being careful with the amount of higher-fat foods you choose.

How Do You Begin Healthy Eating for Life?

If you are to have a healthy balanced diet then you need to eat food in the correct proportions: 50% of your calories in the form of carbohydrates; 35% from fat and 15% from protein. When you look at your plate half the plate should be taken up with carbohydrate foods such as rice, pasta, bread or potatoes. A little over one-sixth should be a protein source such as meat, fish, cheese or eggs and the remainder should only contain fruit or vegetables as the calories required from fat will be used in cooking or hidden fats within other foods.

Make Healthy Eating Part of Your Lifestyle:

ENJOY A VARIETY OF FOODS FROM EACH GROUP EVERY DAY

Your body needs over 50 different nutrients every day. You won't find that in a meal replacement drink or bar! In order to make sure you are getting all the nutrients you need, choose different foods from each food group and vary your choices within each group. The easiest way to get variety in your diet is to include different food groups at each meal.

CHOOSE LOWER-FAT FOODS MORE OFTEN

Everyone needs to eat some fat to stay healthy, but the reality is that most people eat too much. Dietary fat is linked to the development of chronic diseases such as heart disease, cancer, hypertension and obesity. Calories from fat in the British diet is, and has been, since the mid '70s around 41% although the quantity of saturated fat is falling. Current recommendations are that adults should get 35% of calories from fat.

About the Food Groups

There are four main food groups in any Healthy Eating Plan: Grain Products, Vegetables & Fruit, Milk Products, Meats & Alternatives. We should be striving to eat more foods from the Grain Products and Vegetables & Fruit groups than ever before. That's because foods in these two groups are high in carbohydrates, fibre and nutrients. Milk Products and Meats & Alternatives are also important, but they should make up a smaller part of your healthy eating pattern and most of the choices you make should be lower in fat.

What and How Much from Each Group?

The number of servings you need from each group varies depending on your age, sex, size, activity level and if you are pregnant or breast feeding. These guidelines are suitable for all over the age of five*. Young children and older women can choose the lower number of servings. Male teenagers and very active people can choose the higher number of servings from each group.

A word of warning: don't throw up your hands and say these suggestions are more than you could

---

* For fat guidelines for infants and children, see ** page 17.

eat before you note the size of servings. A plate of pasta with sauce can equal 3 to 4 servings of Grain Products, 2 Vegetables & Fruit servings and 1 Meat & Alternatives serving.

BREAD, CEREAL, POTATO GROUP: 5 to 11 servings per day

Choose whole grain and high fibre products more often. Whole grain products made from whole wheat, oats, barley or rye are suggested because they are high in complex carbohydrates and fibre. Try multigrain breads, wholewheat pasta, breakfast cereals or porridge.

1 serving = 3 tbsp (45 ml) breakfast cereal;
1 slice bread or toast;
½ bread bun or roll;
1 small pitta bread or Chapati;
3 crackers;
1 egg sized potato;
2 tbsp (30 ml) rice, pasta, noodles;
2 tbsp (30 ml) green banana, plantain or sweet potato

VEGETABLES & FRUIT: 5 to 9 servings per day

Choose dark green and orange vegetables and orange fruit more often.
   These foods are high in important nutrients such as vitamin A (beta carotene), C and folate. Choose broccoli, spinach, squash, sweet potatoes, carrot, cantaloupe melon or orange juice.

1 serving = 2 tbsp (30 ml) vegetables;
small salad with mixed leaves;
1 medium sized vegetable or fruit (apple, banana, orange, carrot);
2 tbsp (30 ml) stewed or tinned fruit;
4 fl oz (100 ml) fruit juice

MILK & DAIRY PRODUCTS: 2 to 3 servings per day

Choose lower-fat milk products more often. Lower-fat milk products provide protein and calcium essential to healthy eating with less fat and calories. Look on the labels and choose milk, yogurt or cottage cheese with 2% fat or less, often marked as virtually-fat-free or fully skimmed products; for cheese choose 15% fat or less.

1 serving = 200 ml (⅓ pt) milk;
small pot of yogurt;
1½ oz (40 g) cheese (small match-box size);
cottage cheese or fromage frais.

MEAT & ALTERNATIVES: 2 to 3 servings per day

Choose leaner meats, poultry and fish, as well as beans and lentils more often. Many leaner choices of meats, poultry, fish and seafood are now available to help you eat less fat without losing important nutrients. Trim visible fat and try baking, grilling, roasting or microwaving instead of frying. Remove extra fat after cooking. Choose a meat alternative such as baked beans or pea soup to help you eat less fat and more fibre.

1 serving = 2 tbsp (30 ml) peanut butter;
3½ oz (100 g) tofu;
3½-7 oz (100-200 g) baked beans;
1 to 2 eggs (up to 4 per week);

2-4 oz (55-115 g) canned fish;
2-3 oz (55-75 g) beef, pork, ham, lamb, liver, kidney, chicken or oily fish;
4-5 oz (115-150 g) white fish (not fried in batter);
3 tbsp (45 ml) pulses, lentils or dhal;
1½ oz (40 g) cheese (small match-box size); 2 tbsp (30 ml) nuts

What About Foods That Don't Fit a Food Group?

Many foods and beverages are not part of the four food groups I listed in a plan for healthy eating. These are called 'other foods': fats (butter, margarine, oils and salad dressings); sugars (jam, honey, syrup, sweets); snack foods that are high in fat and/or salt (crisps, pretzels); beverages (water, tea, coffee, alcohol and soft drinks); and condiments (pickles, ketchup). We all include 'other foods' in our diet because we like them. The main thing is to choose high-fat or high-calorie foods in moderation.

WATER
When you are thirsty, choose water. Have water often, especially in hot weather or when you are very active.

ALCOHOL
The government recommendations are that moderate drinking can carry health benefits, i.e. 1-2 units a day (One unit approx equals half pint of beer, small glass of wine, single measure spirits). Men who drink 3-4 units and women 2-3 units a day do not face a significant health risk but more is not advised. After heavy drinking, 48 hours without alcohol is recommended but alcohol-free days are of no proven benefit to moderate drinkers. Pregnant women should not drink more than 1-2 units a week.

CAFFEINE
You may use caffeine in moderation. It's found in coffee, tea or cola soft drinks, foods that contain cocoa and in some medications.

How Do These Food Guidelines Fit Into a Day's Menu?

Following a food groups guide to healthy eating is easy.

Consider the following day's menu, using this key:

G   = Grain products serving;   O   = Other foods, Fats and Fatty and Sugary foods;
F   = Fruit & Vegetable serving;   C   = Bread, Cereal, Potato Group;
M   = Milk products serving;   V   = Vegetable and Fruit Group
MA = Meats & Alternatives serving;

Breakfast	Lunch
Orange juice (4 fl oz/125 ml) = 1F	2 slices wholemeal bread = 2G
Bran Flakes (1⅛ oz/30 g) = 1G	Tuna, canned in water (3 oz/85 g) = 1MA
Plain yogurt low-fat (6 fl oz/175 ml) = 1M	Light mayonnaise (2 tbsp/30 ml) = O
Brown sugar (1 tbsp/15 ml) = O	Alfalfa sprouts (2 oz/55 g) = ½F
	Fig bars (2) = ½F, ½G

Dinner

Honey Garlic Roast Pork (page 127) = 1MA
Spanish Rice with Coriander (page 169) = 1½G, 1F
Baked Squash (¼ acorn squash) = 1F
   Margarine or butter (1 tbsp/5 ml) = O
Green Beans (2 oz/55 g) = 1F
Wholemeal bread (1 slice) = 1G
   Margarine or butter (1 tsp/5 ml) = O
Milk (8 fl oz/225 ml) = 1M
Banana = 1F

For one day, this adds up to: G=6, F=6, MA=2, M=2

Some people need to eat more. For example, growing teens, depending on their size, would add 1 to 4 more servings of either fruits and vegetables and 1 to 6 servings of grain products, 1 to 2 more servings of milk products and may choose another serving of meat and alternatives.

In my house, my university student sons would have double the portions of the rice, a peanut butter sandwich for a snack, another glass each of juice and of milk, then maybe raid the biscuit tin. This all fits into a healthy diet for growing, active students and follows the Department of Health's recommendations for healthy eating.

Make More Lower-fat Choices

Healthy eating means making lower-fat choices more often. Adults should aim for not more than 35% of calories coming from fat rather than the current 41%.

It is amazing to see how seemingly minor changes in our meals can affect the amount of fat in our diet. For example, in the above day's menu, the total calories = 1680; grams of fat = 42; and % calories from fat = 23.

For example, in the above menu, a clinical, very low-fat diet would include some of these changes: skimmed milk and low-fat yogurt; yogurt instead of mayonnaise mixed with tuna; no margarine or butter on bread or on beans. Total calories = 1501; grams of fat = 21; % calories from fat = 12.*

If you're not careful, the fat can easily be too high, as you can see if you make these higher-fat choices: Full-cream milk and yogurt, tuna canned in oil; standard mayonnaise, plus 1 tbsp (15 ml) butter (for sandwich); 2 tsp (10 ml) butter or margarine on bread and on beans. Total calories = 2125; grams of fat = 94; % calories from fat = 40.

When you add snacks, depending on your choices, the total amount of calories and fat increases but the % calories from fat could stay the same. Most of us would be better off choosing lower-fat snacks. For example, in the higher-fat menu above, you increase your calories and fat if you add snacks of 1 cola drink; 1 bag (2 oz/55 g) potato crisps; 1 sandwich of 2 slices wholemeal bread, 2 tbsp (30 ml) each peanut butter and jam; 4 chocolate chip cookies. Total calories = 3157; grams of fat = 139; % calories from fat = 40.

---

* I'm not recommending this low a fat or calorie diet; this is just an example of how easy it can be to lower (or raise) the fat in our diet. Anyone on a low-fat diet should be under the care of a dietitian. The average woman aged 25 to 49 should have about 1900 calories a day.

VEGETARIAN MEALS

I'm hearing from my friends more and more that their children are now vegetarians. In one family with six children, all of them decided to give up meat. Mothers usually wonder if their kids are getting all the nutrients they need.

Whether you eat meat or not, it's still very important to follow healthy-eating guidelines. Have a variety of foods and include meat alternatives such as tofu, dried beans, peas and lentils and eggs. If one is eating dairy products daily, protein isn't usually a problem. If you are a strict vegetarian consult a dietitian. A vegan diet, which includes no animal products such as eggs, meat or dairy products, is a concern for teens and young children because it may not provide enough energy, vitamins B_{12} and D and calcium.

I know you can get calcium from foods such as kidney beans, broccoli and most tofu. But you have to be careful to eat large amounts of these foods every day. If you are avoiding dairy products, you may need a vitamin D or calcium supplement.

CALCIUM-RICH FOODS

Canned sardines (3 oz/85 g)	393 mg
Yogurt (6 fl oz/175 ml)	355 mg
Milk (8 fl oz/250 ml)	315 mg
Cheddar cheese (1 oz/25 g)	216 mg
Salmon with bones (3 oz/85 g)	183 mg
Scallops or prawns (3 oz/85 g)	104 mg
Vegetarian	
Cooked broccoli (8 oz/225 g)	187 mg
Tofu (4 oz/115 g)	154 mg
Cooked spinach (4½ oz/125 g)	139 mg
Dried figs (4)	108 mg
Cooked beans (Haricot or cannellini)	98 mg

- Teenage girls need 700 to 1000 mg calcium daily.
- Taking calcium supplements at meals and drinking tea inhibit iron absorption.

IRON-RICH FOODS

Calves liver (3 oz/85 g)		13 mg
Trout (3 oz/85 g)		4.5 mg
Veal, pork or beef (3 oz/85 g, cooked)		2 to 3 mg
Most fish (3 oz/85 g, cooked)		1 to 2 mg
Vegetarian		
Iron enriched breakfast cereal	(1½ oz/40 g)	4.7 mg
Bran cereal (1½ oz/40 g)		3.6 mg
Cooked spinach (4½ oz/125 g)		3.5 mg
Cooked dried peas, beans or lentils (3½ oz/100 g)		2 to 4 mg
Broccoli, corn, carrots, peas (5½ oz/150 g, cooked)		1 to 3 mg

- Teenage girls need 12 to 13 mg iron daily.
- Eating vitamin C-rich foods together with iron-rich plant foods helps maximize iron absorption.

Hints for Cooking for Both Vegetarians and Non-Vegetarians:

1. Vegetarian pasta dishes often please everyone. If this isn't the case in your home, plan to have some leftover cooked meats to add to dinner plates.

2. In some dishes, such as the Chinese Vegetable Fried Rice, page 170 (do try it; everyone in my family loves it), the meat can be added after the vegetarians have been served.

3. Often vegetarian dishes are high in fat and cheese. The recipes in this book use simi-skimmed milk and reduced fat cheese and a minimum of fat.

4. Keep on hand lower-fat cheese, tofu, canned chick peas and kidney beans, peanuts or sunflower seeds to add to soups, salads, stir-frys or pasta dishes.

5. Canned pea or lentil soup or beans in tomato sauce, along with toasted wholemeal bread, are easy meal ideas.

6. When you serve meat, also include one of the substantial vegetarian dishes listed below. Include wholemeal bread, a vegetable or salad and milk; the vegetarians can choose not to have the meat and everyone should be happy.

Appetizers
Fresh Tomato Pizza (*Page 45*)
Goat Cheese and Pesto Tortilla Pizzas (*Page 47*)
Cheese and Tomato Quesadillas (*Page 52*)

Soups
Three Grain Vegetable Soup (*Page 65*)
Italian Chick Pea and Pasta Soup (*Page 67*)
Red Bean and Rice Soup (*Page 66*)

Salads
Easy Couscous Vegetable Salad (*Page 77*)
Mediterranean Lentil and Bean Salad (*Page 75*)
Pasta Salad with Tomato Basil Dressing (omit ham) (*Page 163*)
Spicy Noodle Salad (*Page 161*)
Bulgar Salad with Cucumber and Feta (*Page 76*)
Pasta Salad with Sun-Dried Tomatoes (*Page 162*)

Pastas
Pasta with Chick Peas, Tomato and Herbs (*Page 146*)
Light Fettuccine Alfredo with Herbs (*Page 150*)
Macaroni and Cheese (*Page 149*)
Pasta Provençal with Tofu (*Page 154*)
Pasta with Tomatoes, Cheese and Jalapeños (*Page 147*)
Linguine with Mushrooms and Green Peppers (*Page 151*)
Make-Ahead Party Thai Noodles (*Page 157*)
Jiffy Chinese Noodles (*Page 156*)
Singapore Noodles (omit pork) (*Page 154*)

Grains, Legumes and Meatless Main Dishes
Potato, Bean and Tomato Stew (*Page 179*)
Tomato, Aubergine and Courgette Gratin (*Page 185*)
Spinach Rice Casserole (*Page 166*)

Indian Rice with Lentils (*Page 168*)
Green Vegetable Risotto (*Page 167*)
Chinese Vegetable Fried Rice (omit ham) (*Page 170*)
Spanish Rice with Coriander (*Page 169*)
Marinated Baked Tofu (*Page 183*)
Spicy Vegetable Tofu Stir-Fry (*Page 184*)
Bean Casserole (omit sausage) (*Page 178*)
Winter Vegetable Curry with Couscous (*Page 180*)
Crustless Vegetable Quiche (*Page 182*)
Quinoa-Stuffed Peppers (*Page 176*)
Barley and Corn Casserole (*Page 177*)

ALL ABOUT CHOLESTEROL AND FAT

Cholesterol

Cholesterol is still very much in the news because high blood cholesterol levels are a major contributor to heart disease. Knowing the facts is important to help you keep your blood cholesterol levels in a healthy range.

First, it's important to know that we need cholesterol. It is a fat-like substance that is a component of body cells, and it's needed to produce hormones and vitamin D, and also bile acids (which help digest fat).

Part of the confusion surrounding cholesterol is because of the way people talk about the cholesterol you eat and the cholesterol in your blood. In fact, these are different things.

Dietary cholesterol is the cholesterol we get from eating foods of animal origin. Meat, fish, poultry, eggs and dairy products all contain cholesterol. Only foods of animal origin contain cholesterol.

Blood cholesterol exists as a natural component of our blood fats. The cholesterol in our blood comes from both our liver and from foods that we eat. About 80% of the cholesterol in our blood is produced by the liver, while the remaining 20% comes from what we eat.

Many people believe that the cholesterol from foods is the main cause of high blood cholesterol and heart disease. We now know that dietary cholesterol doesn't affect blood cholesterol nearly as much as saturated fat.

The best dietary way to reduce the amount of cholesterol our body makes is to reduce the total amount of fat we eat – particularly saturated and partially hydrogenated fats – and to eat more foods containing carbohydrates and fibre.

A word of warning: for people diagnosed with high blood cholesterol levels, limiting high-cholesterol foods to limit include egg yolks, liver, kidney and fish roe.

Fat and Your Health

For most people, eating less fat is the most important dietary change they can make. That's because high-fat diets contribute to heart disease, cancer, high blood cholesterol levels and obesity. The following information will help you sort out the facts about fat.

WHERE DOES THE FAT WE EAT COME FROM?

Many foods contain fat, including foods from each of the four food groups. The main sources of fat in our diet are fats (butter, margarine, lard), oils, higher-fat meats, poultry and dairy products, salad dressings, gravies, sauces, fried foods, croissants and other pastries, biscuits and chocolate.

Some fats, such as the skin on poultry and the fat on meat and bacon, are quite visible. Other fats that you eat are hidden in foods such as peanut butter, dairy products, meat products, snack foods like crisps, nuts and seeds, cake and biscuits and rich desserts. Fat also gets into your diet when you add it to foods when preparing, serving or eating them. These fats include butter, margarine, oils, salad dressing and rich sauces, which should be your primary target for lowering your fat intake.

THERE ARE DIFFERENT KINDS OF FAT

All fats are made up of a combination of fats. You may have heard about saturated, monounsaturated and polyunsaturated fats and trans fatty acids. All of these fats have different effects on your blood cholesterol levels.

Saturated fats have been shown to increase LDL* ('bad') cholesterol in blood. Saturated fats come from foods of animal origin including meats, dairy products (butter, cream, ordinary cheese, full-cream milk), egg yolks, lard, and some vegetable products such as coconut or palm kernel oil, hard margarine or cooking fat and hydrogenated vegetable oils.

Monounsaturated fats may help to lower harmful LDL cholesterol in blood. Olive, avocado, rapeseed and peanut oils, some fish and some nut oils are included in this category. Olive oil has been found to contain some antioxidants which may protect against heart disease.

Polyunsaturated fats also tend to lower LDL cholesterol levels, but not as much as saturated fats do. The process of hydrogenation changes some unsaturated fatty acids to trans fatty acids that act like saturated fats. Some research shows that trans fatty acids may also lower HDL cholesterol. Most of the trans fatty acids that we eat come from partially hydrongenated vegetable oils, which are found in most margarines, cooking fats, some packaged biscuits, crackers, snack foods, pastries, cakes, breaded and fried chicken and fish, and other deep-fried foods. Check labels for the words partially hydrogenated or hydrogenated fats and oils.

CONTROL TOTAL FAT

The bottom line here is to find ways to eat less of all types of fat. We should strive to keep our total fat intake to less than 35% of a day's calories.** This figure doesn't apply to each food or meal that you eat; it's meant as a guideline for your total fat allowance at the end of the day. That means sometimes you can have a higher-fat meal and balance it off with lower-fat choices for the rest of the day. It also means making choices. I have found it easiest to cut out butter or margarine by having cereal rather than toast some mornings, or by just using jam. I don't spread butter or margarine on bread when making a sandwich, but use either light mayonnaise or mustard, and I add sliced cucumber so it won't be dry. I eat both lower-fat and higher-fat cheeses.

---

* LDL and HDL: Cholesterol is transported in our blood by a fat and protein compound called lipoprotein. Too much low-density lipoprotein-cholesterol (LDL) in the blood is directly linked to clogged arteries or coronary artery disease. High-density lipoprotein-cholesterol (HDL) returns cholesterol back to the liver where it is removed from the blood. When you have your blood cholesterol checked, have it done for LDL and HDL as well as for total blood cholesterol. The higher the HDL the better, for it doesn't stay around and clog arteries.
** This guideline has some flexibility for growing children. Parents should not restrict the amount of fat that children under the age of two eat. Infants and children need fat in their diets to provide energy and nutrients for growth and development. Infants need fat to help form the nervous system. Because of this, skimmed and semi-skimmed milk are not recommended during the first two years of life. Children need to progress from a diet that contains about 50% of calories from fat (breast milk) to a lower-fat diet of an adult (35% of calories from fat).

WHAT DOES 35% OF CALORIES FROM FAT REALLY MEAN?

An average woman, age 25 to 49, should keep her daily fat intake to about 75 grams of fat or less (based on 1900 calories). An average man, age 25 to 49, should keep his daily fat intake to about 105 grams of fat or less (based on 2700 calories).

This means that if you have this many calories:	1800	2000	2200	2400	2600	2800
You should have not more than this many grams of fat daily:	70	78	86	94	101	109

COMPARE THE FAT

Higher-Fat Menu

(2420 calories, 50% calories from fat)

Breakfast	*Fat (g)*
Orange juice	0
Croissant	12
1 tbsp (15 ml) butter or margarine	11
Milk full-cream (8 fl oz/225 ml)	9
Total	**32**

Lunch	
Ham and cheese sandwich	
2 slices wholemeal bread	2
1 oz (25 g) Cheddar cheese	10
1 oz (25 g) lean ham	2
2 tsp (10 ml) butter or margarine	8
2 tsp (10 ml) mayonnaise	8
Carrot cake (2¼ oz/60 g) with cream cheese icing	13
Total	**43**

Dinner	
1 chicken breast breaded and fried with skin (5 oz/140 g)	18
Baked potato	0
1 tsp (5 ml) butter or margarine	4
2 tbsp (30 ml) soured cream	6
Carrots	0
1 tsp (5 ml) butter or margarine	4
Green salad	0
Oil and vinegar dressing (1 tbsp/15 ml)	11
Wholemeal bread (1 slice)	1
2 tsp (10 ml) butter or margarine	8
Vanilla ice cream (4 fl oz/125 ml)	10
Total	**62**

Daily total	**137 grams of fat**

COMPARE THE FAT

Lower-Fat Menu

(1714 calories, 28% calories from fat)

Breakfast	*Fat (g)*
Orange juice	0
2 slices wholemeal toast	2
2 tsp (10 ml) butter or margarine	8
Jam	0
Milk semi-skimmed (8 fl oz/225 ml)	5
Total	**15**

Lunch	
Ham and cheese sandwich	
2 slices wholemeal bread	2
1 oz (25 g) skimmed milk cheese (7% fat)	2
1 oz (25 g) lean ham	2
2 tsp (10 ml) light mayonnaise	4
2 oatmeal cookies with raisins	4
1 banana	0
Milk semi-skimmed (8 fl oz/225 ml)	5
Total	**19**

Dinner	
1 chicken breast, baked without skin	3
1 baked potato	0
2 tbsp (30 ml) virtually-fat-free natural	
fromage frais	0
Carrots	0
1 tsp (5 ml) butter or margarine	4
Green salad	0
1 tbsp (15 ml) lower-fat dressing	5
Whole wheatmeal bread (1 slice)	1
1 tsp (5 ml) butter or margarine	4
Lime sorbet (4 fl oz/125 ml)	1
Total	**18**

Snacks	
1 bran muffin (small)	4
1 apple	0
Daily total	**56 grams of fat**

Tips to Cut Back on Fat

1. Use the recipes in this book because they are all lower in fat.

2. Have starchy carbohydrate products like bread, cereal, pasta and rice at every meal. Use high-fat spreads, toppings or sauces in smaller amounts, or try lower-fat alternatives.

3. Eat lots of vegetables and fruit, but watch out for cream sauces, butter or margarine and deep-fat frying.

4. Choose lower-fat milk products such as skimmed or semi-skimmed milk and skimmed- milk yogurt. Try a lower-fat cheese that contains less than 15% fat. Use milk in your coffee instead of cream.

6. Use smaller amounts of full-fat salad dressing or mayonnaise or try a reduced-fat type instead.

7. Prepare foods with herbs, spices, salsa, lemon juice, garlic and mustard for enjoyable flavours without extra fat.

8. Limit high-fat snack foods such as crisps, chips, chocolates, biscuits, cakes and pastries. Instead, choose unbuttered popcorn, pretzels, fruit, vegetable sticks, low-fat yogurt, fresh bread, breakfast cereals, fruit bread and muffins more often.

How to Choose Your Fat Spreads

Butter and margarine both contain 70 calories and 8 g of fat per 2 tsp (10 ml). What you should be concerned about is the amount of saturated fat and hydrogenated or 'trans' fat because these are linked with increased blood cholesterol levels. Butter is high in saturated fat. If you have high blood cholesterol levels, you should choose a soft tub or light margarine with the lowest amount of trans fat and saturated fats. To date, trans fats don't have to be declared on labels in the UK, although some manufacturers voluntarily do so.

	Saturated fat and/or trans fat (grams)	Total fat (grams)	Calories (kcal)
Butter vs Margarine: Here's what's in a 2 tsp (10 ml) serving			
Butter	5	8	70
Margarine (hard)	4	8	70
Half-fat dairy spread	2 to 3	4	35
Soft tub margarine PUFA* (healthier brand, see below)	1 to 2	8	70
Other soft tub margarines	3 to 4	8	70
Reduced fat or very low fat spread	1	2.5	30

To make sure you are buying a healthier margarine, read the fat information listed on the nutrition information panel. If the margarine package doesn't have a nutrient label, don't buy it. Add the grams of polyunsaturated and monounsaturated fat only. The total of these two fats should equal 6 g of fat or more for margarine, or 3 g of fat or more for low fat spread per 2 tsp (10 ml) serving.

Which Oil to Choose

Choose one that suits your taste but make sure that it's high in monounsaturated or polyunsaturated fat. I use safflower and rapeseed oil for cooking and baking because they meet this criteria and are

*Polyunsaturated margarine.

bland in flavour. In salad dressings and pasta sauces when I want good flavour, I often use extra-virgin olive oil. I also use a teaspoon or so of sesame oil for its strong nutty taste in stir-frys (add at the end of cooking), some pasta dishes and salad dressings.

GETTING ENOUGH FIBRE FOODS

Eating more foods that are high in fibre is another positive healthy-eating change. Besides helping to keep you regular, a high-fibre diet may help reduce blood cholesterol levels and reduce your risk for colon and other cancers.

Adults in this country generally have a diet that is relatively low in fibre. That's one of the reasons why the Department of Health suggests that we increase the number of grain products, vegetables and fruit that we eat. Because most high-fibre foods are high in complex carbohydrates and vitamins and low in fat and calories, they play a very important part in a healthy eating pattern.

Where Does Fibre Come From?

Fibre is found in foods of plant origin only. Grains, cereals, vegetables, fruit, beans, peas, lentils, nuts and seeds are all high in fibre.

Types of Fibre

There are two main types of fibre, soluble and insoluble. Each has different health benefits. All plants provide both soluble and insoluble fibre; some sources have more of one than the other. In order to get a good combination of the different types of fibre, choose a variety of high-fibre foods.

Insoluble fibre is the type of fibre known to keep your digestive system working and help keep you regular. It may also play a preventive role, protecting against colon and rectal cancers. Insoluble fibre is found in wheat bran, bran cereals, bran muffins, whole grain products and some vegetables such as broccoli, carrots and peas and fruit skins.

Soluble fibre has been shown to help reduce blood cholesterol levels and to slow down the rate at which sugar is absorbed by the body. Beans, lentils, oat bran, barley and some vegetables and fruit contain soluble fibre.

How Much Fibre Should You Eat?

The average person in this country consumes around 12 g of fibre per day. The recommended daily intake is 18 g but some international experts suggest we need more, around 25 to 35 g of fibre per day. However, because sudden increases in fibre intake can cause abdominal discomfort, you should try to increase your fibre intake gradually.

Tips to Increase Your Fibre Intake

1. Have 5 to 11 servings of whole grain breads, cereals and other grain products every day. For instance, if you choose 4 slices of wholemeal bread instead of white, you add 4 g of fibre.

2. Eat 5 to 9 servings of vegetables and fruit each day. Keep the skins on and choose vegetables and fruit more often than juice. For instance, if you add 3 oz (85 g) cooked green peas to your serving of macaroni and cheese, you add an extra 4 g of fibre. If you have 2 oz (55 g) of spinach salad instead of leaf lettuce, you add an extra 3 g of fibre.

3. Try meals made with dried peas, beans and lentils more often. If you add 3½ oz (100 g) cooked kidney beans to your serving of vegetable soup or green salad, you add 7 g of fibre.

4. Choose high-fibre snacks such as carrots, apples, berries, wholemeal rolls and sandwiches, currant buns, scones, tea-breads, high-fibre breakfast cereals.

5. Add dried fruit to breakfast cereals, desserts, salads and casseroles.

6. Drink plenty of water and other fluids. They help your body use fibre properly.

Fibre Content of Some Common Foods

Food Item	Calories (kcal)	*Fibre (g)	Fat (g)
All-Bran-type cereal, 1½ oz (40 g)	105	10.0	0.8
Baked beans, 6 oz (175 g)	240	6.5	1.0
Prunes, dried, uncooked (10)	201	3.0	tr
Lentils, cooked, 8 oz (225 g)	224	4.3	1.0
Apricots, dried, 2½ oz (70 g)	165	4.5	tr
Raisin bran-type cereal, 1¼ oz (35 g)	145	4.7	0.6
Peas, green, boiled, 3 oz (85 g)	70	4.0	tr
Bran flakes-type cereal, 1¼ oz (35 g)	125	5.2	0.6
Potato, baked with skin (1 medium)	225	4.6	tr
Apple, with skin (1 medium)	80	1.8	tr
Banana (1 large)	105	1.3	tr
Broccoli, boiled, 3 oz (85 g)	25	2.3	tr
Carrot, raw (1 medium)	30	2.2	tr
Tomato, raw (1 medium)	25	1.5	tr
Bread, wholemeal (1 slice)	60	1.7	0.8
Peanut butter, smooth, 1 tbsp (15 ml)	95	0.8	8.1
Bread, white (1 slice)	75	0.4	0.9
Rice, white, long grain, 3½ oz (100 g)	90	0.1	0.1
Sole, baked without fat, 3 oz (85 g)	85	0.0	1.0
Beef, lean, fillet steak, grilled, 3½ oz (100 g)	163	0.0	3.9

THE LATEST NEWS ON VITAMINS

There is a great deal of hype these days about the power of vitamins, especially vitamin C, beta carotene and vitamin E. New research shows that they may help fight heart disease, cancer and even boost the immune system of the elderly, but all the facts aren't in yet. There is also very important news about preconceptual and pregnant women's need for increased folate in order to prevent neural tube defects such as spina bifida.

Department of Health (1993) recommends all women should be taking 0.4 g of folic acid daily as a supplement pre-conceptually and for the first 12 weeks of pregnancy.

Antioxidants

Some scientists believe that antioxidant vitamins (C, E and beta carotene) can help lower your risk for

---

* Fibre is also known as Non-starch polysaccharides (NSP).

cancer and heart disease by protecting you from free radicals. These antioxidants are thought to work by preventing the formation of, or destroying, disease causing compounds known as free radicals. Free radicals are unstable chemicals that form in our bodies at all times. If free radicals aren't inactivated or destroyed by an antioxidant, they can damage cells and contribute to blood vessel wall changes or start disease processes.

Certain nutrients can make free radicals harmless, particularly the antioxidant vitamins C and E and beta carotene (the plant form of vitamin A). Dark green and orange vegetables and orange fruit are good sources of these antioxidant vitamins as well as sources of other non-nutritive substances such as indoles, phenols, flavones and isothiocyantes which may have this protective effect.

Research is not complete, but there are indications that these vitamins, along with other non-nutritive food substances found in fruits and vegetables, are natural antioxidants that help protect against cancer.

The following foods are good sources of antioxidant vitamins and other non-nutritive substances:

Vitamin C
Grapefruit, oranges, papaya, kiwi fruit, green peppers, fresh berries, tomatoes and potatoes, canteloupe melon and broccoli.

Vitamin E
Sunflower seeds, wheat germ, fortified cereals, assorted nuts, olive oil, polyunsaturated vegetable oils such as sunflower or corn oil and dried apricots.

Beta Carotene
Carrots, sweet potatoes, yellow squash, spinach, kale and cantaloupe.

Folate
New research indicates that folate, one of the B vitamins, is very important in the few months before pregnancy and for the first month after conception. Increased folate at these times greatly reduces the risk of neural tube birth defects such as spina bifida. While it's helpful to choose foods that are high in folate, most women who are considering becoming pregnant may need more than their diet can provide. These women are advised to speak to their dietitian or physician about a folic acid supplement.

Foods high in folate include dark green vegetables (broccoli, brussels sprouts, spinach, peas), fortifed breakfast cereal, beans and lentils, melons, oranges and orange juice.

Sould You Take Supplements?
Not necessarily. All the fibre supplements or pills in the world won't make up for a high-fat, high-salt diet that's lacking enough vegetables and fruit. Also they don't contain all the trace nutrients and fibre that your body needs to stay healthy or the non-nutritive substances found in high-fibre foods that may act as protective agents. Until we know for sure exactly what it is in these high-fibre foods that may act as protective agents, we should be eating the foods, not taking supplements.

While there's no harm for most of us in taking one multivitamin pill a day, there are potential toxic effects from taking some supplements in too large an amount (especially vitamin A and D). Also, until we have more proof that supplemental amounts of the antioxidant vitamins (beta carotene, vitamins C and E) or fibre supplements are beneficial, you should rely on food sources of these nutrients, such as vegetables and fruit.

Some supplements may benefit certain groups in the population such as preconceptual and pregnant women who have increased nutrient needs. The elderly who contract a lot of infections may need supplements to improve their nutritional status. There is some concern that people on a very low-fat diet may not get enough vitamin E. People who think they need supplements should check with their GP (Family Doctor) for advice.

The best way to get all the vitamins you need is to choose a well-balanced diet, emphasizing vegetables, fruit and grain products and eating a variety of foods from each of the four food groups each day.

DIETING – WHO NEEDS IT!

Dieting for many people is a short-term solution to help them lose weight, but it may cause long-term problems with weight gain. The reason – diets don't work. About 95% of people who lose weight regain it within 5 years and that weight gain is often higher than it was before. You don't need a special diet to help you attain or maintain a healthy weight. In fact, if you're dieting now, you should stop and take a new approach to eating and thinking about your weight.

Most often diets restrict calorie intake and offer only limited choices of foods. Because of that people get bored and feel deprived and return to their ususal way of eating. The key is to modify some of your usual food choices to a healthier eating pattern, make changes that you can follow for a lifetime and make physical activity part of your daily life.

Body Mass Index (BMI)

Many people don't realize that they may already be at a healthy weight, and there really is no need for them to lose weight at all. Health experts now use the Body Mass Index (BMI) to determine healthy weights, but it is not intended to be used with children, pregnant and breast-feeding women, highly muscular people or people over the age of 65. To find out your BMI, follow these steps.

BMI = Body Weight (kg) $\div$ Height (metres)^2

Example: For a person who is 10 stone (140 lb) and 5′ 6″:

1. Find out your weight in kilograms (divide weight in pounds by 2.2).
   $140 \div 2.2 = 63.64$

2. Find out you height in metres (multiply height in inches by 0.025).
   $66 \times 0.025 = 1.65$

3. Multiply your height in metres by itself to square it.
   $1.65 \times 1.65 = 2.72$

4. Divide weight in kilograms by height in metres squared.
   $63.64 \div 2.72 = 23.39$ This person's BMI is about 23

HOW DOES YOUR BMI RATE?

BMI 20: May contribute to health problems due to being underweight.

BMI 20 – 25: Good, this is a healthy weight range.

BMI 25 – 27: Caution. Watch your weight. A BMI like this may lead to health problems for some people.

BMI above 27: The higher your BMI goes above 27, the greater your risk of developing health problems such as heart disease, some cancers, diabetes and high blood pressure.

Tips to Maintaining a Healthy Weight

1. Follow a varied and balanced diet and pay special attention to serving sizes. Part of healthy eating means choosing foods in appropriate amounts.

2. Follow the 'Tips to Cut Back on Fat' on page 19.

3. Keep physically active. Participating in some form of physical activity every day can help you control your weight. It also benefits your heart, lungs and muscles. Choose activities that can become part of your regular day, such as walking, and those that you can do well into your later years, such as hiking, swimming and cycling.

By eating well, being active and feeling positive about who you are and how you look, you should be able to throw away the diet books forever.

SHOPPING AND EATING OUT

Whether you are shopping for foods or eating out, it is important to make sure that your food choices follow healthy-eating guidelines. Aim for foods that are lower in fat and sodium. Choose these foods more often:

- whole grain;

- green and orange vegetables and orange fruit;

- lower-fat milk products; and

- leaner meats, poultry, fish, dried peas, beans and lentils.

Shopping Means Reading Labels

Checking the information on a food label is the best way to find out what's inside. For example, labels can tell you if a food contains whole grain, provides hydrogenated or saturated fat, or if it is high in salt or sodium. Here's what you'll find on a food label:

INGREDIENT LIST

Every packaged food must contain a list of the ingredients. They are listed in decreasing order by weight. If you are looking for a wholemeal bread, that means choosing one that has whole wheat flour listed first.

CLAIMS (SUCH AS 'LOW FAT,' 'HIGH FIBRE,' 'LOW SALT')

Nutritional claims are used on food packages to point out a key nutrition feature of the food. These claims are defined and regulated by the government. For example, foods labelled

- 'low in fat' must contain less than 5 g of fat per normal serving;

- 'high in source of fibre' must contain at least 3 g of dietary fibre per normal daily serving;

- 'souce of/contains' (for a vitamin or mineral) must contain at least 15% of the recommended daily intake per serving.

Most claims can help you choose healthier foods, such as the ones that say low in fat or sodium. Other claims may be misleading and you should watch out for them. For example, potato crisps may claim to contain no cholesterol, but the small print on the nutritional information panel tells you that they do contain fat.

When a claim is made, information will be given on how much of that nutrient is in a serving of that food.

NUTRITION INFORMATION PANEL
The nutrition information panel is optional information on food labels. This panel tells you the nutrient content for a single serving of food. It can help you figure out how many grams of fat or how much sodium there is in a product. Check the serving size and compare with what you normally eat.

Eating Out

Eating out can challenge your skill at maintaining a healthy eating pattern, but it can be done. If you eat out regularly:

- be sure to choose places that offer a variety of lower-fat, higher-fibre choices for a variety of foods;

- be sure to get enough vegetables and fruits – if eating lunches out every day you may have to bring some from home;

- avoid menu items that have been deep-fried, or are served with high-fat salad dressings or rich sauces;

- don't hesitate to ask for the lower-fat dressing (i.e. an oil-free dressing), grilled rather than fried items and for a lower-fat sauce;

- remember moderation and balance are the keys to healthy eating. If you do have some high-fat foods, choose smaller amounts or balance them by making lower-fat choices at your other meals.

WHERE TO GO FOR HELP

If you need information on healthy eating there are a number of places you can go to or contact for help. In the blue information pages at the front of your phone book there are numbers for Health, Help and Support including the Health Information Service on 0800 665544. Your local health authority will also have a helpline and/or a centre; find them in the phone book under Health.

Major supermarkets produce excellent nutrition leaflets and have their own Food Advice Service. If you have a particular dietary concern or would like your own diet planned, the nurse at your local GP or medical centre will be able to advise you. If necessary your GP can refer you for help from the dietician.

About the Nutritional Information on the Recipes

Unless otherwise stated, the recipes were tested and analyzed using skimmed milk, low-fat yogurt, semi-skimmed cottage cheese and 17% (reduced-fat) hard cheeses because these are the most commonly available. However, you can save even more on fat and calories by substituting lower-fat choices. Minced meat was assumed to be completely browned and thoroughly drained. Calculations of meat and poultry recipes, including those where fat or skin was not removed before cooking, assumed that only the lean portion was eaten. Calculations were based on the first ingredient listed where there was a choice and did not include optional ingredients. Unspecified amounts of salt (pinch or to taste) were not included in the analysis.

Nutrient values greater than 0.4 were rounded to the nearest whole number. Following criteria outlined in the *Guide for Food Manufacturers and Advertisers, Revised Edition 1988* (Consumer and Corporate Affairs), the recipes were also evaluated as sources of vitamins A and C, folate, iron and calcium. Other vitamins and minerals were not evaluated.

Fibre: It is recommended that we have 25-35 of fibre each day.

Sodium: Many people consume too much sodium and lower levels of intake are recommended. Most of the recipes in this book are relatively low in sodium; where the levels are high, suggestions for reducing the sodium have been given to help those on sodium-restricted diets.

Potassium: Potassium is thought to have a positive effect on hypertension and strokes. A diet promoting foods high in potassium, emphasizing fruits and vegetables is recommended.

Daily Total Protein, Fat and Carbohydrate Intake

(based on 15% of calories from protein, 35% pf calories from fat and 50% of calories from carbohydrate) according to Department of Health as taken from COMA report 1994.

Calories/day	Protein (g)	Fat (g)	Carbohydrate (g)
1800	68	70	225
2100	79	82	262
2300	86	90	287
2600	98	101	324
2900	109	113	362
3200	120	125	400

Menus

Nutritional information is based on servings as follows: appetizers, 2 pieces; milk, semi-skimmed, 8 fl oz (225 ml); breads, 1 slice with 1 tsp butter or margarine; salads with 1 tbsp dressing; vegetables, plain, 3 oz (85 g) with ½ tsp butter or margarine; dips, spreads and dessert sauces, 2 tbsp; biscuits and cakes, 1 piece; fruit, 3 oz (85 g) or 1 piece; ice cream, 5-7% fat, 4 fl oz (125 ml); open-faced sandwiches, ½ of each type. See notes for children's and teens' parties on page 30.

Special Sunday Breakfast
Upside-Down Apple Pancake (*page 190*)
Apricot, Orange and Fig Compote (*page 227*)
Citrus Double-Bran Muffins (*page 192*)

Calories 501; Total Fat 13 g; % Calories from Fat 23

Autumn or Winter Brunch
Hot Spiced Cider (*page 54*)
Crustless Vegetable Quiche (*page 182*)
Green Bean Salad with Buttermilk Dressing
(*page 79*)
Cherry tomatoes
Jalapeño Cornmeal Muffins (*page 193*)
or Lemon Poppy Seed Muffins (*page 194*)
Deep-Dish Pear Pie with Apricots and Ginger
(*page 220*)

Calories 730; Total Fat 23 g; % Calories from Fat 29

Spring Lunch
White Sangria Punch (*page 56*)
Seafood Pasta Salad (*page 164*)
Asparagus and Mushroom Salad (*page 78*)
Muesli Soda Bread (*page 197*)
Easy Berry Flan (*page 214*)

Calories 730; Total Fat 17 g; % Calories from Fat 22

Summer Weekend Lunch
Pasta and Ham Salad with Tomato Basil
Dressing (*page 163*)
Sliced cucumber
Toasted bagels/Herbed Cheese Spread (*page 38*)
Gingerbread Cake (*page 204*)
Apple Cinnamon Cookies (*page 202*)
Fresh strawberries

Calories 834; Total Fat 21 g; % Calories from Fat 23

Patio Picnic
Fruit Spritzers (*page 55*)
Open-Faced Sandwiches (*page 50*)
Nectarine and Orange Compote (*page 226*)
Apricot Streusel Cake (*page 203*)

Calories 863; Total Fat 18 g ; % Calories from Fat 18

Autumn Lunch
Mariners' Chowder (*page 69*)
Open-Faced Sandwiches (*page 50*)
Fruit platter (grapes, melon wedges,
strawberries, pear wedges)
Apple Cinnamon Cookies (*page 202*)
Light Lemon Squares (*page 200*)

Calories 1022; Total Fat 27 g; % Calories from Fat 24

Winter Holiday Family Lunch for 12
Cheese and Tomato Quesadillas (*page 52*)
Italian Chick Pea and Pasta Soup
(*page 67*)
Platter of celery, carrots, courgette strips
Muesli Soda Bread (*page 197*)
Pumpkin Spice Cake (*page 205*)
Tangerines/ice cream

Calories 980; Total Fat 27 g; % Calories from Fat 25

Spring Dinner Party
Oriental Noodle and Chicken Soup
(*page 63*)
Baked Whole Salmon Stuffed with Mushrooms
and Artichokes (*page 116*)
Asparagus
Lemon Parsley Rice Pilaf (*page 173*)
or Green Vegetable Risotto (*page 167*)
Rhubarb Fool with Fresh Strawberries
(margin, page 224)

Calories 750; Total Fat 22 g; % Calories from Fat 26

Summer Barbecue Dinner
Chilled Cucumber Mint Soup
(*page 58*)
Thai Barbecued Turkey Escalopes
(*page 108*)
Grilled sweet red peppers and yellow courgettes
Tiny new potatoes with fresh dill
Nectarines, blueberries and raspberries
with Vanilla Cream (*page 231*)

Calories 485; Total Fat 12 g; % Calories from Fat 22

Easy Barbecue Suppers
Each meal includes 1 slice fresh bread, and milk

Barbecue Salmon Fillets (*page 115*)
Baby beets and greens
Sliced tomatoes with basil
New potatoes with fresh dill
Strawberries

Calories 725; Total Fat 26 g; % Calories from Fat 32

Barbecue Trout with Light Tartare Sauce
(*page 114*)
Barbecue Potato Packets
(*page 150*)
Ginger Stir-Fried Courgettes
(*page 147*)
New carrots with fresh dill

Calories 831; Total Fat 29 g; % Calories from Fat 31

Grilled Chicken Breast Burger
with Sun-Dried Tomatoes (*page 91*)
on wholemeal bun
Easy Couscous Vegetable Salad
(*page 77*)
on a bed of lettuces
Peaches

Calories 706; Total Fat 17 g; % Calories from Fat 22

Chinese Chicken Burgers
(*page 90*)
Corn-on-the-cob
Tossed Green Salad
with Tomato Basil Dressing
(*page 86*)
Ice Cream
Orange Hazelnut Biscotti
(*page 201*)

Calories 816; Total Fat 27 g; % Calories from Fat 30

Barbecued Curried Chicken Breast
(*page 100*)
Lemon Parsley Rice Pilaf
(*page 173*)
Green beans
Sliced tomatoes
Apples
Cheese (1 oz/30 g 17% b.f.)

Calories 701; Total Fat 22 g; % Calories from Fat 28

Easy Family Menus
Chinese Chicken Burgers (*page 90*)
in hamburger bun
Purple Vegetable Slaw (*page 83*)
Sliced Tomato
Apple
Milk

Calories 691; Total Fat 22 g; % Calories from Fat 28

Potato, Bean and Tomato Stew (*page 179*)
Easy Couscous Vegetable Salad (*page 77*)
Wholemeal bread
Orange
Milk

Calories 778; Total Fat 23 g; % Calories from Fat 26

Thai Noodles with
Chicken and Broccoli (*page 159*)
Sesame Carrots (*page 134*)
Strawberries
Milk

Calories 716; Total Fat 23 g; % Calories from Fat 29

Lemon Tarragon Sole Fillets (*page 111*)
Bulgur with Red Onion and Pimiento
(*page 174*)
Spinach with Lemon and Nutmeg (*page 138*)
Tossed Salad Greens with
Mustard Garlic Vinaigrette (*page 88*)
Kiwifruit
Milk

Calories 570; Total Fat 19 g; % Calories from Fat 30

Summer Make-Ahead Buffet For a Crowd
Chinese Chicken Balls
with Dipping Sauces (*page 41*)
Clam Dip with Herbs and Crudités (*page 35*)
Thai Pork Skewers (*page 49*)
Grilled Salmon Ribbons with Sesame
and Coriander (*page 48*)
Spicy Noodle Salad (*page 161*)
Oriental Coleslaw (*page 82*)
Couscous, Tomato and Basil Salad (*page 77*)
Fresh Plum Flan (*page 215*)

Calories 873; Total Fat 29 g; % Calories from Fat 30

Make-Your-Own
Summer Pizza Party
White Sangria Punch (*page 56*)
Goat Cheese and Pesto Tortilla Pizzas
(*page 47*)
Easy Berry Flan (*page 214*)

Calories 513; Total Fat 17 g; % Calories from Fat 29

End-of-Summer Dinner
Chilled Purée of Tomato Soup
with Basil (*page 59*)
Herb and Buttermilk Barbecued Chicken
(*page 93*)
Field Mushrooms
with Sweet Peppers (*page 140*)
Barley and Corn Casserole (*page 177*)
Amaretto Custard Sauce (*page 230*)
over sliced peaches

Calories 492; Total Fat 15 g; % Calories from Fat 27

Summer/Autumn Vegetarian Dinner
Fresh Tomato Pizza (*page 45*)
Marinated Baked Tofu (*page 183*)
served on Purple Vegetable Slaw (*page 83*)
Jiffy Chinese Noodles (*page 156*)
Fresh Plum Flan (*page 215*)

Calories 1012; Total Fat 31 g; % Calories from Fat 27

Autumn Dinner Party Menu
Thai Prawn Salad in Pitta (4 each)
(*page 43*)
Hot and Sour Soup (*page 62*)
Honey-Garlic Roast Pork (*page 127*)
Rice with Black Beans and Ginger
(*page 172*)
Sherried Green Beans with Sweet Peppers
(*page 136*)
Apple-Pecan Fillo Crisps (*page 217*)

Calories 831; Total Fat 28 g; % Calories from Fat 30

Make-Ahead Winter Dinner Party
Leek and Mushroom Soup (*page 61*)
Moroccan Rabbit Tagine (*page 132*)
Quick and Easy Spiced Couscous
(*page 181*)
Lemon Mousse with Raspberry Sauce
(*page 213*)

Calories 1019; Total Fat 27 g; % Calories from Fat 24

Winter Sunday Dinner
Chicken and Vegetable Stew with
Parsley Dumplings (*page 101*)
Buttermilk Mashed Potatoes (*page 143*)
Baked Pear Bread Pudding with
Honey Almond Sauce (*page 216*)

Calories 1040; Total Fat 18 g; % Calories from Fat 16

Winter Vegetarian Dinner Party
Cheese and Tomato Quesadillas (*page 52*)
Winter Vegetable Curry with Couscous (*page 180*)
Tossed Green Salad with
Yogurt Herb Dressing (*page 87*)
Chocolate Marbled Cheesecake (*page 211*)

Calories 840; Total Fat 25 g; % Calories from Fat 26

Make-Ahead Winter Buffet
Clam Dip with Herbs (*page 35*) and crudités
Prawn and Chicken Jambalaya (*page 118*)
Salad Greens with Mustard Garlic Vinaigrette
(*page 88*)
Wholemeal rolls
Deep-Dish Pear Pie with Apricots and Ginger
(*page 220*)

Calories 941; Total Fat 21 g; % Calories from Fat 20

Dinner with Teens
Carrot and Corn Chowder (*page 68*)
Chalupas (*page 124*)
Chocolate Mocha Ice Cream Pie (*page 210*)

Calories 1050; Total Fat 22 g; % Calories from Fat 19

After-Bridge Supper
Salmon Salad Fajitas (*page 120*)
Elizabeth Baird's Chocolate Angel Food Cake
(*page 206*)

Calories 494; Total Fat 16 g; % Calories from Fat 30

Oriental Evening
Hoisin Sesame Chicken Platter (*page 96*)
Chinese Vegetable Fried Rice (omit ham)
(*page 170*)
French bread
Easy Berry Flan (*page 214*) and
Nectarine and Orange Compote (*page 226*)

Calories 988; Total Fat 21 g; % Calories from Fat 19

Easy But Different Dinner Party
Hot and Sour Soup (*page 62*)
Asian Chicken (*page 98*)
Light Lemon Squares (*page 200*)
Nectarine and Orange Compote (*page 226*)

Calories 759; Total Fat 13 g; % Calories from Fat 15

Children's or Teens' Party[*]
Jiffy Salsa Dip (*page 34*) with raw veggies
Chicken Fingers (*page 40*) with
Apricot Dipping Sauce (*page 41*)
Herbed Cheese Spread (*page 38*)
on Crostini (*page 39*)
Tortilla Pizza Triangles (*page 46*)
Candied Corn (*page 53*)
Make-Your-Own Ice Cream Sundaes
with Three Sauces
Chocolate Sauce (*page 209*),
Butterscotch Sauce (*page 232*),
Raspberry Sauce (*page 213*)

Calories 985; Total Fat 28 g; % Calories from Fat 25

Teenagers' Buffet Birthday Dinner
Marinated Baked Tofu (*page 183*)
Spicy Noodle Salad (*page 161*)
or Jiffy Chinese Noodles (*page 156*)
Caesar salad
Hot herb bread or buns
Orange Chocolate Refrigerator Cake (*page 212*)

Calories 897; Total Fat 31 g; % Calories from Fat 31

Special Birthday Dinner
Seafood Vegetable Chowder (*page 69*)
Honey Garlic Roast Pork
(*page 127*)
Asparagus or green beans
Field Mushrooms with
Sweet Red Peppers (*page 140*)
Quick and Easy Spiced Couscous (*page 181*)
or new potatoes with dill
Elizabeth Baird's Chocolate Angel Food Cake
(*page 206*)
with Vanilla Cream (*page 231*) and strawberries

Calories 1036; Total Fat 25 g; % Calories from Fat 22

---

* Nutritional information based on: 8 pieces of chicken;
8 pieces pizza triangles; 250 ml candied corn; 175 ml
ice cream; 1 tbsp (15 ml) each sauce.

Buffet Dinner for 24

Sun-Dried Tomato and Onion Toasts
(page 44)
Roasted Aubergine Dip (page 37) with crudités
Lemon Grass Marinated Leg of Lamb
(page 129)
Make-Ahead Party Thai Noodles
(page 157)
Sugar-Snap Peas with Mushrooms (page 135)
Tossed Green Salad with Asian Vinaigrette
(page 85)
Meringues with Lemon Cream (page 222)

Calories 800; Total Fat 21 g; % Calories from Fat 24

Cocktail Party

Thai Prawn Salad in Mini Pittas (page 43)
Chinese Chicken Balls with Dipping Sauces
(page 41)
Mushrooms and/or cherry tomatoes stuffed with
Herbed Cheese Spread (page 38)
Sun-Dried Tomato and Onion Toasts
(page 44)
Goat Cheese and Pesto Tortilla Pizza Triangles
(page 47)
Roasted Red Pepper and Basil Dip (page 36)
with crudités
Smoked Turkey-Wrapped Melon Balls
(page 42)

Calories 411; Total Fat 15 g; % Calories from Fat 32

Easy Friday Night Dinner

Miso Soup with Tofu (page 64)
Linguine with Scallops and Leeks (page 153)
or Summer Prawn and Tomato Pasta
(page 152)
Wholemeal French bread
Berries with Orange Cream (page 228)

Calories 978; Total Fat 20 g; % Calories from Fat 19

Holiday Family Reunion Dinner

Jiffy Salsa Dip (page 34) with vegetables
Chutney-Glazed Ham (page 128)
Rosemary Garlic Roasted Potatoes (page 142)
Sesame Broccoli and Carrots (page 134)
Tossed Salad with Yogurt Herb Dressing
(page 87)
Gingerbread Cake (page 204) with fresh fruit
and Vanilla Cream (page 231) or frozen yogurt

Calories 682; Total Fat 19 g; % Calories from Fat 24

New Year's Eve Dinner Party

Warm Scallop Salad (page 73)
Sherry Chicken Breasts Stuffed with
Courgettes and Carrots (page 94)
Spinach with Lemon and Nutmeg
(page 138)
Sweet Potato and Apple Purée
(page 144)
Chocolate Crêpes with
Banana Cream Filling
and Chocolate Sauce
(page 208)

Calories 889; Total Fat 26 g; % Calories from Fat 27

Christmas Dinner

Cranberry Lime Punch (page 56)
Crudités and Clam Dip with Herbs
(page 35)
Thai Prawn Salad in Pitta Pockets
(page 43)
Roast Turkey with Giblet Gravy
(page 104)
Sausage Apple and Herb Stuffing
(page 105)
Buttermilk Mashed Potatoes (page 143)
Sweet Potato and Apple Purée
(page 144)
Green Beans with Herbs and Pine Nuts
(page 137)
Pumpkin Pie with Orange Yogurt Cream
(page 218)
or Winter Berry Trifle (page 221)

Calories 1062; Total Fat 27 g; % Calories from Fat 23

Christmas Eve Dinner

Herbed Cheese Spread (page 38) with
melba toasts (top with slice of smoked salmon)
Pork Tenderloin Teriyaki (page 122)
or Honey-Garlic Roast Pork (page 127)
Bulgur with Red Onion and Pimiento
(page 174)
or Barley and Corn Casserole (page 177)
or Make-Ahead Party Thai Noodles
(page 157)
Broccoli or Green Beans or Sugar-Snap Peas with
Mushrooms (page 135)
Chocolate Mocha Ice Cream Pie
(page 210)

Calories 806; Total Fat 23 g; % Calories from Fat 26

INFORMATION ON INGREDIENTS

CHILLI PASTE OR SAUCE
Used in Asian cooking, red in colour and made from chilli peppers, salt and often garlic, this adds hotness to dishes. I use the Indonesian chilli paste called *sambal oelek*; Chinese chilli sauce or Thai chilli paste are others to use.

CHILLI PEPPERS
People are now enjoying chilli peppers – fresh, canned and bottled – on everything from pizza to pasta and Mexican to Thai cooking. Start with green chilli, the mildest, work your way up to jalapeño and serrano. When your mouth can stand it and you want some punishment, try Scotch Bonnet, the hottest.

CILANTRO OR CORIANDER
Cilantro is the leaf part of the coriander plant. Often called Chinese parsley or fresh coriander, it has a distinct, pungent flavour that most people either love or hate. It is available in many supermarkets and most greengrocers. The dry leaf cilantro is not a good substitute.

FISH SAUCE
This staple in Thai and Vietnamese cooking has a salty taste and awful smell but adds wonderful flavour to sauces. You'll find it, bottled, in Oriental and specialty food stores and in some supermarkets.

GARLIC
Because garlic cloves vary so much in size, I give a measure in teaspoons of chopped garlic rather than the number of cloves if I use more than one clove in a recipe. I do not suggest that you use bottled chopped garlic; fresh chopped garlic is much superior. If you would rather not measure, just estimate one medium-large clove per teaspoon (5 ml) of chopped garlic.

GINGER
Fresh root ginger adds wonderful flavour to vegetables, salads, sauces, stir-frys and marinades. Buy smooth, shiny, firm root ginger; not shrivelled or mouldy. Peel the ginger with a vegetable peeler or paring knife. Dried powdered ginger is a poor substitute.

HOISIN SAUCE
Made from soybeans, vinegar, sugar and spices, this thick brown sauce adds flavour and a touch of sweetness to dishes. It is available bottled or canned.

LEMON GRASS
This contributes a wonderful lemon flavour to dishes and is becoming more easily available at greengrocers and Asian markets in bigger cities. Fresh lemon grass has pale green straw-textured stalks about the size of green onions. The top two-thirds and outer leaves are discarded. Dried lemon grass is sold in bags at some markets; soak in hot water for 15 minutes before using.

OYSTER SAUCE
Made from oysters and soy sauce but without a fishy taste, this thick brown sauce is used in Chinese dishes. It is sold bottled in Chinese grocery stores and some supermarkets.

SESAME OIL
A dark, strong-flavoured oil made from roasted sesame seeds, this is used in small amounts to add wonderful flavour to stir-fries, vegetable dishes, salad dressings and marinades. Don't buy the light sesame oil as it is light in flavour, not in fat; instead buy ones from Asia.

Appetizers, Snacks and Beverages

Jiffy Salsa Dip
Clam Dip with Herbs
Roasted Red Pepper and
Fresh Basil Dip
Roasted Aubergine Dip
Herbed Cheese Spread
Crostini
Chicken Fingers
Chinese Chicken Balls with
Dipping Sauces
Smoked Turkey-Wrapped
Melon Balls
Thai Prawn Salad in
Mini Pitta Pockets
Sun-Dried Tomato and
Onion Toasts
Fresh Tomato Pizza
Tortilla Pizza Triangles
Goat Cheese and Pesto Tortilla
Pizzas
Grilled Salmon Ribbons with
Sesame and Coriander
Thai Pork Skewers
Open-Faced Sandwiches
Cheese and Tomato Quesadillas
Spicy Popcorn
Candied Corn
Tofu Blender Drink
Hot Spiced Cider
Fruit Spritzers
White Sangria Punch
Cranberry Lime Christmas Eve
Punch

Salsa

Sometimes I chop a tomato, some cucumber and fresh coriander leaves and add to bought salsa.

When I have time I make my own:

Finely chop and combine: 1 large tomato, 3 inch (7.5 cm) piece cucumber, 1 green (mild) or jalapeño (hot) pepper, 2 tbsp (30 ml) chopped onion, 1 tbsp (15 ml) wine vinegar, chopped fresh coriander leaves to taste and one small clove garlic. Makes 18 fl oz (500 ml).

Low-Fat Dips

Check out your local stores for low-fat dips to keep on hand: look for tzatziki (yogurt, cucumber and garlic), salsa or puréed sweet red peppers.

Jiffy Salsa Dip

This easy-to-make dip is low in fat and calories. Serve with some raw vegetable sticks, bread sticks or reduced fat tortilla chips.

4 fl oz	salsa	125 ml
4 fl oz	virtually-fat-free natural fromage frais	125 ml
4 tbsp	chopped fresh coriander	60 ml

1. In small bowl, stir together salsa, sour cream and coriander. Makes about 8 fl oz (225 ml).

Make ahead

Dip can be covered and refrigerated for up to two days.

PER SERVING	1 tbsp/15 ml
calories	6
g protein	1
g total fat	0.01
g saturated fat	0
mg cholesterol	1
g carbohydrate	1
g dietary fibre	0
mg sodium	51
mg potassium	44

Dip Bases		
Compare 8 fl oz (225 ml)	**Fat (g)**	**Calories**
Yogurt (1.5% fat)	4	154
Cottage cheese (low-fat)	4	202
Half-fat crème fraîche	33	416
Virtually-fat-free fromage frais	0.5	104
Soured cream	45	456
Light cream cheese (23%)	53	572
Cream cheese (35%)	81	809
Light mayonnaise	73	726
Mayonnaise	176	1604

Clam Dip with Herbs

This lightened-up version of an old favourite is much lower in fat and calories than a dip made with cream cheese, sour cream or mayonnaise – yet is just as good. Serve with vegetables for dipping.

8 oz	low-fat cottage cheese*	225 g
1	can (5 oz/142 g) clams	1
4 tbsp	chopped fresh parsley	60 ml
3 tbsp	low-fat yogurt*	45 ml
2 tbsp	coarsely chopped fresh basil or dill (or 1 tsp/5 ml dried basil or dill)	30 ml
1 tbsp	finely chopped onion	15 ml
1 tbsp	lemon juice	15 ml
Dash	hot pepper sauce	Dash

1. In blender or food processor, blend cottage cheese until smooth.

2. Drain clams, reserving 1 tbsp (15 ml) liquid.

3. In bowl, combine cottage cheese, clams, parsley, yogurt, basil, onion, lemon juice, reserved clam juice and hot pepper sauce.

4. Cover and refrigerate for at least 1 hour.
Makes about 18 fl oz (500 ml).

Make ahead
Dip can be refrigerated for up to two days.

PER SERVING	1 tbsp/15 ml
calories	11
g protein	2
g total fat	0.2
g saturated fat	0.1
mg cholesterol	2
g carbohydrate	1
g dietary fibre	0
mg sodium	33
mg potassium	28

* Nutrient information is based on cottage cheese and yogurt with 2% fat content.

Stuffed Mushrooms
Prepare dip recipe. Wash mushrooms quickly in small amount of water; dry on towels. Remove stems and spoon about 1 tsp (5 ml) dip into each cavity. Cover and refrigerate for up to 4 hours. Makes 72 pieces.

Roasted Red Pepper and Fresh Basil Dip

Serve this delicious dip when red peppers are plentiful and fresh basil is easy to find.

2	sweet red peppers	2
1½ oz	light ricotta cheese	40 g
2½ oz	soft goat cheese (chèvre)	70 g
3 tbsp	virtually-fat-free fromage frais	45 ml
5 tbsp	chopped fresh basil*	75 ml
Pinch	cayenne pepper	Pinch
	salt and pepper	

1. On baking sheet, bake red peppers in 400°F (200°C) Gas Mark 6 oven for 30 minutes, turning once or twice, or until peppers are blackened and blistered. (Or barbecue until blistered.) Let cool and scrape off skin; discard seeds. Purée in food processor until smooth to make almost 6 fl oz (175 ml).

2. Add ricotta cheese, goat cheese, fromage frais, basil and cayenne pepper; process until well blended. Season with salt and pepper to taste. Makes 12 fl oz (350 ml).

Make ahead
Dip can be covered and refrigerated for up to two days.

PER SERVING	1 tbsp/15 ml
calories	19
g protein	1
g total fat	1
g saturated fat	1
mg cholesterol	4
g carbohydrate	1
g dietary fibre	0.2
mg sodium	24
mg potassium	23

* If you can't find fresh basil, substitute 5 tbsp (75 ml) chopped fresh parsley, and ½ tsp (2.5 ml) dried basil or more to taste.

Roasted Aubergine Dip

For the best flavour, barbecue the aubergine. Aubergine can be baked in the oven, but don't microwave it for this recipe. Garnish with sprigs of parsley and serve with small pitta rounds or raw vegetables for dippers.

4 fl oz	low-fat yogurt (not set) (or 4 tbsp/60 ml low-fat fromage frais)	125 ml
2	medium aubergines (each 1 lb/450 g)	2
4 tbsp	chopped fresh parsley	60 ml
3 tbsp	lemon juice	45 ml
2	spring onions, finely chopped	2
1	clove garlic, chopped	1
1 tsp	sesame oil or olive oil	5 ml
½ tsp	each ground cumin and salt	2.5 ml
	pepper	

1. In cheesecloth-lined sieve set over bowl, drain yogurt in refrigerator for 4 hours or until yogurt is 2 fl oz (50 ml). Discard liquid. (Do not drain fromage frais.)

2. Prick aubergines with fork. Grill over high heat for 1 hour or until black and blistered. (Or bake on baking sheet at 400°F [200°C] Gas Mark 6 for 40 to 45 minutes or until softened, turning once during baking.) Cut in half and drain; scoop out flesh. Purée in food processor or mash until smooth to make about 12 fl oz (350 ml).

3. Stir in yogurt, parsley, lemon juice, onions, garlic, sesame oil, cumin, salt, and pepper to taste. Transfer to serving dish. Makes 18 fl oz (500 ml).

Make ahead
Dip can be covered and refrigerated for up to two days.

PER SERVING	1 tbsp/15 ml
calories	10
g protein	0.4
g total fat	0.3
g saturated fat	0.1
mg cholesterol	0
g carbohydrate	2
g dietary fibre	1
mg sodium	39
mg potassium	67

Herbed Cheese Mushrooms
Remove stems from mushrooms. Spoon Herbed Cheese Spread into caps. Garnish with a strip of smoked salmon, tiny prawn or a sprig of fresh herb. Makes about 50 pieces.

Yogurt Herbed Cheese Spread
Instead of quark, use 8 fl oz (225 ml) extra-thick or pressed yogurt or ¾ pt (425 ml) low-fat yogurt and 8 oz (225 g) low-fat cottage cheese. Drain regular yogurt in cheesecloth-lined sieve set over bowl in refrigerator for 4 hours or until 8 fl oz (225 ml). Discard liquid. Press cottage cheese through sieve into bowl. Stir in 1 tbsp (15 ml) lemon juice, drained yogurt and fresh herbs and garlic as in recipe.

Herbed Cheese Spread

Quark, a low-fat soft cheese, is an ideal base for this herbed spread. If it's unavailable, use the yogurt variation described in the margin. Spread this on Crostini (page 39) or melba toast rounds and garnish with a thin strip of red pepper and a sprig of fresh basil or dill. Or spoon it into cherry tomatoes or chicory spears.

18 fl oz	plain quark (7% fat)	500 ml
4 tbsp	chopped fresh parsley	60 ml
4 tbsp	chopped fresh dill or basil	60 ml
2	small cloves garlic, crushed	2
2 tbsp	chopped chives or spring onions	30 ml
½ tsp	salt	2.5 ml
	pepper	

1. In bowl, combine quark, parsley, dill, garlic, chives, salt, and pepper to taste; mix well. Makes 18 fl oz (500 ml).

Make ahead
Spread can be covered and refrigerated for up to two days.

PER SERVING	1 tbsp/15 ml
calories	19
g protein	2
g total fat	1
g saturated fat	1
mg cholesterol	4
g carbohydrate	1
g dietary fibre	0
mg sodium	36
mg potassium	5

About Quark

Quark is a creamy, smooth, unripened soft cheese. It is a fresh cultured product that, depending on how it is made and packaged, can have a shelf life in the refrigerator of up to 6 months. It can be used in dips, spreads and baked desserts. It ranges in fat content from 7% or higher to less than 1%. The lower-fat variety can sometimes have a slightly bitter taste. Quark is available at some supermarkets, cheese stores, delicatessens and dairies. Use the plain, not the flavoured, variety in recipes.

At fast food chains

- Chilli
- Burger (keep it regular-size and avoid the cheese, "special sauce" and bacon)
- Grilled chicken sandwich
- Pizza with vegetable toppings and small amount of cheese
- Baguette sandwich with lean turkey or ham (not salami), lower-fat dressing, all the vegetables you want but no spread
- Burrito or tostada with vegetables (skip the sour cream, avocado and guacamole)
- Frozen yogurt, milk

At salad bars

- Spinach, vegetables, chick peas, bean salad, light dressing
- Fresh fruit salad

At delis

- Sandwiches: sliced turkey, chicken, beef, on wholemeal bread with tomato, cucumber or lettuce (but no butter or mayonnaise)
- Soups

Crostini

Crostini are Italian-style toasted bread rounds and are a nice change from crackers to top with your favourite spread. They vary slightly from one area of Italy to another. For a fat-restricted diet, omit oil and simply rub toasted bread rounds with cut clove of garlic.

1 tbsp	olive oil	15 ml
1	small clove garlic, crushed	1
1	baguette (French bread stick)	1

1. Combine oil and garlic; set aside.

2. Cut bread into ½-inch (1-cm) thick slices (if large, cut slices in half); place on baking sheet.

3. Brush with oil and toast in 350°F (180°C) Gas Mark 4 oven for 5 to 8 minutes or until crisp. Makes about 36 slices.

Make ahead

Crostini can be covered and stored at room temperature for up to three days.

PER SERVING	(1 Slice)
calories	31
g protein	1
g total fat	1
g saturated fat	0.1
mg cholesterol	0
g carbohydrate	5
g dietary fibre	0.2
mg sodium	55
mg potassium	9

Use Leaner Spreads on Your Bread

Compare the calories and fat in these spreads with those in butter.

1 tbsp (15 ml):	Calories	Fat (g)	Protein (g)
1% fat cottage cheese	12	trace	2
Low-fat cheese spread	30	1	4
Light cream cheese	36	3	1
Cheddar cheese spread	46	3	3
Cream cheese	51	5	1
Jam	54	0	0
Peanut butter	93	8	4
Butter or margarine	101	11	trace

Cajun Chicken Fingers
Follow recipe for Chicken Fingers but omit breadcrumb mixture. Instead, use 4 tbsp (60 ml) fine dry breadcrumbs, ½ tsp (2.5 ml) each dried basil, oregano, thyme, pepper and dried parsley, ¼ tsp (1.25 ml) each salt and onion and garlic powders.

Chicken Fingers

This is a hit with my teenagers and their friends for snacks or a meal.

8 oz	boneless skinless chicken breasts	225 g
1	small clove garlic, chopped	1
4 tbsp	fine dry breadcrumbs	60 ml
1 tbsp	freshly grated Parmesan cheese	15 ml
1 tbsp	finely chopped fresh parsley	15 ml
½ tsp	paprika	2.5 ml
¼ tsp	dried oregano	1.25 ml
	pepper	
4 tbsp	skimmed milk	60 ml

1. Cut chicken into 2½- × ½-inch (6 × 1 cm) strips.

2. Combine garlic, breadcrumbs, cheese, parsley, paprika, oregano, and pepper to taste. Dip chicken into milk; roll in crumbs. Place in single layer on lightly greased baking sheet.

3. Bake in 425°F (220°C) Gas Mark 7 for 5 minutes; turn and bake for 2 minutes longer or until chicken is no longer pink inside. Serve hot. Makes 16 pieces.

Make ahead
To the end of step 2, cover and refrigerate for up to two hours. Best when prepared and eaten hot from the oven.

PER PIECE	
calories	27
g protein	4
g total fat	0.5
g saturated fat	0.2
mg cholesterol	9
g carbohydrate	2
g dietary fibre	0.1
mg sodium	31
mg potassium	50

PER SERVING	(1 Ball)
calories	32
g protein	4
g total fat	2
g saturated fat	0.4
mg cholesterol	21
g carbohydrate	1
g dietary fibre	0
mg sodium	35
mg potassium	41

Chinese Chicken Balls with Dipping Sauces

Meatballs are always a favourite, and these juicy ones will be particularly popular, especially with the dipping sauces.

1	recipe Chinese Chicken Burgers (page 90)	1
	Minted Coriander Dipping Sauce	
	Spicy Apricot or Plum Sauce	

1. Mix ingredients for chicken burger recipe; shape mixture into twenty-four 1-inch (2.5 cm) balls. Place on baking sheet.

2. Grill for 6 to 8 minutes or until browned and no longer pink inside. Serve with dipping sauces. Makes 24 pieces.

Make ahead
Chicken balls can be covered and refrigerated for up to one day.

PER SERVING	½ tsp/2.5 ml
calories	2
g protein	0.1
g total fat	0
g saturated fat	0
mg cholesterol	0
g carbohydrate	0.2
g dietary fibre	0
mg sodium	2
mg potassium	7

Minted Coriander Dipping Sauce

4 fl oz	low-fat yogurt	125 ml
2 tbsp	each chopped fresh coriander and mint	30 ml
	salt and pepper	

1. Combine yogurt, coriander and mint; stir in salt and pepper to taste. Makes 4 fl oz (125 ml).

Spicy Apricot or Plum Sauce

4 oz	apricot or plum jam	115 g
2 tbsp	lemon juice	30 ml
¼ tsp	crushed red pepper flakes or hot chilli paste to taste	1.25 ml

1. Combine jam, lemon juice and red pepper flakes; mix well. Makes ¼ pt (150 ml).

Make ahead
Coriander Sauce can be covered and refrigerated for up to one week; Apricot Sauce for one month.

PER SERVING	½ tsp/2.5 ml
calories	7
g protein	0
g total fat	0
g saturated fat	0
mg cholesterol	0
g carbohydrate	2
g dietary fibre	0
mg sodium	0
mg potassium	3

**Tips to Avoid
Overeating at Parties**

- Just as you shouldn't go grocery shopping when you're hungry, don't go to parties on an empty stomach. Rather than starve all day then gorge at the party, have a glass of milk and a light snack before you go out. This way you'll have the willpower to eat reasonably.

- Go easy on pastry-based appetizers, crisps and deep-fried foods; instead, choose items such as marinated vegetables, prawns and salsa dip. Skip the butter on the rolls. And ask for small servings, especially for dessert.

- Don't skip meals; when you know you will have a special lunch, plan for light suppers and vice versa.

- On occasions where you eat more than usual, try to get a little extra exercise.

Smoked Turkey-Wrapped Melon Balls

These juicy snacks make a nice addition to an hors d'oeuvres platter. They are delicious on their own or with Minted Coriander Dipping Sauce (page 41). Prosciutto or thinly sliced ham can be used instead of turkey.

1	large cantaloupe melon	1
8 oz	thinly sliced smoked turkey	225 g

1. Cut melon in half; scoop out seeds. Using melon baller, scoop out melon rounds.

2. Cut turkey into strips about 1 inch (2.5 cm) wide and 5 inches (13 cm) long. Wrap each strip around melon ball; fasten with cocktail stick. Makes about 48 pieces.

Make ahead
Melon balls can be covered and refrigerated for up to six hours.

PER PIECE	
calories	10
g protein	1
g total fat	0.4
g saturated fat	0.1
mg cholesterol	3
g carbohydrate	1
g dietary fibre	0.1
mg sodium	35
mg potassium	25

Prawns
These shellfish are very low in fat but high in cholesterol. This recipe combines the prawns with other ingredients so the total cholesterol is low and fits into a healthy diet.

Thai Prawn Salad in Mini Pitta Pockets

Perfect for a cocktail party menu or with drinks before dinner, these easy-to-make hors-d'oeuvres are one of my new favourites, mainly because of the fabulous flavour combination of fresh mint and fresh coriander. Instead of mini pittas, you can use Crostini (page 39) or cucumber cups (hollowed-out cucumber rounds).

2 tbsp	light mayonnaise	30 ml
1 tbsp	lemon juice	15 ml
1 tsp	finely chopped root ginger	5 ml
Dash	hot pepper sauce	Dash
8 oz	cooked peeled prawns	225 g
4 oz	bean sprouts	115 g
2 oz	grated carrot	55 g
4 tbsp	coarsely chopped fresh mint	60 ml
4 tbsp	chopped fresh coriander	60 ml
14	wholemeal mini pittas, halved	14

1. In bowl, whisk together mayonnaise, lemon juice, ginger and hot pepper sauce.

2. Add prawns, bean sprouts, carrot, mint and coriander; mix gently.

3. Spoon prawn mixture into pitta halves. Makes 28 pieces.

Make ahead
To the end of step 2, cover and refrigerate early in the day. To end of step 3 for up to two hours.

PER PIECE	
calories	24
g protein	2
g total fat	1
g saturated fat	0.1
mg cholesterol	10
g carbohydrate	3
g dietary fibre	0.4
mg sodium	41
mg potassium	28

Sun-Dried Tomatoes
Sun-dried tomatoes are available at supermarkets and speciality food stores. They come packed in oil or dry packed. To keep fat at a minimum, buy the dry ones and soak them in hot water for ten minutes to soften before using as a pizza topping (Goat Cheese and Pesto Tortilla Pizzas, page 47) or in a salad such as the pasta salad on page 162.

Soaking isn't necessary when cooking in liquid as in this recipe.

Sun-Dried Tomato and Onion Toasts

Tender-sweet onions, full-flavoured dried tomatoes and balsamic vinegar make a delightful flavour combination. To save time, slice the onions in a food processor.

1 lb	cooking onions, thinly sliced	450 g
8 fl oz	chicken stock	225 ml
4 tbsp	chopped dry-packed sun-dried tomatoes	60 ml
2 tsp	granulated sugar	10 ml
4 tbsp	chopped fresh parsley	60 ml
5 tbsp	freshly grated Parmesan cheese	75 ml
4 tsp	balsamic vinegar	20 ml
	salt and pepper	
1	baguette (French bread stick)	1
2	cloves garlic, halved	2

1. In a frying pan, bring onions, chicken stock, tomatoes and sugar to the boil; reduce heat to low and simmer, uncovered, for 45 minutes or until onions are tender and only 1 tbsp (15 ml) liquid remains.

2. Stir in parsley, half of the Parmesan, vinegar, and salt and pepper to taste.

3. Meanwhile, slice bread into ½-inch (1 cm) thick rounds. Toast in 350°F (180°C) Gas Mark 4 for 5 minutes. Rub one side of each round with cut side of garlic.

4. Spread each round with about 1 tsp (5 ml) onion mixture. Sprinkle with remaining cheese. Arrange on baking sheet.

5. Grill for 2 to 3 minutes or until hot. Makes about 36 pieces.

Make ahead
To end of step 3 (except omit parsley), cover and refrigerate for up to two days. To end of step 4, adding parsley, up to three hours ahead.

PER PIECE	
calories	43
g protein	2
g total fat	1
g saturated fat	0.3
mg cholesterol	1
g carbohydrate	8
g dietary fibre	1
mg sodium	103
mg potassium	65

Pizza Toppers

There's a wide choice of delicious low-fat, low-calorie pizza toppings. On top of the tomatoes, sprinkle one or two of the following:

- chopped jalapeño peppers
- chopped sweet peppers
- prawns
- slivers of barbecued chicken or meats
- canned artichoke hearts
- lightly cooked asparagus or broccoli
- goat cheese
- wild or button mushrooms

Frozen Ready-Made Pizza

Compare the serving size and nutrient information on the label, then choose ones that are lower in fat.

Fresh Tomato Pizza

Using Armenian or Italian-style flatbread, or a ready-made pizza base, means easy homemade pizza. This one has far less fat than the pepperoni-and-cheese variety. To serve as an appetizer, cut into bite-size squares.

1	12-inch (30 cm) pizza crust or flatbread round	1
4 oz	mozzarella cheese, grated	115 g
2 oz	onion, very thinly sliced (preferably Spanish or sweet)	55 g
2 tbsp	chopped fresh basil (or 1 tsp/5 ml dried)	30 ml
½ tsp	dried oregano	2.5 ml
2	large tomatoes, thinly sliced	2
2 tbsp	freshly grated Parmesan cheese	30 ml

1. On baking sheet, sprinkle pizza crust with mozzarella cheese, onion and half of the basil and oregano.

2. Arrange tomato slices over top; sprinkle with Parmesan, remaining basil and oregano.

3. Bake in 450°F (230°C) Gas Mark 8 for 15 minutes or until cheese is bubbly. Makes 4 servings.

Make ahead

To end of step 2, cover and set aside at room temperature for up to one hour or refrigerate for up to three hours.

PER SERVING	
calories	386
g protein	20
g total fat	10
g saturated fat	4
mg cholesterol	18
g carbohydrate	55
g dietary fibre	3
mg sodium	801
mg potassium	331
Good: Vitamin A, Calcium	

Tortilla Chips
Using scissors, cut tortillas into crisp-sized pieces. Arrange in single layer on baking sheet. Sprinkle with grated Parmesan cheese (optional). Bake in 375°F (190°C) at Gas Mark 5 for 3 minutes or until crisp.

Tortillas
Soft flour tortillas are available in most supermarkets. Look for them in the speciality food section. They make a delicious, crisp pizza base.

Tortilla Pizza Triangles

You can make these cocktail titbits in a jiffy using your favourite pizza toppings.

2	soft 9-inch (23 cm) flour tortillas	2
4 fl oz	tomato sauce (for pasta)	125 ml
½ tsp	dried oregano	2.5 ml
½ tsp	dried basil	2.5 ml
2 oz	Mozzarella, grated or crumbled goat cheese	55 g
2	mushrooms, sliced	2
4	black olives, cut in strips	4
Quarter	sweet green pepper, cut in thin strips	Quarter

1. Using scissors or knife, cut tortillas into 2-inch (5 cm) triangles; place on baking sheet.

2. Combine tomato sauce, oregano and basil; spread about 1 tsp (5 ml) over each triangle.

3. Sprinkle with cheese, mushrooms, olives and green pepper.

4. Bake at 400°F (200°C) Gas Mark 6 for 3 to 5 minutes or until cheese melts. Serve hot. Makes about 32 pieces.

Make ahead
To end of step 3 for up to three hours.

PER PIECE	
calories	17
g protein	1
g total fat	1
g saturated fat	0.3
mg cholesterol	1
g carbohydrate	2
g dietary fibre	0.2
mg sodium	54
mg potassium	24

**Goat Cheese and
Pesto Tortilla Hors d'Oeuvres**
Prepare and bake as for pizza
but cut into quarters after
baking.

Roasted Peppers
Buy bottled roasted red
peppers or roast your own:
Place peppers on barbecue or
under the grill or in the oven at
400°F (200°C) Gas Mark 6 for
20 to 30 minutes (turning when
one side is blackened) or until
skins are blistered and peppers
are soft. Let cool. Scrape skin
from peppers; discard seeds.

Field Mushrooms
See margin, page 140, for
details on this meaty
mushroom.

Goat Cheese and Pesto Tortilla Pizzas

I first had these fabulous crisp thin-crust pizzas at a barbecue at
my friend Marilyn Short's house in Toronto. In the summer, I put
out the toppings in small bowls, then let guests make their own
pizzas and cook them on the barbecue. (Pictured opposite page
64.)

8	soft 6-inch (15 cm) flour tortillas	8
1 tsp	olive oil	5 ml
3 oz	mushrooms, sliced	85 g
8	dry-packed sun-dried tomatoes	8
8	medium asparagus spears	8
4 tbsp	pesto sauce	60 ml
4 oz	mozzarella cheese, grated	115 g
2 oz	goat cheese (chèvre), diced	55 g
1	roasted sweet red pepper (homemade or bottled), cut in thin strips	1
1 tbsp	sesame seeds	15 ml

1. Place tortillas on ungreased baking sheet. Bake at 350°F (180°C)
Gas Mark 4 for 5 minutes. Set aside.

2. In nonstick frying pan, heat oil over medium-high heat; cook
mushrooms for 5 to 8 minutes or until tender, stirring often. In a
bowl, pour boiling water over tomatoes; let stand for 5 minutes.
Drain well; cut into strips.

3. Steam or boil asparagus for 3 minutes or until tender-crisp;
drain. Cool under cold water; drain. Cut in 2-inch (5 cm) lengths.

4. Spread a little pesto sauce on each tortilla round; sprinkle with
mushrooms, tomatoes, asparagus, mozzarella cheese, goat
cheese, red pepper and sesame seeds.

5. Barbecue over medium-high heat, covered, for 5 minutes or
until cheese melts. Or, bake on baking sheet at 400°F (200°C)
Gas Mark 6 for 8 minutes. Makes 8 servings.

Make ahead
To end of step 3 for up to six hours; refrigerate mushrooms and
asparagus.

PER SERVING	
calories	223
g protein	11
g total fat	10
g saturated fat	3
mg cholesterol	11
g carbohydrate	24
g dietary fibre	3
mg sodium	355
mg potassium	297

Good: Calcium, Iron
Excellent: Vitamin C, Folate

Grilled Salmon Ribbons with Sesame and Coriander

Serve these as an appetizer or main course. Easy to eat without cutlery, they are great for a buffet.

1 lb	skinless salmon fillet (1-inch/2.5 cm thick)	450 g
3 tbsp	lemon juice	45 ml
1 tbsp	dark sesame oil	15 ml
2 tbsp	chopped fresh coriander	30 ml
1 tbsp	sesame seeds	15 ml

1. Soak 16 wooden skewers in water to cover for at least 10 minutes to prevent scorching. Cut salmon into ¼-inch (5 mm) thick slices to make sixteen 6- × 1-inch (15 × 2.5 cm) strips. Thread salmon on to skewers. Place in single layer in shallow dish.

2. Combine lemon juice and sesame oil; pour over salmon. Sprinkle with coriander. Let marinate for 15 minutes.

3. Arrange salmon on lightly greased grill or barbecue rack; sprinkle with sesame seeds. Grill or barbecue 6 inches (15 cm) from heat for 3 to 5 minutes or until opaque. Makes 16 appetizer pieces or 4 main-course servings.

Make ahead
To end of step 2, cover and refrigerate for up to four hours.

PER SERVING AS APPETIZER (AS MAIN COURSE)	
calories	43 (173)
g protein	6 (23)
g total fat	2 (8)
g saturated fat	0.3 (1)
mg cholesterol	16 (62)
g carbohydrate	0.1 (0.3)
g dietary fibre	0 (0)
mg sodium	13 (51)
mg potassium	141 (564)

Beef, Chicken or Turkey Skewers
Substitute 1 lb (450 g) of beef, chicken or turkey for pork.

Buying Pork
Buy pork either very thinly sliced or 1-inch (2.5 cm) thick and cut crosswise. Cut strips to fit length of skewer or cocktail sticks. For a barbecue main course, use longer pieces of meat. For ease-of-eating with cocktails, you might want bite-sized lengths.

Thai Pork Skewers

These strips of spicy meat are wonderful for cocktail snacks or buffets when you want something that's easy to eat without using a knife. For a dinner party appetizer, serve with peanut sauce. Fresh coriander adds wonderful flavour; if it's unavailable, substitute fresh parsley and 1 tsp (5 ml) dried coriander leaves.

1 lb	thinly sliced pork	450 g
3 tbsp	chopped fresh coriander	45 ml
2 tbsp	dry sherry or lime juice	30 ml
1 tbsp	wine vinegar	15 ml
1 tbsp	fish sauce or hoisin sauce	15 ml
1 tbsp	dark sesame oil	15 ml
1 tbsp	honey	15 ml
1 tbsp	sodium-reduced soy sauce	15 ml
1 tbsp	grated root ginger	15 ml
1	large clove garlic, crushed	1
Pinch	crushed red pepper flakes	Pinch

1. Trim fat from pork; slice pork into thin strips (short pieces if for cocktail snacks; 6-inch/15 cm long pieces if for buffet or first course).

2. In bowl, combine coriander, sherry, vinegar, fish sauce, sesame oil, honey, soy sauce, ginger, garlic and red pepper flakes. Add pork, stirring to coat. Cover and marinate in refrigerator for at least 2 or up to 24 hours.

3. Soak wooden skewers or cocktail sticks in water for 15 minutes. Thread pork strips on to skewers.

4. Place on grill rack in single layer and grill for 3 to 5 minutes or until browned. Makes about 30 pieces on skewers, 48 on cocktail sticks.

Make ahead
To end of step 2 for up to one day. To end of step 3 (pour remaining marinade over), cover and refrigerate for up to four hours.

PER SERVING ON SKEWER (ON COCKTAIL STICK)	
calories	27 (17)
g protein	3 (2)
g total fat	1 (1)
g saturated fat	0.2 (0.1)
mg cholesterol	8 (5)
g carbohydrate	1 (1)
g dietary fibre	0 (0)
mg sodium	36 (22)
mg potassium	53 (33)

PER PIECE (BRUSCHETTA)	
calories	193
g protein	9
g total fat	9
g saturated fat	6
mg cholesterol	28
g carbohydrate	19
g dietary fibre	1
mg sodium	359
mg potassium	122

Bridge Party Lunch
- Open-Faced Sandwiches
- Raw Vegetables with Clam Dip with Herbs (page 35)
- Apricot Streusel Cake (page 203)

PER PIECE (GREEK SALAD)	
calories	333
g protein	10
g total fat	12
g saturated fat	4
mg cholesterol	16
g carbohydrate	48
g dietary fibre	4
mg sodium	1022
mg potassium	484

Good: Vitamin C, Calcium, Iron
Excellent: Foliate

Open-Faced Sandwiches

A large platter of colourful open-faced sandwiches is an easy, make-ahead, no-fuss way to entertain. Each type of sandwich makes four pieces and when you assemble the whole platter, you'll have enough for eight people.

Bruschetta

4	thick slices Italian bread	4
4 oz	soft mild goat cheese (chèvre) or light cream cheese	115 g
8 oz	tomato, diced	225 g
	salt and pepper	
	chopped fresh basil	

1. Toast bread; spread one side with cheese. Cover with tomato. Sprinkle with salt and pepper to taste. Just before serving, sprinkle basil over top. Makes 4 pieces.

Greek Salad

	Focaccia bread*	
2 tsp	olive oil	10 ml
1	small clove garlic, crushed	1
2	tomatoes, sliced	2
1	small red onion, thinly sliced	1
2 oz	crumbled feta cheese	55 g
2	drained canned or marinated artichoke hearts, sliced	2
12	black Greek-style olives, stoned	12
	salt and pepper	
	chopped fresh or dried oregano	

1. Cut bread into four 5- × 3-inch (13 × 7.5 cm) portions. Combine olive oil and garlic; brush over bread.

2. Cover each with 2 or 3 overlapping slices of tomato, then 3 red onion rings. Top each with feta cheese, artichoke slices and 3 olives. Sprinkle with salt, pepper and oregano to taste. Makes 4 pieces.

* Use prepared fresh pizza crust-type bread if focaccia is unavailable

PER PIECE (SMOKED TURKEY)	
calories	214
g protein	17
g total fat	7
g saturated fat	1
mg cholesterol	32
g carbohydrate	26
g dietary fibre	5
mg sodium	615
mg potassium	440

Good: Vitamin C, Iron
Excellent: Folate

Smoked Turkey with Asparagus

12	asparagus spears	12
2 tbsp	light mayonnaise	30 ml
1 tbsp	Dijon mustard	15 ml
4	slices pumpernickel bread	4
6 oz	thinly sliced smoked turkey	175 g
1 tsp	skimmed milk	5 ml

1. Cook asparagus in boiling water until tender-crisp, 3 to 5 minutes. Refresh under cold water; drain and pat dry. Mix mayonnaise with mustard; spread some of the mixture over bread. Cover with turkey. Top with asparagus.

2. Just before serving, mix milk into remaining mayonnaise mixture; drizzle over each sandwich. Makes 4 pieces.

Grilled Chicken Breast with Mango Salsa

2	boneless skinless chicken breasts	2
	salt and pepper	
2	hamburger buns, halved or 4 French bread slices	2
4 tsp	light mayonnaise	20 ml
Mango Salsa		
1	chopped peeled mango or 2 peaches	1
Half	sweet red pepper, chopped	Half
2 tbsp	chopped fresh coriander	30 ml
2 tbsp	lime juice	30 ml

PER PIECE (GRILLED CHICKEN)	
calories	215
g protein	16
g total fat	5
g saturated fat	1
mg cholesterol	37
g carbohydrate	27
g dietary fibre	2
mg sodium	219
mg potassium	262

Excellent: Vitamin A, Vitamin C

1. Mango Salsa: In bowl, combine mango, red pepper, coriander and lime juice.

2. Grill chicken until no longer pink inside, 5 to 8 minutes on each side. Sprinkle with salt and pepper to taste; let cool. Cut into 1/3-inch (9 mm) thick slices.

3. Spread buns with mayonnaise. Cover with chicken and top with salsa. Makes 4 pieces.

Make ahead

All sandwiches can be covered and refrigerated for up to three hours; remove from refrigerator 20 minutes before serving.

Quesadillas
Quesadillas are folded tortillas filled with melted cheese and usually chilli peppers. Any cooked meats or chopped vegetables can also be added.

Grilled or Barbecued Quesadillas
Grill under medium heat or over hot coals for 2 to 3 minutes on each side or until golden and cheese melts.

Oven-Baked Quesadillas
Bake on baking sheet at 400°F (200°C) Gas Mark 6 for 10 minutes or until golden and cheese melts.

Cheese and Tomato Quesadillas

I keep a jar of pickled jalapeño peppers in the refrigerator to use in this zesty recipe.

4	soft 9-inch (23 cm) flour tortillas	4
3 oz	low-fat Gouda or Mozzarella cheese	85 g
1 oz	soft mild goat cheese (chèvre), diced	25 g
1	medium tomato, diced	1
1	spring onion, chopped	1
2 tsp	chopped pickled jalapeño pepper	10 ml
4 tbsp	chopped fresh coriander	60 ml

1. Sprinkle half of each tortilla with grated cheese and goat cheese, tomato, spring onion, jalapeño pepper and coriander. Fold uncovered half over filling and press edges together.

2. Heat ungreased frying pan over medium heat; cook quesadillas for 3 to 4 minutes on each side or until golden and cheese melts. To serve, cut each into 3 wedges. Makes 12 pieces.

Make ahead
To end of step 1, cover and refrigerate for up to three hours.

PER PIECE	1 tbsp/15 ml
calories	75
g protein	4
g total fat	3
g saturated fat	1
mg cholesterol	6
g carbohydrate	9
g dietary fibre	1
mg sodium	118
mg potassium	55

Snacks

Choose snacks that are lower in fat. All fruits and vegetables (except avocados) are good choices. This chart will help.

	Fat (g)
Peanuts 2½ oz (70 g)	36
Potato crisps (2 oz/55 g bag)	20
Popcorn, microwave butter flavour (3½ oz/100 g)	35
Popcorn (plain) air-popped (3½ oz/100 g)	0
Pretzels (5 sticks or 3 rings)	trace
Biscuits (1) Small chocolate chip cookie	3
Sandwich-type with cream	3
Oatmeal or chocolate marshmallow	2
Fig/Gingersnap	1
Rich Tea/Arrowroot	1

PER SERVING	
calories	65
g protein	1
g total fat	3
g saturated fat	0.4
mg cholesterol	0
g carbohydrate	8
g dietary fibre	1
mg sodium	230
mg potassium	39

Spicy Popcorn

When it comes to healthy eating, my downfall isn't dessert, but salty, crisplike snacks. Popcorn is usually my solution.

3 oz	popped corn	75 g
2 tsp	soft margarine or butter, melted	10 ml
½ tsp	chilli powder	2 ml
¼ tsp	each ground cumin and salt	1.25 ml

1. Place popcorn in plastic bag. In small dish, stir together margarine, chili powder, cumin and salt; pour over popcorn and shake to mix. Makes 3 servings.

Candied Corn

This is really tasty and uses only a minimum of sugar and fat. For variation, add ¼ tsp (1.25 ml) cinnamon to the sugar mixture.

1 oz	brown sugar	25 g
½ oz	soft margarine or butter	15 g
1 tbsp	corn or golden syrup	15 ml
4 oz	popped corn	115 g

PER SERVING	
calories	106
g protein	1
g total fat	3
g saturated fat	1
mg cholesterol	0
g carbohydrate	18
g dietary fibre	1
mg sodium	44
mg potassium	52

1. In a small microwaveable dish, combine sugar, margarine and syrup. Microwave on Medium power (50%) for 20 seconds; stir. Microwave on Medium for another 30 seconds; stir.

2. Pour over popcorn and toss to mix. Spread on baking sheet. Bake in 275°F (140°C) Gas Mark 1 for 20 minutes, stirring every 5 minutes. Makes 4 servings.

Make ahead
Popcorn can be kept in an airtight container up to one day.

PER DRINK	
calories	242
g protein	13
g total fat	7
g saturated fat	1
mg cholesterol	0
g carbohydrate	37
g dietary fibre	3
mg sodium	15
mg potassium	762
Excellent: Vitamin C, Folate, Calcium, Iron	

Tofu Blender Drink

The recipe for this creamy-tasting orange drink is from Vancouver vegetarian dietitian and author Vasanto Crawford. I think it's one of the best-tasting and easiest ways to use tofu, which is a good source of protein, calcium, iron, phosphorous and some B vitamins. This is great for breakfast or a snack.

10 oz	tofu, drained	300 g
8 fl oz	frozen orange juice concentrate	225 ml
13 fl oz	water	380 ml
1	ripe banana	1

1. In blender or food processor, combine tofu, orange juice, water and banana; blend until smooth. Makes 4 servings.

Make ahead
Drink can be covered and refrigerated for up to one day; stir before serving.

Party Quantities
For 32 servings, double the recipe. For 64 servings, use 14 pts (8 L) cider, 2 lemons, 12 whole cloves, 8 whole allspice, 8 sticks cinnamon, and 1 bottle (700 ml) Calvados (if using). When making large quantities, tie spices in cheesecloth bag; remove before serving.

Hot Spiced Cider

This old-fashioned favourite provides all the warmth you'll need on a wintry day. If children are part of the gathering, leave out the brandy and use apple juice; the drink is still as heartwarming.

3½ pts	cider or apple juice	2 L
1	lemon, thinly sliced	1
6	whole cloves	6
4	whole allspice	4
4	sticks cinnamon	4
8 fl oz	Calvados or brandy (optional)	225 ml

1. In large saucepan, combine cider, lemon, cloves, allspice and cinnamon sticks. Cover and simmer for 15 to 30 minutes or until hot and fragrant.

2. Just before serving, strain. Stir in Calvados (if using). Makes 16 servings, 4 fl oz (125 ml) each.

Make ahead
To end of step 1 for up to one day.

PER SERVING	
calories	62
g protein	0.1
g total fat	0
g saturated fat	0
mg cholesterol	0
g carbohydrate	17
g dietary fibre	0
mg sodium	4
mg potassium	148

For a Party
Combine 8 fl oz (225 ml)
nectar concentrate and 4 fl oz
(125 ml) lemon juice up to 24
hours in advance. At serving
time, pour 3 tbsp (45 ml) into
wine glass; top with crushed
ice and soda. Makes 8 drinks.

Non-Alcoholic Drinks
- Fruit Spritzer variations:
  mix fruit juices such as
  apple, pineapple,
  grapefruit, passion fruit or
  fruit nectars with soda
  water, adding a slice of fruit
  or twist of citrus peel and
  ice.
- Virgin Bloody Mary; to make
  juice, Worcestershire sauce
  and a dash of Tabasco.
- Soda water with a dash of
  angostura bitters and slice of
  lemon or lime.

Fruit Spritzers

You won't miss the wine in these refreshing drinks. However, you could add an ounce of dry white wine and still be drinking much less alcohol than in a glass of wine or a regular spritzer.

2 tbsp	peach, pear or blackcurrant nectar concentrate or cordial	30 ml
1 tbsp	lemon juice	15 ml
2 fl oz	soda water	50 ml
	crushed ice	

1. In wine glass, combine peach nectar concentrate and lemon juice; stir to mix.

2. Add soda water and ice. Makes 1 drink.

Make ahead
To end of step 1 for up to three hours.

Juices

Fruit juice versus fruit drinks
When buying juice, be label-wise. Look for the word *juice* rather than *drink, cocktail, punch or blend*. Packaged fruit-flavoured drinks might contain Vitamin C but not the potassium, folate and other nutrients that real fruit juice provides. *Note*: Both fresh and processed long-life juices provide similar nutrients.

Too much of a good thing
For children, too much fruit juice can contribute to tooth decay, lack of appetite at mealtimes and, in some cases, diarrhoea.

The real thing or its juice?
While juices and their nutrients are often a concentrated source of vitamins and part of a healthy diet, whole fruits and vegetables are higher in fibre and some nutrients than the juice alone. Variety in our diet means we should have both.

PER DRINK	
calories	90
g protein	0.1
g total fat	0
g saturated fat	0
mg cholesterol	0
g carbohydrate	24
g dietary fibre	0
mg sodium	16
mg potassium	17

Variation
If you are making the alcoholic version, add an ounce of brandy for extra flavour.

PER SERVING	
calories	52
g protein	1
g total fat	0.1
g saturated fat	0
mg cholesterol	0
g carbohydrate	13
g dietary fibre	0.1
mg sodium	16
mg potassium	119

Garnish
Garnish with sliced lime.

Variation
For an alcoholic version, add either rum or wine to taste.

PER SERVING	
calories	102
g protein	0.1
g total fat	0.1
g saturated fat	0
mg cholesterol	0
g carbohydrate	27
g dietary fibre	0
mg sodium	19
mg potassium	54
Good: Vitamin C	

White Sangria Punch

Make this light punch with white grape juice, white wine or an alcohol-free white wine.

1¾ pts	white grape juice (or 1 bottle/750 ml white wine)	1 L
	juice of 1 lemon and 1 lime	
1	lime, sliced	1
1	bottle (750 ml) soda water, chilled	1

1. In large jug, combine grape juice, lemon and lime juice and sliced lime. Refrigerate until chilled.

2. Just before serving, add soda water. Makes 12 servings, each 6 fl oz (175 ml).

Make ahead
To end of step 1 for up to three hours.

Cranberry Lime Christmas Eve Punch

We often have this punch that both children and adults enjoy. If ginger beer is unavailable, substitute ginger ale.

3 pts	cranberry juice drink	1.7 L
¾ pt	lime juice cordial	425 ml
18 fl oz	pineapple juice	500 ml
1½ pts	ginger beer, chilled	850 ml
2¾ pts	soda water, chilled	1.5 L
	ice	

1. In punch bowl, combine cranberry juice, lime cordial, pineapple juice and ginger beer.

2. Just before serving, add soda water and ice. Makes 28 servings, each 6 fl oz (175 ml).

Make ahead
To end of step 1 for up to two hours.

Soups

Curried Cauliflower Soup

Chilled Cucumber Mint Soup

Purée of Tomato Soup with Fresh Basil

Broccoli Soup

Leek and Mushroom Soup with Fresh Basil

Hot and Sour Soup

Oriental Noodle and Chicken Soup

Miso Soup with Tofu

Three-Grain Vegetable Soup

Red Bean and Rice Soup

Italian Chick Pea and Pasta Soup

Carrot and Corn Chowder

Mariners' Chowder

Hearty Scotch Broth

PER SERVING	
calories	133
g protein	7
g total fat	5
g saturated fat	2
mg cholesterol	11
g carbohydrate	16
g dietary fibre	2
mg sodium	486
mg potassium	623

Good: Calcium
Excellent: Vitamin C, Folate

Curried Cauliflower Soup

Cool and creamy, this is a wonderful soup for a warm day.

Half	cauliflower, cut in chunks (about 1 lb 4 oz/550 g)	Half
6 oz	potato, peeled and sliced	175 g
1½ pts	semi-skimmed milk	850 ml
½ oz	soft margarine or butter	15 g
1 tsp	each salt, curry powder and ground cumin	5 ml
2 tbsp	chopped fresh chives or spring onion	30 ml

1. In saucepan, combine cauliflower, potato and milk; bring to the boil. Reduce heat; cover and simmer for 20 minutes or until tender. Purée in food processor or blender.

2. Stir in margarine, salt, curry powder and cumin.

3. Cover and refrigerate for 2 hours or until cold. If desired, thin with additional milk. Garnish with chives. Makes 6 servings, about 6 fl oz (175 ml) each.

Cucumbers
For this soup, peel the cucumber only if the skin is waxed or very thick.

Chilled Cucumber Mint Soup

Refreshing and easy to make, this soup is a nice way to start a summer meal.

1	cucumber, seeded	1
2	spring onions, chopped	2
4 tbsp	chopped fresh mint	60 ml
2 tbsp	chopped fresh coriander or parsley	30 ml
12 fl oz	semi-skimmed milk	350 ml
4 fl oz	light Greek yogurt	125 ml
4 fl oz	low-fat yogurt	125 ml

1. In food processor, purée cucumber, onion, mint and coriander; add milk and Greek yogurt and process to mix.

2. Stir in low-fat yogurt. Season with salt and pepper. Refrigerate for at least 1 hour. Makes 6 servings, about 6 fl oz (175 ml) each.

Make ahead
Both soups can be covered and refrigerated for up to two days.

PER SERVING	
calories	78
g protein	5
g total fat	3
g saturated fat	2
mg cholesterol	10
g carbohydrate	9
g dietary fibre	1
mg sodium	64
mg potassium	288

Good: Calcium

Best Flavour Tomatoes
For the most flavour, don't refrigerate tomatoes; store at room temperature or in a cool place, but not as cold as the refrigerator.

Purée of Tomato Soup with Fresh Basil

This is one of my husband's favourite soups; he likes it cold and says it's better than gazpacho. Make it in the summer when home-grown tomatoes and basil are at their best.

2 lb	ripe tomatoes	900 g
1 tbsp	olive oil	15 ml
Half	Spanish onion, thinly sliced	Half
2 tsp	chopped fresh garlic	10 ml
2 tbsp	chopped fresh basil	30 ml
¼ tsp	salt	1.25 ml
	pepper	
2 tbsp	low-fat fromage frais or light crème fraîche (optional)	30 ml
2 tbsp	chopped fresh chives	30 ml

1. Peel tomatoes by blanching in boiling water for 1 minute; peel off skins. Cut in half, then squeeze or scoop out seeds.

2. In a frying pan, heat oil over medium heat; cook onion and garlic until tender, about 5 minutes.

3. In food processor or blender, purée tomatoes and onion mixture until smooth; stir in basil, salt, and pepper to taste; reheat but don't boil. Or cover and refrigerate for at least 30 minutes.

4. Garnish each bowlful with fromage frais (if using) and chives. Makes 6 servings, about 4 fl oz (125 ml) each.

Make ahead
To end of step 3, cover and refrigerate for up to two days.

PER SERVING	
calories	56
g protein	2
g total fat	3
g saturated fat	1
mg cholesterol	1
g carbohydrate	7
g dietary fibre	2
mg sodium	111
mg potassium	293
Good: Vitamin C	

Broccoli

Broccoli is packed with nutrients: it has many vitamins, including folate, Vitamin C and beta carotene; it has minerals, including calcium and iron; it even has some protein and is a high source of fibre.

Broccoli Soup

This is one of the easiest and most nutritious ways to make soup – throw everything into the pot and cook until tender. This method keeps all the nutrients rather than draining them away in the cooking water; it doesn't use any fat to first cook the onions, and it thickens with a potato rather than with a flour-and-butter mixture. Since there isn't any other fat, I like to use semi-skimmed milk.

12 oz	fresh broccoli	350 g
1	onion, chopped	1
12 oz	potatoes, peeled and diced	350 g
1	clove garlic, crushed	1
12 fl oz	vegetable stock or water	350 ml
½ tsp	dried thyme	2.5 ml
¼ tsp	pepper	1.25 ml
Pinch	nutmeg	Pinch
12 fl oz	milk	350 ml
	salt	

1. Peel broccoli stems; chop coarsely. Separate florets to make 8 oz (225 g); set aside. Coarsely chop remaining florets.

2. In saucepan, combine chopped stems and florets, onion, potatoes, garlic, stock, thyme, pepper and nutmeg; bring to the boil. Reduce heat, cover and simmer for 10 minutes or until potatoes are very tender.

3. Meanwhile, steam reserved florets for 5 minutes or until tender-crisp; set aside.

4. In blender or food processor, purée soup in batches until smooth; return to pan. Add milk; heat through but do not boil. Season with salt to taste.

5. Divide broccoli florets among 5 soup bowls; pour soup into bowls. Makes 5 servings, about 8 fl oz (225 ml) each.

Make ahead

To end of step 4, cover and refrigerate for up to two days. Reheat gently.

PER SERVING	
calories	118
g protein	6
g total fat	2
g saturated fat	1
mg cholesterol	5
g carbohydrate	21
g dietary fibre	3
mg sodium	66
mg potassium	591

Good: Vitamin A
Excellent: Vitamin C, Folate

Washing Leeks
Trim off root ends of leeks and most of dark green. Split leeks lengthwise and hold under running water to remove any grit.

Leek and Mushroom Soup with Fresh Basil

Fresh basil adds wonderful flavour to the mild tastes of mushrooms and leeks. This soup is nice for a first course at dinner or for lunch. Use the white of leek and just a little of the tender green part.

1 tbsp	olive oil	15 ml
5	(medium) leeks, chopped	5
10 oz	mushrooms, coarsely chopped	280 g
1	potato, peeled and chopped	1
16 fl oz	water or chicken or vegetable stock	450 ml
1 pt	milk (semi-skimmed or whole)	600 ml
4 tbsp	chopped fresh basil*	60 ml
½ tsp	salt	2.5 ml
¼ tsp	pepper	1.25 ml

1. In large saucepan, heat oil over medium heat; cook leeks for 5 minutes, stirring occasionally. Add mushrooms and potato; cook for 2 minutes, stirring often.

2. Add water and bring to boil; reduce heat, cover and simmer for 15 minutes or until vegetables are tender. Purée in blender or food processor; return to pan. Add milk, basil, salt and pepper; heat until hot. Makes 6 servings, about 8 fl oz (225 ml) each.

Make ahead
To end of step 2, except omit basil; cover and refrigerate for up to two days, or freeze for up to one month. Reheat, adding basil just before serving.

PER SERVING (USING SEMI-SKIMMED MILK)	
calories	117
g protein	5
g total fat	5
g saturated fat	2
mg cholesterol	8
g carbohydrate	15
g dietary fibre	2
mg sodium	251
mg potassium	425

* If fresh basil is not available, substitute chopped fresh parsley plus ½ tsp (2.5 ml) dried basil or more to taste, or chopped fresh dill.

Adding an Egg
Usually an egg is swirled into this soup, which adds body but can make the soup cloudy.
I omit the egg because I usually serve the soup as an appetizer and I prefer a clear one. If you want to add an egg, gradually stir in one beaten egg after step 3.

Hot and Sour Soup

As its name implies, this soup tastes hot (chilli paste) and sour (vinegar). The sharpness of ginger and saltiness of soy sauce also contribute to the soup's wonderful flavour. If you like a fiery hot soup, you will want to add more chilli paste to taste.

6	dried Chinese mushrooms	6
2¾ pts	chicken stock	1.5 L
4 oz	lean boneless pork, cut in thin 1 inch (2.5 cm) long strips	115 g
1 tbsp	grated root ginger	15 ml
3 oz	bamboo shoots, julienned	85 g
8 oz	diced firm tofu	225 g
3 tbsp	rice vinegar	45 ml
2 tbsp	sodium-reduced soy sauce	30 ml
1 tbsp	dark sesame oil	15 ml
1 tsp	chilli paste*	5 ml
2 tbsp	cornflour	30 ml
½ tsp	granulated sugar	2.5 ml
2	spring onions, thinly sliced	2

1. Soak dried mushrooms in enough warm water to cover for 15 minutes or until softened. Drain. Remove and discard stems; cut mushrooms into thin strips.

2. In a large saucepan, bring stock to boil. Add mushrooms, pork and ginger; simmer, covered, for 10 minutes. Add bamboo shoots and tofu.

3. In a small bowl, combine vinegar, soy sauce, oil and chilli paste; stir in cornflour and sugar until smooth. Stir into soup; bring to boil. Reduce heat and simmer, stirring, for 2 minutes.

4. Sprinkle each serving with spring onions. Makes 8 servings, about 6 fl oz (175 ml) each.

Make ahead
To end of step 3, cool, cover and refrigerate for up to two days.

PER SERVING	
calories	129
g protein	12
g total fat	6
g saturated fat	1
mg cholesterol	8
g carbohydrate	8
g dietary fibre	1
mg sodium	718
mg potassium	349
Good: Calcium	
Excellent: Iron	

* See Information on Ingredients, page 32.

Oriental Noodle and Chicken Soup

This light soup is a combination of Vietnamese and Thai cooking and is a nice way to start a dinner party, especially if some of the other dishes are Oriental. Make most of the soup a day or two in advance, then it's easy to assemble just before serving.

6	stalks fresh lemon grass*	6
1½ lb	chicken necks, backs, wings	675 g
5 tbsp	chopped root ginger	75 ml
3½ pts	water	2 L
5 oz	rice vermicelli or rice noodles	140 g
4 tbsp	bottled Thai fish sauce*	60 ml
2 tbsp	lime juice	30 ml
	pepper	
1 oz	fresh coriander leaves*	25 g
3	spring onions, chopped	3

1. Remove and discard top half of lemon grass stalk. Trim off outside leaves and roots; cut remaining stalk into ½-inch (1 cm) thick slices.

2. In large pot, simmer chicken, ginger, lemon grass and water, covered, for 45 minutes. Remove chicken from broth and let cool; remove meat from bones and shred. Strain broth and return to pot. Skim any fat from surface.

3. Cut rice vermicelli into about 3-inch (7.5 cm) pieces.

4. Bring broth to simmer and add fish sauce and lime juice; simmer for 2 minutes. Add rice vermicelli, shredded chicken, and pepper to taste; simmer for 1 minute.

5. Ladle into soup bowls; top each with coriander and onions. Makes 8 servings, about 6 fl oz (175 ml) each.

Make ahead
To end of step 3, cover and refrigerate for up to two days. Remove any fat from top of broth.

PER SERVING	
calories	145
g protein	10
g total fat	4
g saturated fat	1
mg cholesterol	31
g carbohydrate	17
g dietary fibre	1
mg sodium	280
mg potassium	128

* See Information on Ingredients, page 32.

Soy Sauce
Make your own sodium-
reduced soy sauce by mixing
regular naturally brewed soy
sauce with an equal amount of
water. It has just as much
flavour if not more than the
bottled sodium-reduced soy
sauce, and it's half the cost.

Miso
Miso, packed with protein and
taste, is a staple in Japanese
cooking. It is made from soya
beans and wheat, barley or
rice. It will keep refrigerated for
up to a year.

Miso Soup with Tofu

This Japanese light soup is from Heather Epp, a recipe tester at
Canadian Living magazine. Miso is delicious as a soup base paste,
and is available at health food stores in a wide variety of flavours.
Heather prefers a barley or brown rice miso for this soup. I used
a brown soya bean miso, and my family liked it.

1 tsp	sesame oil	5 ml
Half	onion, chopped	Half
1	large carrot, thinly sliced	1
26 fl oz	water	750 ml
2 tbsp	miso	30 ml
½ tsp	sodium-reduced soy sauce	7.5 ml
3	spring onions, diagonally sliced	3
3 oz	firm tofu, diced	85 g

1. In a saucepan, heat oil over medium heat; cook onion and
carrot, stirring occasionally, for 5 to 7 minutes or until tender.

2. Add water and bring to the boil; reduce heat and simmer for
3 minutes.

3. Remove from heat; stir in miso until dissolved. Add soy sauce,
spring onions and tofu. Serve hot. Makes 4 servings, about 6 fl oz
(175 ml) each.

Make ahead
Soup can be covered and refrigerated for up to two days; reheat
over medium heat but don't boil.

PER SERVING	
calories	78
g protein	5
g total fat	4
g saturated fat	1
mg cholesterol	0
g carbohydrate	8
g dietary fibre	2
mg sodium	458
mg potassium	163

Good: Calcium; Iron
Excellent: Vitamin A

Right:
Goat Cheese and Pesto Tortilla
Pizza (page 47)

What's in a Rice?

Brown and/or whole grain rice are the best choice nutritionally in terms of B vitamins, iron and fibre. Parboiled, or converted, rice sold as 'easy-cook' undergoes processing before the milling (which removes the bran layer), which forces the nutrients in the outer bran layer to the centre of the grain. They are a more nutritious choice than plain white rice.

It's a different story if you use flavoured rice mixes: they are often extremely high in sodium and call for added fats when cooking.

Three-Grain Vegetable Soup

This easy soup is economical, low calorie and packed with nutrients. You can use this recipe as a base and add a ham bone or a chicken carcass or other vegetables. I use whatever vegetables I have on hand, but always like to include swede, for it adds a great deal of flavour. I like to use a combination of grains and legumes, but you can use one or two to make a total of 3½ oz (100 g). Sometimes I add fresh herbs, such as basil, rosemary or dill, or sprinkle each serving with grated Parmesan cheese.

½ oz	soft margarine or butter	15 g
1	large onion, chopped	1
1 tbsp	crushed fresh garlic	15 ml
2¾ pts	chicken or vegetable stock	1.5 L
2 tbsp	each pearl barley, bulgur, brown rice and green lentils	30 ml
2	carrots, diced	2
12 oz	swede, diced	350 g
6 oz	cabbage, thinly sliced	175 g
2 tsp	dried basil	10 ml
4 tbsp	chopped fresh parsley	60 ml
	salt and pepper	

1. In a large saucepan, melt margarine over medium heat; cook onion until tender, about 5 minutes.

2. Add garlic, stock, barley, bulgur, rice, lentils, carrots and swede; bring to the boil. Reduce heat, cover and simmer for 30 minutes.

3. Add cabbage and basil; simmer for 10 to 15 minutes or until vegetables and grains are tender.

4. Add parsley, and salt and pepper to taste. Makes 6 servings, about 8 fl oz (225 ml) each.

Make ahead

Soup can be covered and refrigerated for up to two days; add parsley when reheating.

PER SERVING	
calories	152
g protein	8
g total fat	4
g saturated fat	1
mg cholesterol	0
g carbohydrate	22
g dietary fibre	5
mg sodium	833
mg potassium	567

Good: Vitamin C, Folate
Excellent: Vitamin A

Left:
Salmon Salad Fajitas (page 120)

Nutritional Note
The combination of rice and kidney beans provides a good source of protein.

Sodium-Restricted Diets
Nutrient analyses of recipes in this book are based on canned stock or stock made from a cube, because most people don't have time to make stocks. However, these products are high in sodium.

To reduce sodium, make your own meat or vegetable stock but don't add any salt. Flavour with bay leaves, parsley, thyme, peppercorns, celery, onion and carrots.

Red Bean and Rice Soup

This thick and warming soup will ward off any winter chills.

1 tbsp	vegetable oil	15 ml
1	onion, chopped	1
2	stalks celery, chopped	2
1	clove garlic, crushed	1
2 tbsp	plain flour	30 ml
18 fl oz	water	500 ml
12 fl oz	chicken or vegetable stock	350 ml
8 oz	chopped tomatoes (fresh or canned)	225 g
4 tbsp	long grain rice	60 ml
2 tsp	chilli powder	10 ml
¼ tsp	salt	1.25 ml
12 oz	cooked kidney beans (or 440 g can, drained)	350 g
1 tbsp	lemon juice	15 ml

1. In a large saucepan, heat oil over medium heat; cook onion, celery and garlic for 5 minutes or until softened. Sprinkle with flour; cook, stirring, for 1 minute.

2. Stir in water, stock, tomatoes, rice, chilli powder and salt; bring to the boil. Reduce heat, cover and simmer for 20 minutes.

3. Stir in beans and lemon juice; heat through. Makes 6 servings, about 8 fl oz (225 ml) each.

Make ahead
Soup can be covered and refrigerated for up to two days.

PER SERVING	
calories	162
g protein	8
g total fat	3
g saturated fat	0.3
mg cholesterol	0
g carbohydrate	26
g dietary fibre	7
mg sodium	522
mg potassium	376
Good: Folate	

Fresh Herbs
Instead of dried herbs in this soup, use 2 tbsp (30 ml) chopped fresh basil and 2 tsp (10 ml) fresh rosemary.

Italian Chick Pea and Pasta Soup

Any kind of cooked beans can be used instead of chick peas in this filling soup. For a thicker soup, purée ½ pt (300 ml) of the soup and stir back into soup.

1 tsp	olive oil	5 ml
1	onion, chopped	1
1 tbsp	crushed fresh garlic	15 ml
1	tomato, chopped	1
1 tbsp	tomato purée	15 ml
7 oz	cooked or canned chick peas	200 g
26 fl oz	chicken or vegetable stock	750 ml
3 oz	small pasta	85 g
1½ tsp	dried basil	7.5 ml
½ tsp	dried rosemary	2.5 ml
4 tbsp	chopped fresh parsley	60 ml
	salt and pepper	
4 tbsp	freshly grated Parmesan cheese	60 ml

1. In a large saucepan, heat oil over medium heat; cook onion and garlic until softened. Stir in tomato and tomato purée; cook for 1 minute.

2. Add chick peas and stock; bring to a boil. Add pasta, basil and rosemary; reduce heat and simmer, uncovered, for 10 to 15 minutes or until pasta is tender yet firm.

3. Add parsley, and salt and pepper to taste. Sprinkle each bowlful with Parmesan. Makes 4 servings, about ½ pt (300 ml) each.

Make ahead
Soup can be refrigerated for up to two days.

PER SERVING	
calories	233
g protein	13
g total fat	6
g saturated fat	2
mg cholesterol	5
g carbohydrate	33
g dietary fibre	2
mg sodium	806
mg potassium	478
Good: Iron	
Excellent: Folate	

Carrot and Corn Chowder

Hannah's Kitchen in Toronto is a favourite lunch spot for surrounding office staff. Here is one of their delicious soup recipes from co-owner Susan Hughes.

1 tsp	olive oil	5 ml
1	onion, chopped	1
1	leek (white part only), thinly sliced	1
12 fl oz	water or vegetable stock	350 ml
1	potato, peeled and diced	1
3	medium carrots, peeled and diced	3
1	sweet potato, peeled and diced	1
1 oz	coarsely chopped fresh parsley	25 g
2 tbsp	plain flour	30 ml
12 fl oz	skimmed milk	350 ml
8 oz	sweetcorn	225 g
	salt and pepper	
1 tbsp	fresh thyme (or 1 tsp/5 ml dried)	15 ml

1. In a large nonstick saucepan, heat oil over medium heat; cook onion and leek, stirring occasionally, for 5 to 10 minutes or until onions are tender. Add a little of the water if necessary to prevent sticking.

2. Add ½ pt (300 ml) of the water, potato, carrots, sweet potato and half of the parsley; cover and simmer until vegetables are tender, about 15 minutes.

3. Mix flour with remaining water; stir into soup.

4. Add milk; bring to a simmer, stirring. Add sweetcorn, and salt and pepper to taste.

5. Add thyme and remaining parsley; simmer for 1 minute. Makes 6 servings, about 6 fl oz (175 ml) each.

Make ahead
To end of step 4, cover and refrigerate for up to two days. Add thyme and parsley when reheating.

PER SERVING	
calories	143
g protein	5
g total fat	2
g saturated fat	1
mg cholesterol	5
g carbohydrate	28
g dietary fibre	3
mg sodium	67
mg potassium	405

Good: Folate
Excellent: Vitamin A

Seafood Vegetable Chowder
Follow recipe for Mariners'
Chowder, but instead of 1 lb
(450 g) fish fillets, substitute
8 oz (225 g) fish fillets and 4 oz
(115 g) each shucked clams
and shelled chopped scallops
or peeled prawns. Use any
liquid from clams plus water to
make 12 fl oz (350 ml).
Garnish with chopped fresh
dill or parsley.

Mariners' Chowder

This is an easy recipe to vary depending on what is in your
refrigerator. The potatoes are necessary because they thicken the
soup. However, the other vegetables add flavour and colour and
can be added to or omitted; add sweet peppers, green beans, or
other vegetables you have on hand.

1 tsp	olive oil	5 ml
1	onion, chopped	1
2	carrots, sliced	2
1	stalk celery, sliced	1
2	cloves garlic, chopped	2
3	potatoes, peeled and cubed	3
12 fl oz	water or fish stock	350 ml
1	small courgette, cubed	1
2½ oz	mushrooms, sliced	70 g
1 lb	sole, cod or haddock fillets (frozen or thawed), cut in chunks	450 g
6 oz	sweetcorn or frozen peas	175 g
¾ pt	semi-skimmed milk	425 ml
½ tsp	dried basil or dill (or 3 tbsp/45 ml chopped fresh)	2.5 ml
	salt and pepper	

1. In a heavy saucepan, heat oil over medium heat; cook onion
for 5 minutes or until softened.

2. Add carrots, celery, garlic, potatoes and water; bring to the
boil. Reduce heat, cover and simmer for 10 minutes. Add
courgette mushrooms, fish and sweetcorn; bring to a simmer.
Cook, covered, for 3 minutes, or until fish is opaque.

3. Add milk and basil; bring to a simmer over medium-low heat.
Season with salt and pepper to taste. Makes 4 servings, about
¾ pt (425 ml) each.

Make ahead
Soup can be covered and refrigerated for up to two days; reheat
gently.

PER SERVING	
calories	330
g protein	30
g total fat	5
g saturated fat	2
mg cholesterol	64
g carbohydrate	43
g dietary fibre	5
mg sodium	197
mg potassium	1255

Good: Folate, Calcium
Excellent: Vitamin A

Lamb

Because lamb has a stronger flavour than beef or poultry, it is particularly good for soups – a little meat will add a lot of flavour. You can use any cut of lamb, however you might as well use less expensive cuts such as shank or shoulder. If using shoulder, use about 1 lb (450 g) as there will be much less bone than in shank.

For fat-restricted diets, make a stock first: bring lamb shank, water, bay leaf and 1 chopped onion to the boil; simmer for 1 hour. Remove lamb and cut meat from bone; reserve. Refrigerate stock for 4 hours or overnight; skim all fat from top. Reheat stock; add remaining onion and continue as in recipe.

PER SERVING	
calories	156
g protein	12
g total fat	3
g saturated fat	1
mg cholesterol	38
g carbohydrate	19
g dietary fibre	4
mg sodium	129
mg potassium	422
Excellent: Vitamin A	

Hearty Scotch Broth

In the winter, I like to serve this hearty soup for supper along with some fresh bread and a salad. It's very handy to have in the refrigerator for those rushed weekday dinners. It's best to make the soup in advance – not only does the flavour improve but when it is cool, you can remove any fat that hardens on top.

8 oz	chopped cooked lamb or 1½ lb (675 g) lamb shanks	225 g
3½ pts	water	2 L
1	bay leaf	1
2	medium onions, chopped	2
2	stalks celery, diced	2
2	medium potatoes, peeled and diced	2
4 tbsp	pearl barley	60 ml
8 oz	swede, diced	225 g
6 oz	cabbage, chopped	175 g
2	medium carrots, grated	2
1 oz	chopped fresh parsley	25 g
¼ tsp	each salt and pepper	1.25 ml

1. In a large pan, combine lamb, water, bay leaf and onions; bring to the boil. Cover, reduce heat and simmer for 1 hour. (If using cooked meat, simmer until onion is tender.) Skim fat from top.

2. Add celery, potatoes, barley and swede; simmer for 15 minutes.

3. Add cabbage and carrots; simmer until vegetables are tender, about 10 minutes.

4. Remove lamb shank; cut meat from bones and return to soup. Discard bay leaf. Add parsley, salt and pepper. Makes 8 servings, about 8 fl oz (225 ml) each.

Make ahead

Soup can be covered and refrigerated for up to two days; skim off any fat; add parsley when reheating.

Salads

Light Tuna Salad
in Tomatoes

Warm Scallop Salad

Chick Pea, Sweet Pepper
and Fresh Basil Salad

Mediterranean Lentil and
Bean Salad

Bulgur Salad with
Cucumber and Feta

Easy Couscous Vegetable
Salad

Asparagus and Mushroom
Salad

Green Bean Salad with
Buttermilk Dressing

Salade Composée

Thai Cucumber Salad

Oriental Coleslaw

Purple Vegetable Slaw

Warm Potato and Tuna
Salad

Tossed Green Salad with
Asian Vinaigrette

Tomato Basil Dressing

Yogurt Herb Dressing

Mustard Garlic Vinaigrette

Tuna Salad Platter
On individual plates, arrange lettuce leaf, grated carrot, sliced cucumber, and drained canned chick peas tossed with lemon juice, parsley and pepper. Place a Light Tuna Salad in Tomato in the centre of each plate.

Light Tuna Salad in Tomatoes

This is a light mixed version of something my mother used to make in the summer for lunch or as part of a hors d'oeuvre at dinner. It's very handy when the refrigerator is bare but the cupboard has a can of tuna on the shelf. Coarsely chopped olives or capers are also good in this. Be sure to buy tuna packed in water.

I	can (6½ oz/184 g) water-packed tuna, drained	1
2	spring onions, chopped	2
1	stalk celery, diced	1
3 oz	sweetcorn	85 g
2 tbsp	light mayonnaise	30 ml
2 tbsp	low-fat yogurt	30 ml
2 tbsp	each chopped fresh coriander and parsley	30 ml
2 tsp	lemon juice	10 ml
	pepper	
3	tomatoes	3

1. Combine tuna, onions, celery, corn, mayonnaise, yogurt, coriander, parsley, lemon juice, and pepper to taste; mix well.

2. Quarter tomatoes, cutting almost but not completely through to bottom. Spoon tuna mixture into centre. Makes 3 servings.

Make ahead
To end of step 1, cover and refrigerate for up to 24 hours.

PER SERVING	
calories	161
g protein	17
g total fat	4
g saturated fat	1
mg cholesterol	9
g carbohydrate	16
g dietary fibre	3
mg sodium	368
mg potassium	611
Excellent: Vitamin C, Folate	

Tuna Types			
Compare tuna:	Calories	Fat (g)	Sodium (mg)
Packed in oil, drained	157	7	334
Packed in water, drained	115	2	331

Rocket
Rocket is an oak-leaf-shaped salad green with a delicious nutty, peppery taste.
If unavailable substitute watercress in this recipe.

Tip
If using frozen scallops, be sure they are completely thawed before using in this recipe.

Warm Scallop Salad

My friend Donna Osler serves this fabulous salad as a first course at dinner parties. It's a good choice: not only does it taste delicious but it serves as both a fish course and a salad.

1	bunch rocket	1
8 oz	torn mixed salad leaves	225 g
2 tsp	vegetable oil	10 ml
1 tbsp	grated root ginger	15 ml
1	clove garlic, crushed	1
4 tbsp	diced sweet red pepper	60 ml
1 lb	large scallops	450 g
4 tbsp	dry sherry	60 ml
4 tbsp	chopped fresh coriander	60 ml
Vinaigrette		
2 tbsp	sesame oil	30 ml
1	clove garlic, crushed	1
1 tbsp	lemon juice	15 ml
1 tsp	sodium-reduced soy sauce	5 ml
¼ tsp	granulated sugar	1.25 ml

1. Vinaigrette: In a large bowl, mix oil, garlic, lemon juice, soy sauce and sugar; add rocket and salad leaves and toss well. Divide among plates.

2. In a frying pan, heat oil over medium heat; cook ginger, garlic and red pepper, stirring, for 2 minutes.

3. Add scallops, sherry and coriander; cover and cook for 3 minutes or until scallops are opaque through to centre, turning once. Using slotted spoon, divide scallops among plates.

4. Increase heat to high and cook until pan liquid is reduced slightly; drizzle over salads. Makes 6 appetizer or 3 main-course servings.

Make ahead
Prepare vinaigrette. Measure out all ingredients up to one day in advance.

PER SERVING (APPETIZER)	
calories	153
g protein	15
g total fat	7
g saturated fat	1
mg cholesterol	25
g carbohydrate	6
g dietary fibre	1
mg sodium	178
mg potassium	617

Good: Vitamin C
Excellent: Vitamin A, Folate

Dried Chick Peas
For the best texture, flavour and lowest cost, cook your own chick peas: Soak dried chick peas overnight or for a minimum of 4 hours. Or quick-soak chick peas by covering with water and bringing to the boil; boil 2 minutes. Remove from heat, cover and let stand for 1 hour; drain.

To cook soaked chick peas, cover with water and bring to the boil; reduce heat, partially cover and simmer for 2 to 2½ hours or until tender. Add more water if necessary. Do not add salt until beans are tender or they will take even longer to cook.

- 8 oz (225 g) dried = about 1 lb (450 g) cooked.

Chick Pea, Sweet Pepper and Fresh Basil Salad

This salad tastes best if made a few hours (or even a day) in advance to allow the flavours to develop and blend. If you don't have time to roast the red pepper, you can use a raw sweet red pepper or a canned red pepper. Cannellini beans instead of chick peas makes a tasty variation.

1	sweet red pepper	1
1	can (440 g) chick peas, drained	1
Half	medium cucumber, diced	Half
4 tbsp	red onion, finely chopped	60 ml
4 tbsp	chopped fresh parsley	60 ml
4 tbsp	chopped fresh basil	60 ml
4 tbsp	lemon juice	60 ml
1 tbsp	olive oil	15 ml
1	clove garlic, crushed	1
	salt and pepper	

1. Roast red pepper under grill or over gas flame for 15 minutes, turning often, or in 400°F (200°C) Gas Mark 6 oven for 40 minutes, or until blackened and soft. Peel and seed pepper; chop coarsely.

2. In a bowl, combine red pepper, chick peas, cucumber, onion, parsley and basil.

3. In a small dish, whisk together lemon juice, olive oil, garlic and salt and pepper to taste; pour over salad and toss lightly. Cover and refrigerate for at least 15 minutes or up to 1 day. Makes 8 servings.

Make ahead
Salad can be covered and refrigerated for up to one day.

PER SERVING	
calories	88
g protein	4
g total fat	3
g saturated fat	0.3
mg cholesterol	0
g carbohydrate	13
g dietary fibre	2
mg sodium	105
mg potassium	138
Good: Folate	
Excellent: Vitamin C	

Summer Salad Supper
Arrange Mediterranean Lentil and Bean Salad, sliced cucumbers, melon wedges and lean ham slices on each plate.

Balsamic Vinegar
Balsamic vinegar has a mellow, sweet taste. If unavailable, substitute 3 tbsp (45 ml) red wine vinegar mixed with 1 tsp (5 ml) granulated sugar in this Mediterranean Salad.

Mediterranean Lentil and Bean Salad

Cook extra red peppers when barbecuing one night to use in this recipe. In the winter, use canned or bottled sweet (not hot) red peppers; however, they won't have the smoky flavour of home-roasted ones. Use canned cannellini beans or haricot beans.

3	sweet red peppers	3
1	can (440 g) brown lentils, soaked overnight	1
1	can (440 g) drained white beans	1
2	celery, diced	2
4 tbsp	each chopped fresh basil and parsley	60 ml
4 tbsp	balsamic vinegar	60 ml
	salt and pepper	

1. Roast red peppers under grill or over a gas flame for 15 minutes, turning often, or in 400°F (200°C) Gas Mark 6 oven for 40 minutes, or until peppers are soft and blackened. Peel and seed peppers; cut into strips.

2. Drain and rinse beans and lentils.

3. In a bowl, combine red peppers, beans, lentils, celery, basil and parsley; toss with vinegar. Season with salt and pepper to taste. Makes 8 servings.

Make ahead
Salad can be covered and refrigerated for up to three days.

PER SERVING	
calories	138
g protein	9
g total fat	1
g saturated fat	0.1
mg cholesterol	0
g carbohydrate	26
g dietary fibre	7
mg sodium	224
mg potassium	438

Good: Vitamin A, Iron
Excellent: Vitamin C, Folate

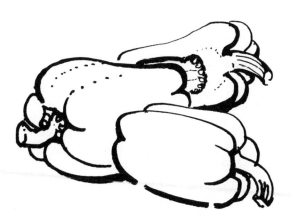

Tomatoes Stuffed with Bulgur Salad
Serve for lunch or as part of a mixed hors d'oeuvre:
Cut tomatoes in half; scoop out seeds and some pulp.
Fill hollow with Bulgur Salad.

Buying Bulgur
Bulgur comes in coarse, medium or fine grind. Medium is best for salads and mixed vegetable dishes. Coarse is often used in pilafs, and fine grind is used in breads.

Bulgur Salad with Cucumber and Feta

This salad is good any time of year for packed lunches, a buffet or with barbecued chicken, meat or fish.

5 oz	bulgur*	150 g
1	medium cucumber, diced	1
2 oz	fresh parsley, chopped	55 g
Half	red onion, finely chopped	Half
2 oz	feta cheese, crumbled	55 g
Dressing		
2	cloves garlic, chopped	2
4 tbsp	lemon juice	60 ml
½ tsp	salt	2.5 ml
4 tbsp	olive oil	60 ml
	pepper	

1. Soak bulgur in 2¾ pts (1.5 L) hot water for 1 hour; drain.

2. In a bowl, combine bulgur, cucumber, parsley, onion and feta.

3. Dressing: In a small bowl, combine garlic, lemon juice and salt; gradually whisk in oil. Season with pepper to taste.

4. Pour over salad; stir to mix. Makes 12 servings.

Make ahead
Salad can be covered and refrigerated for up to two days.

PER SERVING	
calories	101
g protein	3
g total fat	6
g saturated fat	1
mg cholesterol	5
g carbohydrate	11
g dietary fibre	3
mg sodium	159
mg potassium	106

* If you cannot find bulgur and want to use cracked wheat instead, follow package instructions for cooking cracked wheat.

Rice Vegetable Salad
Follow recipe for Easy
Couscous Vegetable Salad
except cook 3 oz (85 g) rice in
8 fl oz (225 ml) boiling water
for 20 minutes or according to
package directions. If using
leftover cooked rice, use about
14 fl oz (400 g).

**Couscous, Tomato and
Basil Salad**
Follow recipe for Easy
Couscous Vegetable Salad,
omitting carrot, sunflower
seeds and cumin.
Add 1 chopped large tomato
and 4 tbsp (60 ml) or more to
taste of chopped fresh basil.

Easy Couscous Vegetable Salad

Couscous is fast to prepare and much cheaper bought in bulk than
by the box. For an appetizing summer lunch, serve with leafy
greens, sliced tomato and a piece of low-fat cheese or lean meat
or hard-boiled egg.

6 fl oz	water	175 ml
3 oz	couscous	85 g
1	celery stalk, chopped	1
1	spring onion, chopped	1
1	medium carrot, grated	1
4 oz	cucumber, diced	115 g
4 tbsp	chopped fresh parsley	60 ml
2 tbsp	sunflower seeds	30 ml
Lemon Cumin Vinaigrette		
2 tbsp	lemon juice	30 ml
1 tbsp	each olive oil and water	15 ml
¼ tsp	ground cumin	1.25 ml
	salt and pepper	

1. In a saucepan, bring water to the boil; add couscous, cover
and remove from heat. Let stand for 5 minutes; fluff with a fork.

2. In a salad bowl, combine couscous, celery, spring onion,
carrot, cucumber, parsley and sunflower seeds.

3. Lemon Cumin Vinaigrette: Whisk together lemon juice, oil,
water, cumin, and salt and pepper to taste; pour over salad and
toss. Makes 4 servings.

Make ahead
Salad can be covered and refrigerated for up to two days.

PER SERVING	
calories	159
g protein	5
g total fat	6
g saturated fat	1
mg cholesterol	0
g carbohydrate	23
g dietary fibre	3
mg sodium	25
mg potassium	239
Good: Folate	
Excellent: Vitamin A	

Green Bean and Mushroom Salad
Substitute green beans for asparagus.

Asparagus and Mushroom Salad

I like this salad for summer barbecues and buffets because it goes with anything, tastes delicious and is easy to make.

1 lb	asparagus	450 g
3	mushrooms, diced	3
Sesame Vinaigrette		
1 tbsp	rice vinegar or white wine vinegar	15 ml
1 tbsp	sodium-reduced soy sauce	15 ml
1 tbsp	sesame oil	15 ml
¼ tsp	granulated sugar	1.25 ml
	salt and pepper	
1 tbsp	toasted sesame seeds*	15 ml

1. Cut or break off tough stem ends of asparagus. Peel stalks if large. In a large pan of boiling water, cook asparagus until tender-crisp, about 4 minutes; drain. Cool under cold water; drain. Dry on paper towels.

2. Sesame Vinaigrette: Whisk together vinegar, soy sauce, sesame oil and sugar.

3. Arrange asparagus on a serving platter; pour vinaigrette over. Add salt and pepper to taste; roll to coat. Sprinkle with sesame seeds and mushrooms. Makes 6 servings.

Make ahead
To end of step 2 for up to 24 hours. Cover asparagus with damp paper towel or plastic wrap and refrigerate. To end of step 3 up to one hour before serving.

PER SERVING	
calories	51
g protein	3
g total fat	3
g saturated fat	1
mg cholesterol	0
g carbohydrate	4
g dietary fibre	1
mg sodium	89
mg potassium	159
Excellent: Folate	

* Toast sesame seeds in nonstick frying pan over medium heat for 3 minutes or until golden.

Green Bean Salad with Buttermilk Dressing

The idea for this salad came from Babette's Feast, a unique catering group in Toronto.

1 lb	green beans, trimmed	450 g
2 oz	fresh parsley, coarsely chopped	55 g
Half	red onion, thinly sliced	Half
1	sweet yellow pepper, thinly sliced	1
3	rashers streaky bacon, cooked and crumbled	3
4 fl oz	Buttermilk Dill Dressing (margin, page 87)	125 ml

1. In a large pan of boiling water, cook beans for 1 minute; drain and rinse under cold water. Drain and pat dry.

2. In a salad bowl, toss together beans, parsley, onion, yellow pepper and bacon.

3. Add dressing and toss. Makes 6 servings.

Make ahead
To end of step 2, cover and refrigerate for up to 24 hours; add dressing up to one hour before serving.

PER SERVING	
calories	78
g protein	3
g total fat	4
g saturated fat	1
mg cholesterol	3
g carbohydrate	9
g dietary fibre	3
mg sodium	172
mg potassium	343

Good: Folate
Excellent: Vitamin C

To Cook Beetroot
Trim stems 1 inch (2.5 cm) from bulb. Cook in a saucepan of boiling water for about 40 minutes or until fork-tender. Drain; rinse under cold running water and slip off skins.

To Cook Potatoes
Cook whole potatoes in a saucepan of boiling water for 20 minutes or until fork-tender; drain. Shake pan over medium heat for about 1 minute to dry potatoes.

Salade Composée

This salad reminds me of our bicycling holidays in France because it is on every French summer menu and was my favourite lunch. I try to cook extra beetroot and potatoes to have on hand for this easy meal. Grated celeriac, sliced cucumber and any cold meat or fish can be added.

	lettuce leaves	
4	medium beetroot, cooked and sliced (about ¾ lb/350 g)	4
4 fl oz	Mustard Garlic Vinaigrette (page 88)	125 ml
8	small new red potatoes (unpeeled), cooked and sliced	8
4	medium carrots, peeled and grated	4
6 oz	cooked or canned sweetcorn	175 g
1	can (440 g) chick peas, drained	1
4 tbsp	chopped fresh parsley	60 ml
2 tsp	ground cumin	10 ml
2 tbsp	balsamic vinegar	30 ml
4	slices smoked turkey (4 oz/115 g)	4

1. Line 4 plates with lettuce.

2. In a small bowl, toss beetroot with 2 tbsp (30 ml) of the dressing; divide among plates. Repeat with potatoes, carrots and corn, arranging attractively on plates.

3. Toss chick peas with parsley, cumin and vinegar; divide among plates.

4. Roll turkey and divide among plates. Makes 4 servings.

Make ahead
Salad can be covered and refrigerated for up to 30 minutes.

PER SERVING	
calories	382
g protein	17
g total fat	13
g saturated fat	2
mg cholesterol	21
g carbohydrate	53
g dietary fibre	8
mg sodium	503
mg potassium	788

Good: Vitamin C
Excellent: Vitamin A, Folate, Iron

Thai Cucumber Salad

This light, tangy salad, from my friend and cookbook author Rose
Murray, is perfect with grilled meats, poultry, fish or as part of an
Oriental meal. For a special meal, garnish with tiny prawns.

1	cucumber	1
4 tbsp	chopped fresh coriander	60 ml
4 tbsp	lime juice	60 ml
2 tbsp	red onion, finely chopped	30 ml
2 tbsp	rice vinegar or cider vinegar	30 ml
1 tsp	granulated sugar	5 ml
¼ tsp	red pepper flakes*	1.25 ml
	round lettuce leaves (optional)	
	chopped peanuts (optional)	

1. Cut cucumber in half lengthwise. By hand or using a food
processor, cut into thin slices.

2. In a bowl, combine coriander, lime juice, onion, vinegar, sugar
and red pepper flakes, stirring to dissolve sugar.

3. Add cucumber and toss gently. Cover and refrigerate for
4 hours.

4. Line individual salad plates or a serving platter with lettuce
leaves (if using). Spoon cucumber mixture in centre; sprinkle with
peanuts (if using). Makes 6 servings.

Make ahead
To end of step 3, cover and refrigerate for up to one day.

PER SERVING	
calories	16
g protein	1
g total fat	0.1
g saturated fat	0
mg cholesterol	0
g carbohydrate	4
g dietary fibre	1
mg sodium	2
mg potassium	129

* You could use 1 small fresh hot pepper, such as a jalapeño or serrano
chilli, seeded and cut into thin strips, or Thai chilli paste instead of red
pepper flakes.

Oriental Coleslaw

My sister-in-law Linda Elliott made this salad for a family dinner using a combination of red and green cabbage. I sometimes use Chinese cabbage instead.

1 oz	flaked almonds	25 g
1 oz	sunflower seeds	25 g
2 tbsp	sesame seeds	30 ml
1 lb	cabbage, thinly sliced (green, red or Chinese leaves)	450 g
6 oz	bean sprouts	175 g
4	spring onions, chopped	4
1	pkg (85 g) dried Oriental soup noodles, crushed*	1

Dressing

4 tbsp	cider vinegar or rice vinegar	60 ml
2 tbsp	granulated sugar	30 ml
2 tbsp	sodium-reduced soy sauce	30 ml
2 tbsp	sesame oil	30 ml
	pepper	

1. Spread almonds, sunflower and sesame seeds on a baking sheet; bake at 350°F (180°C) Gas Mark 4 for 5 minutes. Let cool.

2. In a bowl, combine cabbage, bean sprouts, onions and noodles.

3. Dressing: In a small bowl, combine vinegar, sugar, soy sauce and water; whisk in oil. Add pepper to taste.

4. Toss toasted nuts and dressing with cabbage mixture. Cover and refrigerate for at least 1 hour. Makes 12 servings.

Make ahead
Salad can be covered and refrigerated for up to one day.

PER SERVING	
calories	114
g protein	4
g total fat	6
g saturated fat	1
mg cholesterol	7
g carbohydrate	12
g dietary fibre	2
mg sodium	92
mg potassium	206
Good: Vitamin C, Folate	

* If soup noodles are unavailable, add about 4 oz (115 g) cooked thin noodles, cut in 2-inch (5 cm) pieces.

Coriander

Fresh coriander has a wonderful, distinct flavour. Don't confuse it with coriander seeds or ground coriander, which are totally different. If you can't find fresh coriander leaves, substitute 5 tbsp (75 ml) chopped fresh parsley and 1 tsp (5 ml) dried coriander leaves.

Purple Vegetable Slaw

This salad (pictured opposite page 160) is fabulous to serve with any grilled meats or with Marinated Baked Tofu (page 183), or with soup for a light meal.

5 oz	red cabbage, finely shredded	140 g
	salt	
3½ oz	cooked or canned red kidney beans, drained and rinsed	100 g
3 oz	sweetcorn kernels	85 g
5 tbsp	chopped fresh coriander	75 ml
1	tomato, diced	1
1	spring onion, chopped	1
2 tbsp	balsamic or red wine vinegar	30 ml
1 tbsp	sesame oil	15 ml
¼ tsp	red pepper flakes	1.25 ml
1	clove garlic, finely chopped	1
	pepper	

1. Sprinkle cabbage with ¼ tsp (1.25 ml) salt; set aside.

2. In a bowl, combine kidney beans, corn, coriander, tomato, spring onion, vinegar, oil, red pepper flakes and garlic; mix well.

3. Add cabbage, and salt and pepper to taste. Makes 4 servings.

Make ahead
Salad can be covered and refrigerated for up to 24 hours.

PER SERVING	
calories	92
g protein	3
g total fat	4
g saturated fat	1
mg cholesterol	0
g carbohydrate	13
g dietary fibre	4
mg sodium	223
mg potassium	299
Good: Vitamin C, Folate	

Warm Potato Salad
As a salad accompaniment omit tuna; green beans and red pepper are optional.

Cooking Tips
Don't peel the potatoes; the red skins are attractive and contain fibre and nutrients. To save time, cut the potatoes into ¾-inch (2 cm) pieces so they will cook faster.

To refrigerate salad for up to 24 hours, cook green beans separately; remove from refrigerator 30 minutes before serving and add green beans.

Nutritional Note
To reduce sodium in this salad, use fresh cooked tuna and omit anchovy paste.

Warm Potato and Tuna Salad

This salad is a meal in itself to serve on lettuce leaves with fresh bread and sliced tomatoes or perhaps a bowl of soup.

2 lb	new red potatoes, cut into chunks	900 g
½ lb	green beans, halved	225 g
4	spring onions, chopped	4
2	stalks celery, chopped	2
1	sweet red pepper, chopped (optional)	1
4 tbsp	coarsely chopped fresh parsley	60 ml
1	can (6½ oz/184 g) water-packed tuna, drained and broken into chunks	1
	salt	
Dressing		
3 tbsp	tarragon or cider vinegar	45 ml
2 tbsp	water	30 ml
1 tbsp	Dijon mustard	15 ml
1 tbsp	anchovy paste	15 ml
4 tsp	olive oil	20 ml
1	clove garlic, finely chopped	1
	pepper	

1. In a saucepan, cover potatoes with water; bring to the boil. Reduce heat and simmer until nearly tender, about 5 minutes. Add green beans; cook for 3 to 5 minutes or until tender-crisp; drain.

2. Dressing: Whisk together vinegar, water, mustard, anchovy paste, oil, garlic, and pepper to taste; toss 4 tbsp (60 ml) with hot potato mixture.

3. Add spring onions, celery, red pepper (if using) and parsley. Add remaining dressing and toss.

4. Gently stir in tuna, without breaking up chunks. Add salt and pepper to taste. Makes 4 main-course servings.

Make ahead
Salad can be covered and refrigerated for up to four hours.

PER SERVING	
calories	291
g protein	17
g total fat	6
g saturated fat	1
mg cholesterol	9
g carbohydrate	45
g dietary fibre	5
mg sodium	321
mg potassium	1152
Excellent: Vitamin C, Folate, Iron	

Light Salads
Be careful: salads aren't light if they're drowned in high-fat dressings.

There's a good selection of calorie-reduced or fat-free dressings available – I counted 26 in one supermarket. Be sure to read the nutrition information on the labels: choose the salad dressings with 3 g of fat or less per 1 tbsp (15 ml).

Better yet, mix your own flavourful low-fat salad dressings. They take only minutes to make, taste fresher and are about one-third of the cost of store-bought ones. The secret is adding extra herbs, mustard, garlic or other seasonings for flavour and replacing some of the oil in a traditional dressing with water, buttermilk, low-fat yogurt or juicy tomatoes.

Tossed Green Salad with Asian Vinaigrette

Use any combination of colourful seasonal greens in this tossed salad; here is just a suggestion.

3 handfuls	each torn round lettuce, radicchio, watercress and spinach	3 handfuls

Asian Vinaigrette

4 tbsp	rice vinegar	60 ml
2 tbsp	water	30 ml
2 tbsp	sesame oil	30 ml
2 tbsp	sodium-reduced soy sauce	30 ml
½ tsp	granulated sugar	2.5 ml
1	clove garlic, finely chopped	1
1	spring onion, finely chopped	1

1. In a large salad bowl, combine lettuce, radicchio, watercress and spinach.

2. Asian Vinaigrette: Whisk together vinegar, water, sesame oil, soy sauce, sugar, garlic and onion. Pour half over salad; toss to mix. Add more dressing if desired. Makes 8 servings.

Make ahead
Prepare salad leaves; wrap in towels, place in plastic bag and refrigerate for up to eight hours. Vinaigrette will keep, covered and refrigerated, for up to three days.

PER SERVING	
calories	30
g protein	2
g total fat	2
g saturated fat	0.3
mg cholesterol	0
g carbohydrate	3
g dietary fibre	1
mg sodium	87
mg potassium	268

Good: Vitamin A
Excellent: Folate

Basil
Basil is one of the easiest herbs to grow. I plant some in the garden and more in a pot. I take a pot when I go to the cottage (my husband groans at another thing to pack into an already filled car). In the autumn, I bring the pots indoors and have fresh basil for another few months.

Tomato Basil Dressing

For a starter salad, spoon this dressing over a mixture of lettuces arranged on individual plates. Or toss with a pasta salad.

8 oz	tomatoes, finely chopped	225 g
4 tbsp	chopped fresh basil	60 ml
1	clove garlic, finely chopped	1
2 tbsp	chopped spring onion	30 ml
2 tbsp	olive oil	30 ml
2 tbsp	lemon juice or balsamic vinegar	30 ml
½ tsp	granulated sugar	2.5 ml
¼ tsp	each salt and pepper	1.25 ml

1. In a small bowl, combine tomatoes, basil, garlic, onion, oil, lemon juice, sugar, salt and pepper. Let stand for at least 15 minutes. Makes 8 fl oz (225 ml).

Make ahead
Dressing can be covered and refrigerated for up to one day.

PER SERVING	1 tbsp / 15 ml
calories	19
g protein	0.1
g total fat	2
g saturated fat	0.2
mg cholesterol	0
g carbohydrate	1
g dietary fibre	0.2
mg sodium	37
mg potassium	34

**Potato Salad with
Yogurt Herb Dressing**
Lightly mix 12 oz (350 g)
cooked cubed potatoes with
4 tbsp (60 ml) Yogurt Herb
Dressing. Add sliced radishes
to taste.

Buttermilk Dill Dressing
Prepare Yogurt Herb Dressing
except substitute 8 fl oz (225
ml) buttermilk for the yogurt.

Yogurt Herb Dressing

Use this creamy dressing for pasta salads, green salads and potato salad.

8 fl oz	low-fat yogurt	225 ml
4 fl oz	light mayonnaise	125 ml
5 tbsp	chopped fresh parsley	75 ml
5 tbsp	chopped fresh dill*	75 ml
1	clove garlic, crushed	1
1 tbsp	lemon juice	15 ml
1 tsp	Dijon mustard	5 ml
½ tsp	salt	2.5 ml
	pepper	

1. In a bowl or large measuring jug, combine yogurt, mayonnaise, parsley, dill, garlic, lemon juice, mustard, salt, and pepper to taste. Using a whisk or fork, mix well. Makes 14 fl oz (400 ml).

Make ahead
Dressing can be covered and refrigerated for up to one week.

PER SERVING	1 tbsp/15 ml
calories	20
g protein	1
g total fat	2
g saturated fat	0.2
mg cholesterol	1
g carbohydrate	1
g dietary fibre	0
mg sodium	82
mg potassium	30

* If fresh dill isn't available, substitute ½ tsp (2.5 ml) dried dill.

Pasta Salads
For pasta salads, see pages 160 to 164.

Mustard Garlic Vinaigrette

This is a good all-purpose vinaigrette.

2 tbsp	cider vinegar or white wine vinegar	30 ml
1 tbsp	Dijon mustard	15 ml
½ tsp	granulated sugar	2.5 ml
1	clove garlic, finely chopped	1
5 tbsp	water	75 ml
5 tbsp	olive oil	75 ml
2 tsp	freshly grated Parmesan cheese	10 ml
	salt and pepper	

1. In a small bowl, mix together vinegar, mustard, sugar, garlic and water; gradually whisk in oil. Stir in Parmesan.

2. Season with salt and pepper to taste. Makes about 8 fl oz (225 ml).

Make ahead
Vinaigrette can be covered and refrigerated for up to one week.

PER SERVING	1 tbsp/15 ml
calories	43
g protein	0.2
g total fat	5
g saturated fat	1
mg cholesterol	0
g carbohydrate	0.4
g dietary fibre	0
mg sodium	18
mg potassium	4

Poultry

Chinese Chicken Burgers

Grilled Chicken Breast Burgers with Sautéed Onions and Sun-Dried Tomatoes

Jamaican Jerk Chicken

Herb and Buttermilk Barbecued Chicken

Sherry Chicken Breasts Stuffed with Courgettes and Carrots

Hoisin Sesame Chicken Platter

Chicken and Mange Tout in Black Bean Sauce

Asian Chicken

Asian Sauce

Barbecued Curried Chicken Breasts

Chicken and Vegetable Stew with Parsley Dumplings

Turkey Vegetable Casserole

Roast Turkey with Sausage, Apple and Herb Stuffing

Sausage, Apple and Herb Stuffing

Giblet Gravy

Lemon Pepper Turkey Loaf

Thai Barbecued Turkey Escalopes

Chinese Chicken Burgers

Serve these juicy, delicious burgers in a bun with sliced tomato and lettuce, or as patties along with stir-fried bok choy and rice or Oven-Baked Fries (page 143).

1 lb	lean minced chicken	450 g
1	egg (or 2 egg whites)	1
2	spring onions, chopped	2
1 tbsp	sodium-reduced soy sauce	15 ml
1 tbsp	cornflour	15 ml
2 tsp	root ginger, grated	10 ml
2	cloves garlic, crushed	2
1 tbsp	chopped fresh coriander or parsley	15 ml
	pepper	

1. In a bowl, combine chicken, egg, onions, soy sauce, cornflour, ginger, garlic, coriander, and pepper to taste; mix gently.

2. Form into 4 patties (mixture will be moist) about ½-inch (1 cm) thick.

3. Grill on greased grill rack or baking sheet for 6 minutes or until browned on top; turn and grill for 2 to 3 minutes or until no longer pink inside. Makes 4 servings.

Make ahead
To end of step 2, cover and refrigerate for up to four hours.

PER SERVING	
calories	191
g protein	23
g total fat	9
g saturated fat	2
mg cholesterol	125
g carbohydrate	4
g dietary fibre	0.3
mg sodium	210
mg potassium	245

Grilled Chicken Breast Burgers with Sautéed Onions and Sun-Dried Tomatoes

The idea for this came from Browne's Bistro in Toronto, where they serve the most wonderful grilled chicken sandwich with a sun-dried tomato pesto and sautéed onions. Serve with coleslaw or a tossed salad.

½ oz	soft margarine or butter	15 g
1½ lb	Spanish onions, sliced	675 g
4 tbsp	chopped dry-packed sun-dried tomatoes	60 ml
1	large clove garlic, crushed	1
	water	
4	boneless skinless chicken breasts (about 1 lb/450 g)	4
4	wholemeal baps or burger buns	4

1. In a large nonstick frying pan, melt margarine over medium heat; cook onions, stirring occasionally, for 10 minutes or until tender.

2. Add tomatoes, garlic and 1 tbsp (15 ml) water; cook for 5 minutes, adding another tablespoon (15 ml) water if needed to prevent sticking.

3. Meanwhile, place chicken on a greased grill rack under medium heat or over coals on a barbecue; for about 4 minutes on each side or until no longer pink inside.

4. Toast baps. Spoon some of the onion mixture over bottom halves. Top with chicken, then remaining onion mixture and tops. Makes 4 servings.

Make ahead
To end of step 2, cover and refrigerate for up to one day; reheat to serve.

PER SERVING	
calories	378
g protein	35
g total fat	6
g saturated fat	1
mg cholesterol	73
g carbohydrate	48
g dietary fibre	6
mg sodium	527
mg potassium	762

Good: Iron
Excellent: Folate

Jerk
The term jerk refers to a traditional method of preserving meats: cutting them into strips and drying them in the sun. I use fresh chicken in this recipe.

Low Sodium
For a sodium-restricted diet, omit soy sauce and salt. Sodium will then be 122 mg/serving.

Jamaican Jerk Chicken

This fabulous spicy sauce is traditionally cooked with dried meats in a large pot over an open fire. It is absolutely delicious with chicken or roast pork. I prefer to use a jalapeño pepper instead of the traditional Scotch bonnet or Rocotillo pepper because the jalapeño is not as hot.

1	onion, quartered	1
1	Scotch bonnet* or hot pepper, halved	1
3	cloves garlic, halved	3
4	spring onions, coarsely chopped	4
4 tbsp	orange juice	60 ml
3 tbsp	soy sauce	45 ml
1 tbsp	vegetable oil	15 ml
1 tbsp	wine vinegar	15 ml
1 tsp	each dried thyme and ground allspice	5 ml
¼ tsp	each cinnamon, curry powder, salt and pepper	1.25 ml
2 lb	skinless chicken pieces	900 g

1. In food processor, purée onion, hot pepper, garlic and spring onions. Add orange juice, soy sauce, oil, vinegar, thyme, allspice, cinnamon, curry powder, salt and pepper; process to mix.

2. Pour marinade over chicken pieces; cover and refrigerate for 2 hours, turning occasionally.

3. Grill or barbecue over high heat for about 20 minutes on each side, or bake at 325°F (160°C) Gas Mark 3 for 40 minutes, or until no longer pink inside. Makes 4 servings.

Make ahead
To end of step 2 for up to two days.

PER SERVING	
calories	256
g protein	32
g total fat	8
g saturated fat	1
mg cholesterol	95
g carbohydrate	15
g dietary fibre	3
mg sodium	750
mg potassium	713

Excellent: Vitamin C, Folate, Iron

* A Scotch bonnet pepper is fiery hot. You can substitute jalapeño or serrano and wear rubber gloves when handling. I discard the seeds because they are so hot.

Baked Buttermilk Herb Chicken

Follow recipe for Herb and Buttermilk Barbecued Chicken to end of step 2. Spread 3 oz (85 g) cornmeal on plate. Remove chicken from marinade; coat each piece all over with cornmeal. Bake on baking sheet at 350°F (180°C) Gas Mark 4 for 45 minutes or until juices run clear when chicken is pierced with fork. (Pictured opposite page 96.)

Buttermilk

Despite its name, buttermilk is not high in fat and is wonderful to use in lower-fat cooking and baking.

The dilemma everyone faces is what to do with the rest of the buttermilk in the carton. See index for other recipes using buttermilk.

Herb and Buttermilk Barbecued Chicken

This delicious chicken recipe is from food writer and test kitchen assistant, Vicki Burns. Buttermilk is low in fat yet thick and creamy, perfect for marinating. If it's not available, substitute semi-skimmed evaporated milk.

3 lb	chicken pieces, skinned	1.3 kg
Buttermilk Marinade		
6 fl oz	buttermilk	175 ml
2 tbsp	Dijon mustard	30 ml
2	cloves garlic, crushed	2
2 tsp	each dried oregano, basil, thyme and rosemary	10 ml
¼ tsp	each salt and pepper	1.25 ml

1. Buttermilk Marinade: In a large bowl, combine buttermilk, mustard, garlic, oregano, basil, thyme, rosemary, salt and pepper.

2. Add chicken, turning pieces to coat. Cover and refrigerate for 3 hours, turning occasionally.

3. Place chicken on greased rack over medium heat; cook, turning occasionally, for 30 to 40 minutes or until juices run clear when chicken is pierced. Makes 6 servings.

Make ahead
To end of step 2 for up to 24 hours.

Barbecuing Safely

Recent research shows that whenever fat drips onto a heat source, chemicals form on the outside of the meat, fish or poultry that might increase the risks of some types of cancer. In this country we tend to barbecue in moderation but it is recommended that:
- For meat or poultry that requires a long cooking time, microwave first, then discard juices, and barbecue; or wrap in foil, then cook.
- Prevent flare-ups: raise rack if necessary and keep the water spray bottle handy for dousing. Use a drip can to catch fat, or cover the rack with foil and poke holes in it to let fat drip through.
- Cook meat until medium well done: if too rare, it will be higher in fat and may contain harmful bacteria; if too well done or charred, it will be higher in chemicals.
- Use a **clean** plate for the cooked meat. Don't eat charred parts.

PER SERVING	
calories	152
g protein	25
g total fat	4
g saturated fat	1
mg cholesterol	78
g carbohydrate	3
g dietary fibre	0.1
mg sodium	264
mg potassium	271

Chicken Breasts Stuffed with Mushrooms and Leeks
Omit onion, courgette and carrot from stuffing. Substitute 4 oz (115 g) finely chopped mushrooms and 4 oz (115 g) chopped white of leek.

Sherry Chicken Breasts Stuffed with Courgettes and Carrots

Light yet full of flavour, these make-ahead chicken breasts are perfect for a dinner party.

6	boneless skinless chicken breasts (1½ lb/675 g)	6
1 tsp	soft margarine or butter	5 ml
4 fl oz	sherry	125 ml
12	large spinach leaves	12
Stuffing		
½ oz	soft margarine or butter	15 g
1	onion, chopped	1
2	cloves garlic, crushed	2
5 oz	courgette, coarsely grated	140 g
2 oz	carrot, coarsely grated	55 g
½ tsp	dried thyme	2.5 ml
1 oz	fresh breadcrumbs	25 g
2 tbsp	chopped fresh parsley	30 ml
1	egg white	1
¼ tsp	each salt and pepper	1.25 ml

1. Between sheets of greaseproof paper, beat chicken to ¼-inch (5 mm) thickness.

2. Remove tough stems from spinach; rinse spinach. With just the water clinging to the leaves, cook spinach for 1 minute or just until wilted; drain and set aside.

3. Stuffing: In a nonstick frying pan, melt margarine over medium heat; cook onion and garlic for 3 minutes. Stir in courgette, carrot and thyme; cook, stirring often, for 5 minutes or until tender. Remove from heat. Add crumbs, parsley, egg white, salt and pepper; mix well.

4. Cover top of each chicken breast with 2 spinach leaves; spread stuffing evenly over spinach. Carefully roll up each breast and tie each end with cotton string.

5. In a large nonstick frying pan, melt margarine over medium heat; cook stuffed breasts for 5 minutes, turning often.

6. Pour in sherry; reduce heat to medium-low and cook, covered,

Elegant Dinner For Six
- Warm Scallop Salad (page 73)
- Sherry Chicken Breasts Stuffed with Courgettes and Carrots
- Sugar-snap Peas with Mushrooms (page 135)
- Sweet Potato and Apple Purée (page 144)
- Lemon Mousse with Raspberry Sauce (page 213)

for 10 to 12 minutes or until chicken is no longer pink inside, turning to coat in sauce for last 2 minutes.

7. Let stand for 5 minutes. Untie each roll and slice diagonally into 3 or 4 slices. Makes 6 servings.

Make ahead
To end of step 4, cover and refrigerate for up to eight hours.

PER SERVING	
calories	197
g protein	29
g total fat	4
g saturated fat	1
mg cholesterol	69
g carbohydrate	7
g dietary fibre	1
mg sodium	251
mg potassium	482
Excellent: Vitamin A	

Buying Minced Meat or Poultry

If you're making that late-afternoon dash to the supermarket, quick-cooking minced meat is a good choice for a fast, family-pleasing dinner. But when you're sorting through the labels for the lower-fat products, percentages of fat and terms like *half the fat of standard minced beef, extra lean* or *steak mince* can be confusing.

Minced meat should have a fat content that the consumers find acceptable. Trading standards would take action if the fat content was excessive although there is no legislation governing % of fat. A good supplier will sell regular mince at around 20%, extra lean at 9% and steak mince at 5% fat.

The fat content of minced turkey, chicken, pork, lamb or veal can vary from one pack to the next. Along with the lean ground poultry, both the skin and fat may be included in the grinder. To ensure that you are getting lower-fat minced poultry, choose packages labelled not with just the word lean, but with the actual percentage of fat — 10% or lower is your best choice. Or, buy larger pieces of poultry or meat, remove the fat, bones and skin (if any) and mince it yourself.

Do keep in mind that the percentage of fat on the label is measured by weight and doesn't reflect the percentage of calories from fat. For example, a quarter-pound beef patty made from lean meat, which has 17% fat by weight, actually contains 12 grams of fat when grilled — and that means that 54% of the calories come from fat.

Oven-Baked Chicken
Instead of grilling chicken, place on baking sheet and bake in 375°F (190°C) Gas Mark 5 for 20 to 30 minutes for boneless or 45 minutes with bones or until no longer pink inside.

Easy Entertaining
I got the idea for this dish at an after-tennis dinner at my friend Marg Churchill's. The colourful platter of tossed salad topped with hoisin chicken is a meal in one dish – perfect for elegant yet casual entertaining.

Hoisin Sesame Chicken Platter

Serve this tasty dish with crusty bread, and/or Lemon Parsley Rice Pilaf (page 173).

4 fl oz	Asian Sauce (page 99)	125 ml
6	skinless chicken breasts or 3 lb (1.3 kg) skinless chicken pieces	6
1 tbsp	dark sesame oil	15 ml
1 tbsp	rice vinegar	15 ml
Dash	hot pepper sauce	Dash
8 handfuls	torn mixed lettuces	8 handfuls
	salt and pepper	
8 oz	cherry tomatoes	225 g
6	black olives	6

1. Spread Asian Sauce over chicken; cover and refrigerate for 4 hours.

2. Grill chicken under high heat for 15 to 20 minutes on each side or until no longer pink inside.

3. Meanwhile, combine sesame oil, vinegar and hot pepper sauce; toss with lettuces, and salt and pepper to taste. Arrange on large serving platter.

4. Arrange grilled chicken on lettuces. Garnish with cherry tomatoes and olives. Makes 6 servings.

Make ahead
To end of step 1 for up to one day.

PER SERVING	
calories	225
g protein	29
g total fat	7
g saturated fat	1
mg cholesterol	73
g carbohydrate	12
g dietary fibre	1
mg sodium	419
mg potassium	509

Good: Vitamin C
Excellent: Folate

Right:
Baked Buttermilk Herb Chicken (margin, page 93), Bulgur with Red Onion and Pimiento (page 174), Sugar-snap Peas with Mushrooms (page 135)

Chicken and Mange Tout in Black Bean Sauce

You can find the fermented (or salted) black beans (often in a
plastic bag) in Chinese food stores. If not available, add 4 tbsp
(60 ml) bottled black bean sauce and reduce chicken stock to
4 tbsp (60 ml). Serve with rice or noodles.

1 lb	boneless skinless chicken breasts	450 g
1 tbsp	vegetable oil	15 ml
3 tbsp	Chinese fermented black beans	45 ml
2	cloves garlic, crushed	2
1 tbsp	grated root ginger	15 ml
¼ tsp	crushed red pepper flakes	1.25 ml
7 oz	mange tout, trimmed	200 g
Sauce		
4½ fl oz	chicken stock or water	40 ml
2 tbsp	sodium-reduced soy sauce	30 ml
1 tbsp	sherry	15 ml
2 tsp	granulated sugar	10 ml
1½ tsp	cornflour	7 ml
1 tsp	sesame oil	5 ml

1. Sauce: Combine stock, soy sauce, sherry, sugar, cornflour and
sesame oil; set aside.

2. Slice chicken thinly; set aside.

3. In a large nonstick frying pan or wok, heat oil over high heat;
stir-fry black beans, garlic, ginger and red pepper flakes for 15
seconds.

4. Add chicken; stir-fry for 2 minutes. Add mange tout; stir-fry for
2 minutes.

5. Stir sauce; add to a pan and stir-fry over medium heat for
1 minute or until chicken is no longer pink inside.
Makes 4 servings.

Make ahead
To end of step 2, cover and refrigerate for up to four hours.

PER SERVING	
calories	221
g protein	29
g total fat	6
g saturated fat	1
mg cholesterol	66
g carbohydrate	10
g dietary fibre	2
mg sodium	436
mg potassium	473
Good: Vitamin C	

Left:
Chicken and Vegetable Stew
with Parsley Dumplings (page
101)

Summer Barbecued Asian Chicken

Follow Asian Chicken recipe except: Marinate whole skinless boneless chicken breasts. Grill or barbecue chicken over high heat for about 4 minutes on each side or until meat is no longer pink inside. Cut into strips; place on serving plate.

Mostly Make-Ahead Oriental Dinner

- Hot and Sour Soup (page 62)
- Asian Chicken
- Nectarine and Orange Compote (page 226)
  or
  Fresh Fruit Platter
- Gingerbread Cake (page 204)

Asian Chicken

This is a great dish for casual entertaining or when you want something a little different. Set the table with a dish of chicken, one of lettuce and one with remaining ingredients. Give each person some sauce. Guests make up their own lettuce rolls filled with chicken, noodles and herbs. (Pictured opposite page 128.)

	Asian Sauce (recipe page 99)	
6	boneless skinless chicken breasts, cut in strips	6
½ lb	rice vermicelli noodles	225 g
2	heads soft round lettuce	2
1	cucumber, halved lengthwise and thinly sliced	1
6 oz	bean sprouts	175 g
1 oz	fresh mint leaves	25 g
1 oz	fresh coriander leaves	25 g

1. Spread 5 tbsp (75 ml) of the Asian Sauce over chicken; cover and refrigerate for 4 hours.

2. In a large saucepan of boiling water, cook noodles for 1 minute or according to package directions; drain and rinse under cold water. Drain again and toss with 2 tbsp (30 ml) of Asian Sauce.

3. On a serving plate arrange lettuce leaves. On another plate, arrange cucumber, bean sprouts, mint, coriander and noodles. Divide remaining sauce among 6 small dishes.

4. In a nonstick frying pan or wok stir-fry chicken over high heat for 3 to 5 minutes or until no longer pink inside; transfer to serving plate.

5. Let each person spread some Asian Sauce on a lettuce leaf, then top with some chicken, noodles, bean sprouts, cucumber, mint and coriander leaves. Using fingers, roll up and eat.
Makes 6 servings.

Make ahead
To end of step 2 for up to one day. To end of step 3, cover and refrigerate for up to four hours.

PER SERVING	
calories	377
g protein	32
g total fat	3
g saturated fat	1
mg cholesterol	68
g carbohydrate	56
g dietary fibre	2
mg sodium	704
mg potassium	667
Good: Iron	
Excellent: Folate	

Tip
This sauce is thick and quite sweet. With pasta you might want to add more vinegar to taste.

Asian Sauce

This is delicious as a marinade or as a sauce with chicken, pork, Chinese noodle dishes, prawns or scallops.

4 fl oz	hoisin sauce	125 ml
2 tbsp	soy sauce	30 ml
2 tbsp	rice vinegar	30 ml
2 tbsp	liquid honey	30 ml
1 tbsp	grated root ginger	15 ml
1 tbsp	crushed fresh garlic	15 ml
	crushed red pepper flakes (optional)	

1. Combine hoisin sauce, soy sauce, vinegar, honey, root ginger, garlic, and red pepper flakes to taste, if using. Makes about 8 fl oz (225 ml).

Make ahead
Sauce can be covered and refrigerated for up to two weeks.

Light and Lean Barbecues

Barbecuing is a great way to cook light, low-fat dishes. To keep barbecues lean, follow these easy tips:
- Choose lean cuts of meat:
  Beef: rump, sirloin slices from a topside joint
  Pork: loin chops, leg, tenderloin
  Lamb: loin, leg, tenderloin or fillet
- Thaw completely before cooking to reduce cooking time, and avoid charring food on the outside before it's cooked inside.
- Remove all visible fat from meat.
- Choose marinades with little or no oil or reduce oil to a minimum in your own recipes. In some cases, you can substitute water, stock or fruit juice for most of the oil.
- Keep your accompaniments light. Serve lots of fresh vegetables and salads and forget the butter and mayonnaise. Try Light Tartar Sauce (page 114) on fish.
- Serve meat portions no larger than 3½ ounces (100 g) per person – about the size of a pack of cards.
- Remove skin from chicken, turkey and fish before serving.

PER SERVING	1 tbsp/15 ml
calories	29
g protein	1
g total fat	1
g saturated fat	0
mg cholesterol	0
g carbohydrate	6
g dietary fibre	0
mg sodium	231
mg potassium	12

Baked Spicy Chicken
Marinate chicken as in
Barbecued Curried Chicken
Breasts. Then cover chicken
with fresh brown breadcrumbs
(see margin, page 185); bake at
350°F (180°C) Gas Mark 4 for
45 minutes or until no longer
pink inside.

Chicken Salad
Curried Chicken Breasts are
delicious cold, so in the
summer, I like to cook extra
then slice the meat and serve it
as part of a salad or over salad
greens leaves tossed with Asian
Sauce (page 99).

Barbecued Curried Chicken Breasts

Yogurt and curry powder are the basis for this flavourful marinade.
Serve with Barbecued Potato Packets (page 142) or Potato Salad
with Yogurt Herb Dressing (page 87) and asparagus, green beans
or sliced tomatoes.

4 tbsp	low-fat yogurt	60 ml
2 tbsp	vegetable oil	30 ml
2 tbsp	lime or lemon juice	30 ml
2 tbsp	liquid honey	30 ml
2 tbsp	curry powder	30 ml
1 tbsp	crushed fresh garlic	15 ml
½ tsp	salt	2.5 ml
6	skinless chicken breasts	6

1. Combine yogurt, oil, lime juice, honey, curry powder, garlic
and salt; brush over chicken. Cover and refrigerate for 4 hours.

2. Grill or barbecue chicken at medium heat for 15 to 20 minutes
on each side or until no longer pink inside. Makes 6 servings.

Make ahead
To end of step 1 for up to one day.

PER SERVING	1 tbsp/15 ml
calories	220
g protein	28
g total fat	8
g saturated fat	1
mg cholesterol	74
g carbohydrate	9
g dietary fibre	0.4
mg sodium	264
mg potassium	291

Chicken and Vegetable Stew with Parsley Dumplings

This one-pot chicken dinner (pictured opposite page 97) is a light version of an old-fashioned favourite. Add 4 fl oz (125 ml) white wine to the stew when adding peas, if desired.

4	skinless chicken breasts (2 lb/900 g) or 2 lb (900 g) skinless chicken pieces	4
4	small potatoes, quartered	4
2	each carrots and onions, quartered	2
2	celery stalks, sliced	2
8 oz	swede, cubed	225 g
8 oz	sweet potato, cubed	225 g
1¾ pts	water or chicken stock	1 L
½ tsp	each dried thyme, sage and salt	2.5 ml
¼ tsp	pepper	1.25 ml
6 oz	frozen peas	175 g
Dumplings		
4 oz	plain flour	115 g
2 tbsp	chopped fresh parsley	30 ml
1 oz	soft margarine or butter	25 g
1½ tsp	baking powder	7 ml
¼ tsp	salt	1.25 ml
4 fl oz	skimmed milk	125 ml

1. In a large saucepan, combine chicken, potatoes, carrots, onions, celery, swede, sweet potato, water, thyme, sage, salt and pepper; bring to the boil over high heat. Reduce heat to medium-low; simmer, covered, for 20 minutes. Stir in peas.

2. Dumplings: In a food processor or by hand, combine flour, parsley, margarine, baking powder and salt until mixture is in coarse crumbs. Stir in milk; drop by tablespoonfuls (15 ml) on to hot stew to make 4 to 6 mounds.

3. Cover and simmer (don't boil hard and don't lift lid) for 15 minutes or until dumplings have risen. Makes 4 servings.

Make ahead

To end of step 1 (except peas), cover and refrigerate for up to 24 hours.

Make-Ahead Buffet Menu
- Turkey Vegetable Casserole
- Tossed Salad Leaves with
  Mustard Garlic Vinaigrette
  (page 88)
- Green Bean Salad with
  Buttermik Dressing (page 79)
  or
  Asparagus and Mushroom
  Salad (page 78)
- Fresh Breads
- Chocolate Mocha Ice Cream
  Pie (page 210)
  or
  Lemon Mousse with
  Raspberry Sauce (page 213)

Turkey Vegetable Casserole

This is a delicious way to use up cooked turkey or chicken and makes a great dish for a buffet.

6 oz	long grain rice	175 g
½ tsp	soft margarine or butter	7.5 ml
1 oz	coarsely chopped fresh parsley	25 g
1	onion, chopped	1
3	cloves garlic, crushed	3
6 oz	carrots, finely chopped	175 g
6 oz	celery, chopped	175 g
½ lb	mushrooms, thinly sliced	225 g
1 lb	cooked turkey	450 g
Herb Cream Sauce		
1 oz	soft margarine or butter	25 g
1 oz	plain flour	25 g
1 pt	skimmed milk	600 ml
½ tsp	each dried tarragon, salt and pepper	2.5 ml
¼ tsp	dried thyme	1.25 ml
Topping		
1 oz	fresh wholemeal breadcrumbs	25 g
4 tbsp	chopped fresh parsley	60 ml

1. In a saucepan, bring ¾ pt (425 ml) water to the boil; add rice and a third of the margarine. Reduce heat, cover and simmer for 20 minutes. Toss with 2 tbsp (30 ml) of the parsley; spoon into a greased 13- × 9-inch (33 × 23 cm) baking dish.

2. Meanwhile, in a large nonstick saucepan, melt remaining margarine over low heat; cook onion, garlic and carrots for 5 minutes. Add celery, mushrooms and remaining parsley; cook, stirring, for 5 to 10 minutes or until softened. Stir in turkey.

3. Herb Cream Sauce: In a saucepan, melt margarine over medium-low heat; whisk in flour and cook, stirring, for 1 minute. Gradually add milk, whisking constantly; cook for 1 to 2 minutes or until bubbling and thickened. Add tarragon, salt, pepper and thyme. Stir sauce into turkey mixture; spread over rice.

4. Topping: Combine breadcrumbs and parsley; sprinkle over casserole. Bake at 325°F (160°C) Gas Mark 3 for 40 to 50 minutes or until heated through. Makes 8 servings.

Make ahead
To end of step 3, cover and refrigerate for up to two days, or cool then freeze for up to two weeks. Thaw in refrigerator for two days; let stand at room temperature for 25 minutes before sprinkling with topping and baking.

PER SERVING	
calories	298
g protein	23
g total fat	8
g saturated fat	3
mg cholesterol	49
g carbohydrate	32
g dietary fibre	2
mg sodium	320
mg potassium	558
Good: Folate, Iron	
Excellent: Vitamin A	

Buying Turkey
Avoid pre-basted turkeys or ones injected with fat. You are paying a high price for added fat, which is usually hydrogenated or saturated.

Thawing Turkey
Leave in original wrapper. Cover with cold water and allow 1 hour per pound (450 g); change water occasionally.
   Or, in refrigerator, allow 1 day for every 5 lb (2.25 kg).

Roast Turkey with Sausage, Apple and Herb Stuffing

Traditional roast turkey is still my family's favourite for Christmas and festive dinners. Serve it with flavourful Giblet Gravy (page 106).

14 lb	turkey	6.3 kg
	Sausage, Apple and Herb Stuffing (page 105)	
4	sprigs fresh rosemary or thyme	4

1. Remove neck and giblets from body cavities of turkey. Discard gizzard and heart. Cover and refrigerate neck and liver for gravy. Rinse turkey under cold running water; dry skin and cavities.

2. Loosely stuff neck and body cavities with stuffing. Fold neck skin over cavity and skewer to back. Secure legs by tying with string. Lift wings and fold behind back or tie to sides of turkey with string. Place rosemary sprigs between body of turkey and each leg and wing.

3. Place turkey on a rack in a roasting pan with breast side up. Cover with loose tent of lightly greased foil, dull side out, leaving sides open. Roast in 325°F (185°C) Gas Mark 3 for 5½ to 6 hours or until juices run clear when turkey is pierced and thermometer inserted into thigh reads 185°F (85°C). Remove foil for last 30 minutes of cooking, so turkey can brown.

4. Remove from oven and let stand, covered with foil, for 30 minutes before carving. Makes 14 servings.

PER SERVING 3½ oz/100 g (LIGHT MEAT AND STUFFING)	
calories	229
g protein	33
g total fat	5
g saturated fat	2
mg cholesterol	73
g carbohydrate	12
g dietary fibre	2
mg sodium	245
mg potassium	389
Good: Iron	

Turkey Cooking Times

Roast at 325°F (160°C) Gas Mark 3 for 20 minutes per pound, 40 minutes per kilogram (small turkeys require a little more, large ones a little less) or until meat thermometer inserted into thigh reads 185°F (85°C) or, if stuffed, thermometer inserted into stuffing reads 165°F (75°C).

Many factors affect the cooking time. Fresh turkeys take longer than thawed. A 10 lb (4.5 kg) stuffed turkey takes about 3½ hours, a 20 lb (9 kg) turkey, 6 to 6½ hours. Don't overcook as it will be dry.

Sausage, Apple and Herb Stuffing

In the autumn, I often use McIntosh apples or other russett apples; in the winter, Golden Delicious is easily available. Stuff the bird just before cooking.

4 oz	low-fat turkey sausagemeat	115 g
9	slices day-old wholemeal bread, cubed	9
2 oz	celery, chopped	55 g
2 oz	onion, chopped	55 g
2	small apples, peeled and chopped	2
2 tbsp	each chopped fresh sage and basil (or ½ tsp/2.5 ml each dried)	30 ml
½ tsp	dried savory	7.5 ml
2 tsp	chopped fresh thyme or oregano (or ½ tsp/2.5 ml dried)	10 ml
½ tsp	each salt and pepper	2.5 ml

1. In a small nonstick frying pan, cook sausagemeat over medium heat for 5 to 7 minutes or until no longer pink, breaking up meat with fork.

2. In a large bowl, combine sausagemeat, bread, celery, onion, apples, sage, basil, savory, thyme, salt and pepper. Makes about enough for one 14 lb (6.5 kg) turkey or 14 servings.

Make ahead
Stuffing can be refrigerated in airtight container for up to two days or frozen for up to four weeks. Thaw slightly in refrigerator to stuff the turkey.

PER SERVING	
calories	71
g protein	3
g total fat	2
g saturated fat	1
mg cholesterol	3
g carbohydrate	12
g dietary fibre	2
mg sodium	181
mg potassium	84

Nutritional Note
Avoid eating the skin of turkey
or chicken as it is high in fat.
Light meat has about half the
fat of dark turkey meat.
  Compare:
3½ oz (100 g)
Cooked turkey fat (g)
Light meat.........................3
Dark meat.........................7

Giblet Gravy

Liver adds a delicious flavour to this gravy. Liver is high in cholesterol, but the actual amount per serving in this recipe is very small and not worth worrying about.

	turkey neck and liver	
4 tbsp	pan drippings from turkey	60 ml
6 tbsp	plain flour	90 ml
	water, cooking liquids and pan juices	
	salt and pepper	

1. In a small saucepan, cover neck with water; simmer, covered, for 2 hours. Add liver; simmer for 20 minutes. Drain, reserving cooking liquid in a large measuring jug. Remove meat from neck and chop along with liver; refrigerate.

2. Pour pan juices from cooked turkey into a bowl, leaving all particles in the pan. Let fat rise to top of liquids; skim off fat and pour 4 tbsp (60 ml) of the fat into the roasting pan. Add pan juices to reserved cooking liquid, adding water if necessary to make 1¾ pt (1 L). Sprinkle flour into pan; cook over low heat, stirring to scrape up any brown bits, for 1 minute.

3. Gradually add reserved liquid, whisking continuously until boiling and thickened. Stir in chopped liver and neck meat. Season with salt and pepper to taste. Makes 2 pt (1.2 L).

PER SERVING	2 fl oz/50 ml
calories	57
g protein	4
g total fat	4
g saturated fat	1
mg cholesterol	39
g carbohydrate	2
g dietary fibre	0.1
mg sodium	9
mg potassium	23
Good: Vitamin A	

How Much Turkey to Buy

| Purchased weight | | Number of 3 oz (85 g) |
lb	kg	Servings of cooked turkey
9	4	17
12	5.5	24
14	6.5	29
22	10	42

To Garnish
To garnish loaf, before baking, arrange slices from 1 peeled and thinly sliced lemon over top.

Nutritional Note
Commercial minced chicken or turkey may contain skin, which adds extra fat. For the leanest product, ask your butcher for some made without skin, or buy boneless skinless breast meat and grind your own.

Lemon Pepper Turkey Loaf

This tasty turkey loaf is absolutely delicious served either hot with mashed potatoes, baked pumpkin and green beans, or cold in a sandwich.

10½ oz	frozen spinach, thawed	300 g
1 lb	lean minced turkey	450 g
1	small onion, chopped	1
1	egg, lightly beaten	1
1	slice wholemeal bread, crumbled	1
1	clove garlic, crushed	1
3 tbsp	freshly grated Parmesan cheese	45 ml
2 tsp	grated lemon rind	10 ml
½ tsp	each salt and pepper	2.5 ml
Pinch	nutmeg	Pinch

1. Squeeze spinach dry; chop finely.

2. In a bowl, combine spinach, turkey, onion, egg, breadcrumbs, garlic, cheese, lemon rind, salt, pepper and nutmeg; mix gently.

3. Transfer to 2¾ pt (1.5 L) baking dish, smoothing top.

4. Bake in 350°F (180°C) Gas Mark 4 for 40 minutes or until no longer pink in centre and meat thermometer registers 185°F (85°C). Let stand for 10 minutes. Pour off any liquid.
Makes 4 servings.

Make ahead
To end of step 3, cover and refrigerate for up to three hours.

PER SERVING	
calories	268
g protein	26
g total fat	14
g saturated fat	4
mg cholesterol	114
g carbohydrate	9
g dietary fibre	2
mg sodium	538
mg potassium	440

Good: Calcium, Iron
Excellent: Vitamin A, Folate

Escalopes

Escalopes are thin slices of meat, usually veal. Turkey is an excellent, less expensive alternative and if you can't find turkey escalopes, buy turkey or chicken breast and cut it into thin slices.

Easy Grilled Dinner
- Thai Grilled Turkey Escalopes
- Jiffy Chinese Noodles (page 156)
- Green Beans
- Sliced Tomatoes with Fresh Basil

Thai Turkey Escalopes

Serve these tasty slices with rice or noodles and a salad such as Purple Vegetable Slaw (page 83) or Ginger Stir-Fried Courgettes (page 139).

2 tbsp	chopped fresh coriander or parsley	30 ml
2 tbsp	fish sauce or sodium-reduced soy sauce	30 ml
4 tsp	lemon juice	20 ml
2 tbsp	water	30 ml
1 tsp	granulated sugar	5 ml
1 tsp	vegetable oil	5 ml
¼ tsp	pepper	1.25 ml
¼ tsp	crushed red pepper flakes*	1.25 ml
1 lb	turkey escalopes	450 g

1. Combine coriander, fish sauce, lemon juice, water, sugar, oil, pepper and red pepper flakes; mix well.

2. Place turkey in shallow dish; pour marinade over top. Cover and refrigerate for 1 hour, turning occasionally.

3. Place on greased grill rack under high heat; grill for about 2 minutes on each side or until no longer pink inside.
Makes 4 servings.

Make ahead
To end of step 2 for up to 24 hours.

PER SERVING	
calories	150
g protein	27
g total fat	3
g saturated fat	1
mg cholesterol	61
g carbohydrate	2
g dietary fibre	0.1
mg sodium	301
mg potassium	304

* Or chilli paste to taste.

Fish and Seafood

Steamed Ginger Fish Fillets

Fish Mediterranean

Lemon Tarragon Sole Fillets

Baked Breaded Fish Fillets
with Almonds

Lemon Sesame Tuna Fillets

Barbecued Trout with Light
Tartare Sauce

Barbecued Salmon Fillets

Baked Whole Salmon
Stuffed with Mushrooms
and Artichokes

Creamy Dill Sauce

Prawn and Chicken
Jambalaya

Spicy Scallops

Salmon Salad Fajitas

Steamed Ginger Fish Fillets

If you don't have a steamer, place a rack in a wok or a metal colander in a large pan, add water and bring to a boil. Place fish on a heatproof plate on rack; cover and steam.

12 oz	cod or halibut fillets	350 g
1 tbsp	chopped root ginger	15 ml
3	spring onions, diagonally sliced	3
1 tsp	vegetable oil	5 ml
1 tsp	crushed fresh garlic	5 ml
1 tbsp	sodium-reduced soy sauce	15 ml

1. Place fillets in steamer; sprinkle with ginger and onions. Cover tightly and steam for 5 minutes or until fish is opaque. Transfer to plates.

2. In a small frying pan, heat oil over medium heat; cook garlic for 30 seconds. Stir in soy sauce; drizzle over fish.
Makes 4 servings.

PER SERVING	
calories	89
g protein	16
g total fat	2
g saturated fat	0.2
mg cholesterol	36
g carbohydrate	2
g dietary fibre	0.4
mg sodium	175
mg potassium	218

Fish Mediterranean

Any kind of fish fillet is delicious topped with this zesty sauce. Cooking time will vary depending on the thickness of the fish. (Pictured opposite page 129.)

1 lb	red snapper, sole or other fillets	450 g
Sauce		
½ tsp	olive oil	2.5 ml
1 tbsp	chopped spring onion or shallots	15 ml
½ tsp	crushed fresh garlic	2.5 ml
6 oz	drained canned tomatoes, chopped	175 g
¼ tsp	dried basil (or 1 tsp/5 ml chopped fresh)	1.25 ml
2 tbsp	chopped black olives	30 ml
1½ tsp	capers	7.5 ml
	pepper	

Buying Fish
Fresh fish:
- should not have a strong smell
- should have firm flesh that springs back when touched
- should have clear bright convex eyes (not sunken)

Frozen fish:
If fish is frozen as soon as caught, it is often better than fresh. I like the fillets that have been individually frozen.

Keep higher-fat fish (salmon, mackerel, trout) for a maximum of two months in the freezer; lean fish up to 6 months.

PER SERVING	
calories	132
g protein	24
g total fat	3
g saturated fat	1
mg cholesterol	42
g carbohydrate	3
g dietary fibre	1
mg sodium	175
mg potassium	572

Olives

Olives can be high in fat and sodium so should be used in moderation. Black olives are usually lower in fat and sodium than green olives. Choose ones packed in brine rather than oil.

1. In a pan of gently simmering water, cover and poach fish over medium heat for 5 minutes or until fish is opaque. Drain well; transfer to serving platter and keep warm.

2. Sauce: Meanwhile, in a small saucepan, heat oil over medium heat; cook onion and garlic for 2 minutes. Add tomatoes and basil; simmer for 3 minutes, stirring occasionally. Stir in olives, capers, and pepper to taste.

3. Spoon sauce over fish. Makes 4 servings.

Make ahead

Sauce, step 2, can be made up to one hour before serving and gently reheated.

Lemon Tarragon Sole Fillets

I love this easy way to cook any kind of fish fillets or steaks. It's a lighter version of my mother's method.

2 tbsp	light mayonnaise	30 ml
2 tbsp	low-fat yogurt	30 ml
1 tsp	plain flour	5 ml
½ tsp	dried tarragon	2.5 ml
1 tsp	finely chopped lemon rind	5 ml
1 lb	sole fillets	450 g

1. In a small bowl, mix together mayonnaise, yogurt, flour, tarragon, and lemon rind.

2. Arrange fillets in a single layer on a baking sheet; spread with the mayonnaise mixture.

3. Grill 6 to 8 inches (15 to 20 cm) from heat for 5 to 10 minutes or until fish is opaque. (Time will vary depending on thickness of fish; ¼ inch/5 mm thick fillets will take only 5 minutes.) Makes 4 servings.

Make ahead

To end of step 2, cover and refrigerate for up to two hours.

PER SERVING	
calories	134
g protein	22
g total fat	4
g saturated fat	1
mg cholesterol	61
g carbohydrate	2
g dietary fibre	0.1
mg sodium	148
mg potassium	327

Baked Breaded Fish Fillets with Almonds

You can use any kind of fresh or frozen and thawed fillets in this easy-to-make fish dish. Wholemeal breadcrumbs instead of white breadcrumbs not only add fibre but are much more attractive in colour. (Pictured opposite page 160.)

1	egg, lightly beaten	1
4 tbsp	skimmed milk	60 ml
3 oz	fresh wholemeal breadcrumbs	85 g
1 tsp	dried oregano or basil	5 ml
¼ tsp	each salt and pepper	1.25 ml
1 lb	sole or haddock fillets	450 g
2 tbsp	lemon juice	30 ml
2 tbsp	water	30 ml
½ oz	soft margarine or butter, melted	15 g
3 tbsp	flaked almonds	45 ml
3 tbsp	chopped spring onions	45 ml

1. In a shallow dish, combine egg and milk.

2. On a plate, mix crumbs, oregano, salt and pepper.

3. Dip fish in egg mixture, then in crumbs. Arrange in single layer on a greased baking sheet.

4. Combine lemon juice, water and margarine; drizzle over fish. Sprinkle with almonds. Bake, uncovered, in 425°F (220°C) Gas Mark 7 for 10 minutes or until fish is opaque.

5. Sprinkle with onions. Makes 4 servings.

Make ahead
To end of step 3 for up to 30 minutes, cover and refrigerate.

PER SERVING	
calories	224
g protein	26
g total fat	9
g saturated fat	2
mg cholesterol	110
g carbohydrate	10
g dietary fibre	1
mg sodium	379
mg potassium	549

Grilled Tuna Fillet Burgers
Prepare Lemon Sesame Tuna
Fillets using 4 oz (115 g) fillets
½ inch (1 cm) thick. Grill for 5
to 7 minutes and serve in
toasted wholemeal bun with
lettuce and sliced tomato.

Lemon Sesame Tuna Fillets

Tuna is tender and moist as long as it isn't overcooked, when it becomes dry. Cook until light pink in the centre.

4	tuna fillets or steaks, 1-inch (2.5 cm) thick (1½ lb/675 g)	4
1	spring onion, chopped	1
Pinch	pepper	Pinch

Lemon-Soy Marinade

2 tbsp	lemon juice	30 ml
½ tbsp	soy sauce	7.5 ml
½ tbsp	water	7.5 ml
1 tbsp	sesame or vegetable oil	15 ml

1. Lemon-Soy Marinade: Combine lemon juice, soy sauce, water and oil; pour over tuna fillets in baking dish. Cover and refrigerate for at least 30 minutes.

2. Bake at 400°F (200°C) Gas Mark 6 for 10 to 12 minutes or until fish is opaque and is slightly pink in centre.

3. Sprinkle with spring onion and pepper. Makes 4 servings.

Make ahead
To end of step 1 for up to four hours; remove from refrigerator 10 minutes before cooking.

PER SERVING	
calories	262
g protein	40
g total fat	10
g saturated fat	2
mg cholesterol	65
g carbohydrate	1
g dietary fibre	0.1
mg sodium	128
mg potassium	445
Excellent: Vitamin A	

Cooking Fish

Fish is tender and doesn't require a long cooking time. It is cooked as soon as the flesh becomes opaque throughout.
- Measure fish at the thickest part.
- Allow 10 minutes cooking time per inch (2.5 cm) thickness for fresh fish, 20 minutes per inch if frozen. If wrapped in foil, add 5 minutes for fresh, 10 minutes for frozen. This applies to all fish and all cooking methods (if in oven, cook at 450°F [230°C] Gas Mark 8).
- To Microwave Fish: Place fish on microwaveable dish. Cover and microwave on High for 3 to 5 minutes per pound (450 g). Let stand for 2 to 3 minutes.

Oven-Baked Trout
Prepare trout as in Barbecued Trout recipe. Bake on baking sheet at 450°F (230°C) Gas Mark 8 for 10 minutes for every inch (2.5 cm) of thickness of fish.

Foil-Steamed Trout
Prepare trout as in Barbecued Trout recipe. Wrap in foil and bake as in Oven-Baked Trout, adding 5 minutes to baking time.

Light Tartare Sauce
Light Tartare Sauce is also delicious with any fish or with a chicken or turkey burger.

Barbecued Trout with Light Tartare Sauce

This fish can also be cooked in foil; just peel off the foil after cooking to remove the skin. A few capers or a little Dijon mustard, chopped spring onions or chives can be added to the Tartare Sauce. Garnish trout with lemon slices and fresh dill.

4	sprigs fresh dill	4
4	rainbow trout (about 9 oz/250 g each)	4
	salt and pepper	

Light Tartare Sauce

4 tbsp	low-fat yogurt	60 ml
4 tbsp	light mayonnaise	60 ml
4 tbsp	finely chopped dill pickle	60 ml
2 tbsp	chopped fresh dill	30 ml
	salt and pepper	

1. Light Tartare Sauce: Stir together yogurt, mayonnaise, pickle, dill, and salt and pepper to taste.

2. Place a dill sprig in each trout cavity; sprinkle cavity with salt and pepper.

3. Place trout on greased barbecue rack over high heat; cover and cook, turning once, for 10 to 15 minutes or until fish is opaque. Serve with Tartare Sauce. Makes 4 servings.

Make ahead
To end of step 1, cover and refrigerate for up to three days.
To end of step 2, cover and refrigerate for up to six hours.

PER SERVING	
calories	284
g protein	41
g total fat	11
g saturated fat	2
mg cholesterol	111
g carbohydrate	3
g dietary fibre	0.1
mg sodium	273
mg potassium	1009

Good: Calcium
Excellent: Iron

Barbecuing Salmon
I usually start to cook the salmon skin side down on the barbecue, however, others do the reverse. Each way has advantages, so choose for yourself.

Barbecued Salmon Fillets

Barbecued salmon fillet or steak is one of my favourite summer meals: it's fast, easy and tastes terrific. Sometimes I don't do anything to the salmon; its delicate flavour and smoky taste from the barbecue is all it needs. Sometimes I marinate it in a teriyaki-type sauce; other times I add a little lemon juice, or use this recipe.

2 tbsp	lemon juice or white wine vinegar	30 ml
1 tbsp	vegetable oil	15 ml
1 tsp	crumbled dried rosemary (or 2 tsp/10 ml fresh)	5 ml
4	salmon fillets (about 1½ lb/675 g total)	4
	salt and pepper	

1. Combine lemon juice, oil and rosemary. Pour over salmon; marinate for 15 minutes at room temperature.

2. Spray barbecue or grill rack with nonstick coating or brush with oil; cook salmon about 4 inches (10 cm) from medium-high heat, turning halfway through cooking time, for 10 minutes per inch (2.5 cm) of thickness or until fish is opaque. (If fillet is thin and you put the top down on the barbecue, turning may not be necessary.) Season with salt and pepper to taste. Makes 4 servings.

Make ahead
To end of step 1, cover and refrigerate for up to four hours; remove from refrigerator 10 minutes before cooking.

PER SERVING	
calories	250
g protein	34
g total fat	12
g saturated fat	2
mg cholesterol	94
g carbohydrate	0.2
g dietary fibre	0
mg sodium	75
mg potassium	836

Nutritional Content of Fish

Fish is a good nutritional buy. It's high in protein and low or relatively low in fat, unless it is breaded and fried. It is also a source of many vitamins and minerals.

Fish with 5 g of fat or less per 3 oz (85 g) serving: sole, bluefish, cod, halibut, haddock, hake, red snapper, mullet, plaice, pollock, monkfish, trout, turbot, whiting, witch.

Baked Whole Salmon Stuffed with Mushrooms and Artichokes

This easy-to-prepare fish looks and tastes wonderful. Garnish with fresh dill sprigs or parsley and lemon slices. Use any combination of mushrooms – cultivated, oyster, flat, chestnut. If you're lucky enough to have leftovers, this dish is also delicious cold.

5½ lb	whole salmon, cleaned, scaled, head and tail on	2.5 kg
Stuffing		
1 tsp	olive oil	5 ml
4 oz	each cultivated, brown, shiitake and oyster mushrooms, chopped	115 g
1	can (14 oz/400 g) artichokes, drained and coarsely chopped	1
1 oz	fresh dill, chopped	25 g
	Creamy Dill Sauce (page 117)	

1. Stuffing: In a nonstick frying pan, heat oil over medium-high heat; cook mushrooms, stirring often, for about 5 minutes or until softened. Stir in artichokes; cook for 1 minute. Remove from heat; stir in dill.

2. Lightly stuff cavity of salmon with mushroom mixture. Using heavy needle and thread, stitch opening of fish together.

3. Place fish on ungreased baking sheet. Bake, uncovered, at 450°F (230°C) Gas Mark 8 for 50 minutes or until small cut in centre of fish shows meat is opaque. Serve Creamy Dill Sauce separately. Makes 12 servings.

Make ahead
To end of step 2, cover and refrigerate for up to 6 hours. Remove from refrigerator 30 minutes before baking, or increase baking time 5 to 10 minutes.

PER SERVING	
calories	199
g protein	26
g total fat	8
g saturated fat	1
mg cholesterol	67
g carbohydrate	5
g dietary fibre	1
mg sodium	75
mg potassium	765

Creamy Dill Sauce

Serve with Salmon Stuffed with Mushrooms and Artichokes (page 116) or any grilled or poached fish.

4 fl oz	low-fat yogurt	125 ml
4 fl oz	low-fat quark (7%)*	125 ml
1 oz	fresh dill, chopped	25 g
2 tbsp	capers	30 ml
	salt and pepper	

1. In a small bowl, combine yogurt, quark, dill and capers. Season with salt and pepper to taste. Makes ½ pt (300 ml).

Make ahead
Sauce can be covered and refrigerated for up to two days.

PER SERVING 1 tbsp/15 ml	
calories	12
g protein	1
g total fat	1
g saturated fat	0.3
mg cholesterol	2
g carbohydrate	1
g dietary fibre	0
mg sodium	19
mg potassium	22

Omega-3 Fatty Acids

As long as we stick to 3½ oz (100 g) portions, I don't think the fat content of fish should be of too much concern because of the merits of Omega-3 fatty acids found in fish oils.

Omega-3 fatty acids do not reduce blood cholesterol levels, as some have claimed, but may have a very positive effect in reducing the risk of blood clots, the level of blood triglycerides and help in reducing blood pressures. Health professionals do not recommend taking supplements. Instead, they suggest we get our Omega-3 fatty acids from eating fish.

* See page 38, About Quark. If it's unavailable, purée low-fat cottage cheese for a substitute.

Party Buffet Menu
- Smoked Turkey-Wrapped Melon Balls (page 42)
- Roasted Aubergine Dip (page 37) on Melba Rounds Tossed Salad Leaves with Yogurt Herb Dressing (page 87)
- Prawn and Chicken Jambalaya
- Muesli Soda Bread (page 197) *or* Corn and Jalapeño Muffins (page 188)
- Meringues with Lemon Cream (page 222)

Prawn and Chicken Jambalaya

This make-ahead version of a Creole classic is medium-hot. Add more pepper or hot pepper sauce if you want your mouth on fire. Instead of prawns, you could add ½ lb (225 g) lean smoked cubed ham. This recipe was part of a Christmas buffet menu I developed for *Canadian Living* magazine.

½ oz	soft margarine or butter	15 g
8 oz	onion, chopped	225 g
8 oz	celery, chopped	225 g
1	sweet green pepper, chopped	1
3 oz	smoked ham or sausage, diced (andouille or chorizo)	85 g
1½ lb	boneless skinless chicken breasts, cubed	675 g
1½ tsp	fresh garlic, crushed	7.5 ml
2	bay leaves	2
2 tsp	dried oregano	10 ml
1 tsp	dried thyme	5 ml
½ tsp	each salt, cayenne and black pepper	2.5 ml
1	can (28 oz/800 g) tomatoes	1
8 fl oz	Passata	225 ml
1¾ pts	chicken stock	1 L
1 lb	long grain white rice	450 g
1 lb	medium raw prawns, peeled	450 g
1	sweet red pepper, chopped	1
4	spring onions, chopped	4
8 tbsp	chopped fresh parsley	125 ml

1. In a large flameproof casserole, melt margarine over medium-high heat; cook onion and celery for 3 minutes. Add green pepper, ham, chicken, garlic, bay leaves, oregano, thyme, salt, cayenne and pepper; cook, stirring, for 3 minutes.

PER SERVING	
calories	468
g protein	41
g total fat	6
g saturated fat	1
mg cholesterol	125
g carbohydrate	61
g dietary fibre	4
mg sodium	1186
mg potassium	1040

Excellent: Vitamin A, Vitamin C, Folate, Iron

2. Add tomatoes, passata and stock; bring to boil. Stir in rice and prawns; boil for 1 minute. Bake, covered, at 350°F (180°C) Gas Mark 4 for 25 minutes or until rice is tender. Discard bay leaves.

3. Stir in red pepper and spring onions; sprinkle with parsley. Makes 8 servings.

Make ahead
To end of step 2, cool, cover and refrigerate for up to one day. To reheat, stir in 8 fl oz (225 ml) hot water; bake, covered, at 350°F (180°C) Gas Mark 4 for 1¼ hours or until hot.

Nutritional Note

Scallops are a treat for anyone, but they're especially so for someone on a low-calorie, low-fat or low-cholesterol diet. Three ounces (85 g) of steamed scallops (about 7 scallops) has only 1 gram of fat, 100 calories and 48 mg of cholesterol.

Be careful not to overcook scallops. They cook very quickly and soon become overcooked and dry.

Spicy Scallops

Hot Chinese chilli paste adds a little fiery flavour to scallops. Serve with rice and stir-fried bok choy or broccoli. I like to use the full-sized scallops, not the small queen scallops.

2 tsp	vegetable oil	10 ml
1 tbsp	root ginger, grated	15 ml
3	spring onions, chopped	3
1 lb	scallops	450 g
Sauce		
2 tbsp	sherry	30 ml
1 tbsp	sodium-reduced soy sauce	15 ml
1 tbsp	sesame oil	15 ml
1 tsp	granulated sugar	5 ml
½ tsp	chilli paste or hot pepper sauce	2.5 ml

1. Sauce: Stir together sherry, soy sauce, oil, sugar and chilli paste. Set aside.

2. In a nonstick frying pan, heat oil over high heat; stir-fry ginger and onion for 10 seconds. Add scallops; stir-fry for 1 minute.

3. Stir in sauce; stir-fry for 3 to 5 minutes or just until scallops are opaque throughout. Makes 4 servings.

Make ahead
To end of step 1 for up to one day.

PER SERVING	
calories	166
g protein	19
g total fat	7
g saturated fat	1
mg cholesterol	37
g carbohydrate	5
g dietary fibre	0.2
mg sodium	308
mg potassium	404

Other Fish Recipes
- Mariners' Chowder (page 69)
- Seafood Vegetable Chowder (page 69)
- Fettuccine Alfredo with Salmon (page 150)
- Summer Prawn and Tomato Pasta (page 152)
- Linguine with Scallops and Leeks (page 153)
- Seafood Pasta Salad (page 164)
- Bulgur Pilaf with Prawns and Mange Tout (page 175)

Salmon Salad Fajitas

There is a fabulous combination of flavours and textures in this easy-to-make meal (pictured opposite page 65). Avocados are high in fat and even though it is unsaturated fat, they should be eaten in small amounts.

1	can (7 oz/200 g) salmon, drained	1
4 tbsp	low-fat yogurt	60 ml
2 tbsp	light mayonnaise	30 ml
¼ tsp	chilli powder	1.25 ml
1	medium carrot, grated	1
1	spring onion, chopped	1
1	tomato, diced	1
1	small avocado, peeled and cut in chunks	1
4 tbsp	chopped fresh coriander	60 ml
	salt and pepper	
4	soft 8-inch (20 cm) flour tortillas	4
4	large lettuce leaves	4

1. In a bowl, combine salmon, yogurt, mayonnaise and chilli powder. Add carrot, onion, tomato, avocado and coriander. Season with salt and pepper to taste; stir gently.

2. Stack tortillas; wrap in foil and warm at 350°F (180°C) Gas Mark 4 for 5 minutes.

3. Lay each tortilla flat; top with a lettuce leaf. Spoon salmon mixture down one side of each tortilla; roll up. Makes 4 servings.

Make ahead
To end of step 1, cover and refrigerate for up to two hours.

PER SERVING	
calories	328
g protein	15
g total fat	16
g saturated fat	3
mg cholesterol	13
g carbohydrate	34
g dietary fibre	3
mg sodium	414
mg potassium	695

Good: Folate, Calcium, Iron
Excellent: Vitamin A

Meat

Pork Tenderloin Teriyaki

Lettuce Wrapped Pork

Chalupas

Chick Pea and Pork Curry

Spicy Sausage and
Rice Paella

Honey Garlic Roast Pork

Chutney-Glazed Ham

Lemon Grass Marinated Leg
of Lamb

Onions Stuffed with Lamb
and Spinach

Lamb and Feta Pitta Pockets

Moroccan Rabbit Tagine

Oven-Roasted Pork Tenderloin Teriyaki

In rosting pan or on baking sheet, roast marinated pork at 350°F (180°C) Gas Mark 4 for 40 to 50 minutes or until meat thermometer registers 160°-170°F (70°-75°C). Time is based on meat coming straight from refrigerator. If meat is at room temperature, cooking time will be less.

Pork Tenderloin Teriyaki

Pork tenderloin, one of the leanest cuts of pork, is delicious marinated, then grilled just until moist and juicy. Serve with Grilled Vegetables (page 141).

2 tbsp	sodium-reduced soy sauce	30 ml
2 tbsp	sherry	30 ml
1 tbsp	vegetable oil	15 ml
1 tbsp	finely chopped root ginger	15 ml
1 tsp	granulated sugar	15 ml
1	clove garlic, crushed	1
2	pork tenderloins (about 9 oz/250 g)	2

1. Combine soy sauce, sherry, oil, ginger, sugar and garlic.

2. Place pork in a plastic bag; pour in marinade. Refrigerate for 2 hours.

3. Reserving marinade, place pork on greased rack and grill or barbecue over medium-high heat. Cook for 18 to 25 minutes or until meat thermometer registers 160°F (70°C) for medium or 170°F (75°C) for well done, turning occasionally and brushing with marinade during last 10 minutes.

4. Remove from grill; tent with foil and let stand for 5 minutes. Slice diagonally into thin slices.

Make ahead
To end of step 1, cover and refrigerate for up to two days. To step 2 for up to 24 hours.

PER SERVING	
calories	133
g protein	18
g total fat	5
g saturated fat	1
mg cholesterol	43
g carbohydrate	2
g dietary fibre	0.1
mg sodium	204
mg potassium	358

Oriental Dinner Menu
- Hot and Sour Soup (page 62)
- Lettuce Wrapped Pork
- Thai Noodles with Chicken and Broccoli (page 159)
- Spicy Scallops (page 87)
- Chinese Vegetable Fried Rice (page 170)
- Sugar-snap Peas with Mushrooms (page 135)
- Nectarine and Orange Compote (page 226)

Nutritional Note
Anyone on a sodium-restricted diet can omit the sauce in this recipe and reduce the sodium to less than 350 mg.

Lettuce Wrapped Pork

Whenever we go out for Chinese food in Vancouver, my niece and nephew, Ashley and Jayson Elliott, always pick a dish similar to this. Serve as an appetizer or as part of a main course and let guests wrap their own.

6	dried Chinese mushrooms	6
2 tsp	sesame oil	10 ml
12 oz	lean minced pork	350 g
10	water chestnuts, chopped	10
1	stalk celery, chopped	1
3	spring onions, chopped	3
½ tsp	grated root ginger	2.5 ml
2 tbsp	rice vinegar or sherry	30 ml
2 tbsp	hoisin sauce	30 ml
1 tbsp	sodium-reduced soy sauce	15 ml
12	leaves iceberg lettuce	12
Sauce		
2 tbsp	each hoisin sauce, rice vinegar or sherry and sodium-reduced soy sauce	30 ml
1 tsp	grated root ginger	5 ml

1. Sauce: In a small serving dish, combine hoisin sauce, vinegar, soy sauce and ginger.

2. Remove tough stems from mushrooms. Cover mushrooms with hot water and let soak for 15 minutes; drain and chop.

3. In a nonstick pan or wok, heat oil over high heat; stir-fry pork for 3 minutes; pour off any liquid. Add water chestnuts, celery, onions, ginger and mushrooms; stir-fry until pork is no longer pink. Stir in vinegar, and hoisin and soy sauces.

4. Spoon onto platter; surround with lettuce. Let each person spoon a little pork mixture onto a lettuce leaf, drizzle with sauce and roll up to enclose filling. Makes 4 main-course servings.

Make ahead
To end of step 3, cover and refrigerate for up to one day; reheat in microwave or over medium heat.

PER SERVING	
calories	278
g protein	19
g total fat	13
g saturated fat	4
mg cholesterol	41
g carbohydrate	21
g dietary fibre	2
mg sodium	757
mg potassium	580
Excellent: Folate	

Toppings

Toppings could include individual bowls of chopped lettuce, spring onions, diced tomatoes, chopped green pepper, low-fat yogurt or fromage frais, salsa and grated Cheddar cheese.

Low Sodium

Cooking your own beans instead of using canned, and using lean pork instead of the traditional salt pork or smoked pork hock with beans, means lower sodium.

Chalupas

Actually, in Mexico, Chalupas are round corn tortillas fried with the edges curled up in a little boat shape.

Chalupas

This recipe from my friend Janie Sims is great for a weekend meal after skiing, skating or a winter hike. Let each person pile this spicy bean and pork combination over tortilla chips and top with the traditional Mexican toppings. If pinto beans are unavailable, use kidney beans. Sometimes I also include black beans and haricot beans.

1 lb	lean boneless pork loin	450 g
2¾ pts	boiling water	1.5 L
1 lb	pinto beans	450 g
2	large cloves garlic, crushed	2
2 tbsp	chilli powder	30 ml
1 tbsp	ground cumin or cumin seeds	15 ml
1 tbsp	hot pepper sauce	15 ml
1 tsp	dried oregano	5 ml
16	large flour tortillas	16
	Toppings	

1. In a large casserole dish, combine pork, water, beans, garlic, chilli powder, cumin, hot pepper sauce and oregano. Cover and bake in 250°F (125°C) Gas Mark ½ for 6 hours or until beans are tender and most of the liquid is absorbed and meat falls apart when stirred.

2. Toast tortillas in the oven at 350°F (180°C) Gas Mark 4 for 10 minutes or until crisp; break into crisp sized pieces and place in serving bowl.

3. Let each person spoon some bean mixture over tortilla pieces, then top with toppings. Makes 8 servings.

Make ahead
To end of step 2 for up to two days. Refrigerate bean mixture.

PER SERVING WITHOUT TOPPINGS (WITH TOPPINGS*)	
calories	645 (698)
g protein	34 (38)
g total fat	11 (13)
g saturated fat	3 (4)
mg cholesterol	33 (39)
g carbohydrate	103 (108)
g dietary fibre	15 (16)
mg sodium	502 (668)
mg potassium	1070 (1257)

Good: Vitamin C
Excellent: Folate; Calcium; Iron

* Includes 2 tbsp (30 ml) each chopped green pepper, tomatoes and yogurt and 1 tbsp (15 ml) each salsa and grated Cheddar cheese.

Variations
Minced pork adds flavour and
is inexpensive. Minced beef,
chicken or turkey can also be
used, or for a vegetarian meal,
omit meat and instead sauté
garlic, leek and ginger in 1 tbsp
(15 ml) vegetable oil.

Chick Pea and Pork Curry

Minced beef also works well in this tasty curry. Serve over rice.

8 oz	ground pork	225 g
2 tsp	finely chopped fresh garlic	10 ml
1	white of leek (or 1 onion), chopped	1
2 tsp	grated root ginger	10 ml
1 tbsp	plain flour	15 ml
1 tsp	curry powder	5 ml
¼ tsp	each ground coriander, cumin and salt	1.25 ml
Pinch	cayenne pepper	Pinch
8 oz	butternut squash, cubed	225 g
4 oz	carrot, coarsely grated	115 g
6 oz	potato, cubed	175 g
8 fl oz	water	225 ml
1	can (19 oz/540 ml) chick peas, drained	1
1	apple, cored and chopped	1

1. In a nonstick saucepan, brown pork over medium heat; pour off fat.

2. Add garlic, leek and ginger; cook for 2 minutes.

3. Add flour, curry powder, coriander, cumin, salt and cayenne; cook, stirring, for 1 minute.

4. Add squash, carrot, potato and water; bring to the boil. Reduce heat, cover and simmer for 10 minutes. Add 4 fl oz (125 ml) water if too dry.

5. Add chick peas and apple; cover and cook until vegetables are tender. Makes 4 servings.

Make ahead
Curry can be covered and refrigerated for up to 24 hours.

PER SERVING	
calories	327
g protein	19
g total fat	9
g saturated fat	3
mg cholesterol	27
g carbohydrate	45
g dietary fibre	6
mg sodium	394
mg potassium	634

Good: Iron
Excellent: Vitamin A, Folate

Chicken and Rice Paella
Substitute pieces of skinless chicken (1 lb/450 g) for sausage. Fat per serving would then be cut by about half.

Nutritional Note
Whole-grain rice is a good choice for this dish as it cooks in 20 to 25 minutes and has more nutrients than white rice. If you have time, use brown rice. Cook for 20 minutes, add green pepper and tomatoes, cook another 20 minutes or until rice is tender.

Spicy Sausage and Rice Paella

Hot and spicy Spanish sausage is perfect in this easy rice dish. You can use mild sausage, but then add more hot pepper sauce or a pinch of red pepper flakes to taste.

12 oz	Chorizo sausage, thickly sliced	350 g
1	onion, chopped	1
2	cloves garlic, crushed	2
¾ pt	boiling water or chicken stock	425 ml
6 oz	long-grain rice	175 g
1	sweet green pepper, cut in chunks	1
2	tomatoes, coarsely chopped	2
1	bay leaf	1
¼ tsp	turmeric	1.25 ml
Dash	hot pepper sauce	Dash
6 oz	frozen peas, thawed	175 g
	Salt and pepper	

1. In a large nonstick frying pan, cook sausages over medium heat for 10 minutes or until browned. Pour off fat.

2. Add onion and garlic; cook until softened. Add water, stirring up brown bits from bottom of pan.

3. Stir in rice, green pepper, tomatoes, bay leaf, turmeric and hot pepper sauce; cover and simmer for 20 minutes or until rice is tender.

4. Stir in peas, and salt and pepper to taste. Discard bay leaf. Makes 4 servings.

Make ahead
To end of step 3, cover and refrigerate for up to 24 hours. Reheat in microwave or over medium heat.

PER SERVING	
calories	394
g protein	19
g total fat	13
g saturated fat	4
mg cholesterol	36
g carbohydrate	51
g dietary fibre	4
mg sodium	333
mg potassium	424

Good: Folate
Excellent: Vitamin C

About Pork

Pork used to be cooked until well done to ensure it was safe. Today, trichinosis from pork is virtually nonexistent. This organism, if present, is destroyed when pork is cooked to an internal temperature of 137°F (58°C), well below the recommended 160°F (70°C). Also, because pork is leaner, it should be cooked at a lower oven temperature to medium (internal 160°F/70°C) with just a hint of pink remaining. Cooking to a higher temperature will dry it out and make it tough. Of course, minced pork and sausage should be cooked thoroughly.

Honey Garlic Roast Pork

For easy entertaining, this is one of my all-time favourites. While it's roasting, rich aromas fill your kitchen. Serve with Mango Salsa (page 51) or chutney.

4 lb	boneless pork loin roast	1.8 kg
Marinade		
1 tbsp	sodium-reduced soy sauce	30 ml
2 tbsp	sherry	30 ml
2 tbsp	liquid honey	30 ml
2 tbsp	grated root ginger	30 ml
2	cloves garlic, crushed	2

1. Marinade: Combine soy sauce, water, sherry, honey, ginger and garlic.

2. Trim any fat from meat. Place joint in a large plastic bag and pour marinade over. Tie bag shut and refrigerate for at least 4 hours, turning bag occasionally.

3. Remove the joint from bag, reserving marinade and leaving as much ginger and garlic bits as possible clinging to the meat. Place on rack in a roasting tin. Roast, uncovered and basting occasionally with marinade, at 325°F (160°C) Gas Mark 3 for 2 hours or until meat thermometer registers 160°F (70°C). Let stand for 15 minutes before carving. Makes 12 servings.

Make ahead
To end if step 2 for up to two days.

PER SERVING	
calories	209
g protein	23
g total fat	11
g saturated fat	4
mg cholesterol	53
g carbohydrate	4
g dietary fibre	0.1
mg sodium	139
mg potassium	370

Buffet Dinner for 50 Guests
- Thai Shrimp Salad in Pitta Pockets (triple recipe, page 43)
- Clam Dip with Herbs and crudités (page 35) or any other dip
- Chutney-Glazed Ham (buy a whole semi-boneless ham, about 20 lb/9 kg; double glaze recipe)
- Mango Salsa (page 51)
- Party Thai Noodles, (5 times the recipe, page 157)
- Green Beans (about 5 lb/2.25 kg)
- Tossed Salad Greens with Mustard Garlic Vinaigrette (page 88)
- Elizabeth Baird's Chocolate Angel Food Cake (make 2, page 206)
- Fresh Fruit Salad Vanilla Cream (page 231)
- Light Lemon Squares (make 2, page 200)

PER SERVING	3½ oz/100 g
calories	174
g protein	25
g total fat	6
g saturated fat	2
mg cholesterol	55
g carbohydrate	4
g dietary fibre	0.1
mg sodium	1338
mg potassium	333

Right:
Asian Chicken (page 98)

Chutney-Glazed Ham

I often cook a ham when I want an easy meal to feed a crowd as well as have some leftovers. Ham is a good choice because it is easy (very versatile and you always get succulent cold meat for slicing – which isn't always the case with other meats). Serve with Mango Salsa (page 51) or chutney.

7 lb	part-boned ham joint fillet or knuckle end of leg	3.2 kg
Glaze		
4 oz	brown sugar	115 g
4 tbsp	chutney	60 ml
5 tbsp	plum or peach jam	60 ml
1 tbsp	Dijon mustard	15 ml
1 tbsp	wine vinegar	15 ml
1	clove garlic, finely chopped	1
Dash	hot pepper sauce	Dash

1. Glaze: Combine sugar, chutney, jam, mustard, vinegar, garlic and hot pepper sauce; set aside.

2. Remove skin and all but ¼ inch (5 mm) thick layer of fat on ham. Place, fat side up, in roasting pan. Bake at 325°F (160°C) Gas Mark 3 for 1 hour and 45 minutes for fully cooked ham, or 2 hours and 15 minutes for cook-before-eating ham.

3. Brush with half of the glaze; bake for another 30 minutes. Brush with remaining glaze; bake for 15 minutes or until meat thermometer reaches 130°F (55°C) for ready-to-eat ham or 160°F (70°C) for cook-before-eating ham. Remove from oven and let stand for 10 minutes before slicing. Serve hot or cold. Makes 12 servings.

Make ahead
For cold ham, cover and refrigerate cooked ham for up to two days.

Barbecued Leg of Lamb
Barbecue over hot coals for 15 to 20 minutes on each side for medium-rare, 25 to 30 minutes on each side for well-done.

Lamb Tenderloin or Loin
Marinate up to 2 lb (900 g) of tenderloin in this marinade for 1 hour or up to 2 days. Grill or barbecue over high heat for 3 to 4 minutes for tenderloin, 6 minutes for loin, or until still pink inside, turning once or twice.

Lamb
If buying a leg of frozen lamb, it is best to let it thaw in the refrigerator for 2 days. Lamb is juicy and tender when cooked just until it is pink or medium-rare. If it is overcooked, it will be dried out and not as tender.

PER SERVING	
calories	193
g protein	29
g total fat	7
g saturated fat	3
mg cholesterol	105
g carbohydrate	0.4
g dietary fibre	0
mg sodium	78
mg potassium	198
Good: Iron	

Left:
Fish Mediterranean, made with Red Snapper (page 110)
Lemon Parsley Rice Pilaf (page 173)

Lemon Grass Marinated Leg of Lamb

This is one of my favourite meats for entertaining. As well as having fabulous flavour, it's marinated in advance, it cooks fairly quickly and it's boneless for easy serving. In the summer, we barbecue it; in the winter, we grill. Butterflied simply means boned out and flattened.

1	boneless butterflied leg of lamb (about 3 lb/1.3 kg boned)	1

Marinade

3	stalks lemon grass*	3
1 tbsp	finely chopped onion	15 ml
3 tbsp	lemon juice	45 ml
2 tbsp	fish sauce or sodium-reduced soy sauce	30 ml
1½ tsp	finely chopped fresh garlic	7.5 ml
1 tsp	brown sugar	5 ml
½ tsp	hot pepper sauce	2.5 ml

1. Marinade: Cut off top two-thirds of each lemon grass stalk; trim off outside leaves and roots. Finely chop remaining stalk; combine with onion, lemon juice, fish sauce, garlic, sugar and hot pepper sauce.

2. Trim any fat from lamb; place lamb in a bowl or plastic bag; pour marinade over. Cover and refrigerate for at least 12 hours, turning occasionally.

3. Remove lamb from refrigerator about 1 hour before cooking. Grill about 6 inches (15 cm) from heat for 12 minutes on each side for medium-rare, 15 to 20 minutes on each side for well-done. Meat thermometer should register 150°F (65°C) for medium-rare, 160°F (70°C) for medium or 170°F (75°C) for well-done. Remove from heat; let stand for 10 minutes. Slice thinly across the grain. Makes 8 servings.

Make ahead
To end of step 2 for up to two days.

* See Information on Ingredients (page 32). If fresh lemon grass is unavailable, use 2 tbsp (30 ml) dried, or grated rind from 1 lemon.

Onions Stuffed with Lamb and Spinach

Tender, juicy onions are filled with a tasty Middle Eastern stuffing. Use any kind of large onion – Spanish, red or ordinary cooking onions – 3½ to 4 inches (9 to 10 cm) in diameter (or use 8 medium onions). Serve with couscous, cooked rice or bulgur.

5	large onions	5
8 oz	lean minced lamb	225 g
¼ tsp	each cinnamon, allspice and ground cumin	1.25 ml
6 oz	fresh spinach, chopped	175 g
1	egg	1
2 oz	coarse fresh breadcrumbs	55 g
	salt and pepper	
8 fl oz	hot stock (lamb* or beef)	225 ml

1. Peel onions; cut slice off top, then off root end so they will stand. Cut cone shape into top of onion; remove cone.
Using melon baller or teaspoon, hollow out onion to make ½-inch (1 cm) thick shell; chop 8 oz (225 g) of the removed onion and reserve.

2. Blanch onion shells in boiling water for 5 minutes. Remove and drain upside down on rack.

3. In a nonstick pan, cook lamb over medium heat, stirring to break up, for 3 minutes or until browned; pour off fat.
Add chopped onion, cinnamon, allspice and cumin; cook until onion is tender.

4. Add spinach and cook until wilted. Remove from heat. Stir in egg, breadcrumbs, and salt and pepper to taste. Spoon into onion shells.

5. Pour hot stock into pan. Bake at 375°F (190°C) Gas Mark 5 for 30 minutes. Cover with foil and bake for 10 minutes longer or until onion is tender. Makes 5 servings.

Make ahead
To end of step 4, cover and refrigerate for up to four hours.

PER SERVING	
calories	190
g protein	13
g total fat	8
g saturated fat	3
mg cholesterol	73
g carbohydrate	19
g dietary fibre	3
mg sodium	258
mg potassium	463

Good: Vitamin A, Iron
Excellent: Folate

* See lamb stock recipe (page 70).

Lamb and Spinach with Rice
Instead of a filling for pittas, this is also a quick and easy supper dish served over hot rice. Top the lamb mixture with the diced tomato, then drizzle with yogurt.

Lamb and Feta Pitta Pockets

Pork or beef can also be used in this tasty filling for pittas.

4	6-inch (15 cm) pitta breads	4
12 oz	lean minced lamb	350 g
1	onion, finely chopped	1
2 tsp	finely chopped fresh garlic	10 ml
1	celery stalk, chopped	1
10 oz	chopped frozen spinach, thawed and squeezed dry	280 g
2 tsp	dried oregano	10 ml
	salt and pepper	
3 oz	crumbled feta cheese	85 g
	Lettuce leaves (optional)	
1	tomato, diced	1
4 fl oz	low-fat yogurt	125 ml

1. Cut pittas in half; slide knife into each half to form pocket. Warm in the oven at 325°F (160°C) Gas Mark 3 for 5 minutes.

2. Meanwhile, in large nonstick frying pan, cook lamb, onion, garlic and celery over medium-high heat for 5 minutes or until vegetables are tender. Pour off any liquid.

3. Add spinach, oregano, and salt and pepper to taste; cook for 2 minutes or until heated through.

4. Remove from heat. Crumble in cheese.

5. Line each pitta with lettuce (if using); spoon in lamb mixture. Top with tomato and yogurt. Makes 4 servings.

Make ahead
To end of step 3, cover and refrigerate for up to four hours. Reheat in microwave or over medium heat.

PER SERVING	
calories	427
g protein	27
g total fat	16
g saturated fat	7
mg cholesterol	71
g carbohydrate	44
g dietary fibre	4
mg sodium	521
mg potassium	711

Good: Vitamin C
Excellent: Vitamin A, Folate Calcium; iron

Moroccan Chicken Tagine
Substitute 3 lb (1.3 kg) bone-in skinless chicken pieces for rabbit.

Tagine
A tagine is a North African stew usually served over couscous. I don't know if they make a rabbit tagine, but this one tastes wonderful.

Moroccan Rabbit Tagine

A letter from the Ontario Commercial Rabbit Growers Association telling me of the nutritional benefits of rabbit meat made me want to include a rabbit recipe. This one, unlike most traditional rabbit dishes, is low in added fat and spiked with North African seasonings. Serve with plain couscous (see page 180), rice or bulgur.

2 tsp	vegetable oil	10 ml
2 tsp	chopped fresh garlic	10 ml
2	onions, sliced	2
2 tbsp	chopped root ginger	30 ml
1 tsp	each ground coriander, cumin and turmeric	5 ml
½ tsp	cinnamon	2.5 ml
¼ tsp	each salt and pepper	1.25 ml
1	skinned rabbit (3 lb/1.3 kg), cut in pieces	1
1 lb	sweet potato, peeled and chopped	450 g
10 oz	carrots, chopped	280 g
10 oz	parsnips, chopped	280 g
1	can (28 oz/796 g) tomatoes	1
7 oz	pitted prunes	200 g
4 tbsp	chopped fresh parsley and/or coriander	60 ml

1. In a large flameproof casserole, heat oil over medium-high heat; cook garlic, onions, ginger, ground coriander, cumin, turmeric, cinnamon, salt and pepper, stirring often, for 3 minutes.
2. Add rabbit; cook for 5 minutes or until lightly browned. Add potato, carrots, parsnips and tomatoes; bring to the boil.
3. Cook, covered, at 325°F (160°C) Gas Mark 3 for 35 minutes.
4. Add prunes; cook for 5 minutes or until rabbit is tender, meat easily falls away from bone and vegetables are fork-tender. Stir in parsley and/or coriander. Makes 6 servings.

Make ahead
To end of step 3, cover and refrigerate for up to one day or freeze for up to two weeks. Thaw completely. Reheat at 350°F (180°C) Gas Mark 4, uncovered, for 30 to 40 minutes or until pipping hot.

PER SERVING	
calories	444
g protein	39
g total fat	12
g saturated fat	3
mg cholesterol	98
g carbohydrate	46
g dietary fibre	8
mg sodium	398
mg potassium	1193

Excellent: Vitamin A
Vitamin C, Folate; Iron

Vegetables

Sesame Carrots

Mange Tout with
Mushrooms

Sherried Green Beans with
Sweet Red Pepper

Green Beans with Herbs
and Pine Nuts

Spinach with Lemon and
Nutmeg

Cauliflower with Fresh Dill

Ginger Stir-Fried Courgettes

Field Mushrooms with
Sweet Peppers

Grilled Autumn Vegetables

Barbecued Potato Packets

Rosemary Garlic Roasted
Potatoes

Buttermilk Mashed Potatoes

Sweet Potato and Apple
Purée

Sesame Broccoli and Carrots
Prepare Sesame Carrots recipe, add 1 lb (450 g) broccoli and use 2 tbsp (30 ml) sesame seeds. Trim tough ends from broccoli. Peel stalks and slice diagonally. Separate head into florets. Steam broccoli then toss with carrots and ginger mixture. Makes 8 servings.

Beta Carotene
Carrots, raw or cooked, are an excellent source of beta carotene, an antioxidant vitamin. Health professionals recommend we eat more dark green and orange vegetables as they are rich in vitamins.

Sesame Carrots

The crunch of sesame seeds really adds a delicious dimension to familiar carrots.

6	carrots (1 lb/450 g)	6
1 tbsp	sesame seeds	15 ml
2 tbsp	orange juice	30 ml
1 tsp	grated root ginger	5 ml
1 tsp	sesame oil	5 ml
½ tsp	soy sauce	2.5 ml
	salt and pepper	

1. Peel carrots; cut into sticks.

2. In a small frying pan, cook sesame seeds over medium heat for 2 minutes or until golden, shaking pan occasionally.

3. Combine orange juice, ginger, sesame oil and soy sauce.

4. Steam carrots for about 8 minutes or until tender-crisp.
(Or toss carrots with 2 tbsp/30 ml water; cover and microwave at High for 5 minutes.)

5. Toss with sesame seeds and ginger mixture. Season with salt and pepper to taste. Makes 4 servings.

Make ahead
To end of step 3 for up to three hours.

PER SERVING	
calories	67
g protein	2
g total fat	3
g saturated fat	0.4
mg cholesterol	0
g carbohydrate	10
g dietary fibre	2
mg sodium	99
mg potassium	225
Excellent: Vitamin A	

Vitamins

Vitamins
There is a lot of attention now being paid to the role of vitamins in protecting us against heart disease and certain cancers. It is important to get our vitamins from food and not to rely on supplements, as food contains fibre, energy and other important nutrients not found in supplements. Dark green and orange vegetables and orange fruits are rich sources of vitamins.

Sugar-Snap Peas with Mushrooms

Use any kind or combination of mushrooms in this colourful, easy vegetable dish (pictured opposite page 96). If using dried wild mushrooms, soak in warm water to soften before cooking. A few ounces of dried wild mushrooms mixed with some fresh brown mushrooms is a nice combination.

1 lb	sugar-snap peas	450 g
1 tbsp	olive oil	15 ml
8 oz	mushrooms, thickly sliced	225 g
	salt and pepper	

1. Remove stem and string from sugar-snap peas.

2. In a large nonstick frying pan, heat oil over medium-high heat; cook mushrooms, stirring or shaking pan, for 8 to 10 minutes or until browned, tender and any liquid has evaporated.

3. Blanch sugar-snap peas in boiling water for 2 to 4 minutes or until tender; drain well.

4. Toss sugar-snap peas with mushrooms. Season with salt and pepper to taste. Makes 8 servings.

Make ahead
To end of step 3 for up to four hours. After blanching sugar-snap peas, cool in iced water and drain thoroughly. Reheat in boiling water for 30 seconds. Reheat mushrooms in pan over medium heat before step 4.

PER SERVING	
calories	43
g protein	2
g total fat	2
g saturated fat	0.3
mg cholesterol	0
g carbohydrate	5
g dietary fibre	2
mg sodium	3
mg potassium	200
Good: Vitamin C	

Microwave Method for Sauce
In microwaveable dish, combine water, sherry, soy sauce, ginger and cornflour; microwave at High for 3 to 4 minutes, stirring after each minute, until boiling and thickened. Let cool slightly. Add sesame oil.

Sherried Green Beans with Sweet Red Pepper

This colourful vegetable dish goes well with any meats, fish or poultry.

4½ fl oz	water	140 ml
4 tbsp	dry sherry	60 ml
1 tbsp	sodium-reduced soy sauce	30 ml
1 tbsp	grated root ginger	15 ml
2 tsp	cornflour	10 ml
1 tbsp	sesame oil	15 ml
1½ lb	green beans, ends and strings removed	675 g
1	large sweet red pepper, diced	1

1. In a saucepan, combine water, sherry, soy sauce, ginger and cornflour; cook over medium-high heat, stirring constantly, until boiling and thickened. Remove from heat. Stir in sesame oil.

2. In a separate saucepan of boiling water, cook beans for 6 to 8 minutes or until tender-crisp; drain. Pour hot sauce over beans; mix gently. Transfer to serving dish; sprinkle red pepper on top. Makes 10 servings.

Make ahead
To end of step 1 for up to three hours; reheat over medium-high heat, stirring continuously, or microwave at High for one minute, until hot.

PER SERVING	
calories	44
g protein	1
g total fat	2
g saturated fat	0.2
mg cholesterol	0
g carbohydrate	6
g dietary fibre	2
mg sodium	100
mg potassium	208
Good: Vitamin C	

Green Beans with Herbs and Pine Nuts

Green beans are a tasty and colourful addition to most dinners.

2 tbsp	pine nuts or sunflower seeds	30 ml
1½ lb	green beans, trimmed	675 g
4 tbsp	chopped fresh dill or parsley	60 ml
½ oz	soft margarine or butter, melted	15 g
2 tsp	lemon juice	10 ml
	salt and pepper	

1. Toast nuts in the oven at 350°F (180°C) for 5 minutes or until golden.

2. In a large saucepan of boiling water, cook beans for 5 minutes or until tender-crisp. Drain thoroughly.

3. Add dill and margarine; toss gently. Add lemon juice, and salt and pepper to taste; toss again. Sprinkle with pine nuts.
Makes 10 servings.

Make ahead
To end of step 2; immediately plunge into cold water, then drain. Wrap in clean tea towel and refrigerate for up to six hours. Reheat in boiling water for one minute or until heated through; drain and continue with step 3.

PER SERVING	
calories	45
g protein	2
g total fat	2
g saturated fat	1
mg cholesterol	3
g carbohydrate	6
g dietary fibre	2
mg sodium	14
mg potassium	221

Spinach with Lemon and Nutmeg

Spinach adds a pretty colour to a plate and goes well with almost any fish, meat or poultry. This quick-cooking method maximizes the spinach's nutrients.

10 oz	fresh spinach	280 g
2 tsp	lemon juice	10 ml
1 tsp	soft margarine or butter, melted	5 ml
Pinch	nutmeg	Pinch
	salt and pepper	

1. Rinse spinach and shake off excess water.

2. In a large saucepan, cover and cook spinach with just the water clinging to leaves over medium heat for 2 minutes or just until wilted; drain well.

3. Sprinkle with lemon juice, margarine, nutmeg, and salt and pepper to taste. Makes 3 servings.

PER SERVING	
calories	32
g protein	3
g total fat	2
g saturated fat	0.2
mg cholesterol	0
g carbohydrate	4
g dietary fibre	3
mg sodium	81
mg potassium	427

Good: Iron
Excellent: Vitamin A, Folate

Cauliflower with Fresh Dill

Fresh dill goes well with most vegetables and is very good with cauliflower. This dish is also good served cold and makes a wonderful addition to a summer salad.

1	medium head cauliflower	1
2 tbsp	lemon juice	30 ml
1 tbsp	olive oil	15 ml
5 tbsp	chopped fresh dill	75 ml
	salt and pepper	
	chopped sweet red pepper or tomato (optional)	

1. Remove leaves and stem from cauliflower; cut cauliflower into florets. Cook in large pan of boiling water, covered, for 10 minutes or until tender; drain. Transfer to serving dish.

2. Mix lemon juice with oil; pour over cauliflower and stir to mix. Sprinkle with dill, and salt and pepper to taste. Garnish with red pepper (if using). Makes 6 servings.

PER SERVING	
calories	44
g protein	2
g total fat	2
g saturated fat	0.3
mg cholesterol	0
g carbohydrate	5
g dietary fibre	2
mg sodium	6
mg potassium	310

Good: Folate
Excellent: Vitamin C

Ginger Stir-Fried Courgettes

Add carrots, cauliflower, red onion, bean sprouts or any seasonal
vegetables to this easy stir-fry.

1 tsp	vegetable oil	5 ml
10 oz	courgettes, sliced	280 g
Half	red onion, sliced	Half
2 tsp	chopped root ginger	10 ml
1 tbsp	sodium-reduced soy sauce	15 ml
1 tsp	dark sesame oil	5 ml
	salt and pepper	

1. In a nonstick frying pan, heat oil over medium-high heat; stir-
fry courgette, onion and ginger for 1 minute.

2. Add 1 tbsp (15 ml) water; cover and steam for 1 to 2 minutes
or until tender-crisp, adding more water if necessary to prevent
scorching.

3. Stir in soy sauce and oil. Season with salt and pepper to taste.
Makes 4 servings.

PER SERVING	
calories	51
g protein	1
g total fat	2
g saturated fat	0.3
mg cholesterol	0
g carbohydrate	7
g dietary fibre	2
mg sodium	124
mg potassium	227

Barbecued Field Mushrooms
These are delicious on the barbecue and because of their size, easy to manage. Cut into ¼-inch (5 mm) thick slices; brush lightly with olive oil and cook over medium heat for 4 to 6 minutes or until tender, turning once.

Field Mushrooms
These mushrooms are dark brown with 5- to 10-inch (13 to 25 cm) wide caps with prominent gills underneath. Because mushrooms are open and dirt is often in the gills, they need to be washed by quickly swishing through a bowl of water. When cooked, they turn mostly black.

Field Mushrooms with Sweet Peppers

Huge flat mushrooms have much more flavour than button mushrooms and are easy to cook. Thanks to mushroom lover Dave Nichol and Ontario mushroom farmer Lou Argo, I have a good supply. If unavailable, use large, open cup or brown mushrooms.

1 lb	flat field mushrooms	450 g
2 tbsp	soft margarine, butter or olive oil	30 ml
1	clove garlic, crushed (optional)	1
1	each sweet red and yellow pepper, cut in strips	1
	salt and pepper	

1. Wash mushrooms quickly in a little water; pat dry. Cut into ¼-inch (5 mm) thick slices.

2. In a large nonstick frying pan, heat margarine over high heat; cook garlic, red and yellow peppers and mushrooms, shaking pan or stirring often, for 7 to 10 minutes or until vegetables are tender and any liquid from mushrooms has nearly disappeared.

3. Sprinkle with salt and pepper to taste. Makes 6 servings.

PER SERVING	
calories	58
g protein	2
g total fat	4
g saturated fat	1
mg cholesterol	0
g carbohydrate	5
g dietary fibre	2
mg sodium	52
mg potassium	251
Excellent: Vitamin C	

Barbecued Peppers

These autumn vegetables are delicious barbecued too. Another of my favourite vegetables is barbecued sweet red peppers. The problem is cooking them enough to be tender without burning – the minute you forget to watch they burn.

My husband, Bob, does the barbecuing and has tried a number of ways to barbecue peppers, from cooking over high heat and turning often, to his latest, which is to barbecue peppers cut in quarters about 10 minutes over medium-low heat, turning once. Then he moves them to the side of the barbecue, not over the heat, where they continue to cook gently while he barbecues the meat over the hot coals.

Total cooking time varies with the outdoor temperature but is about 20 to 30 minutes.

Grilled Autumn Vegetables

Steaming the aubergine first shortens the grilling time and keeps it moist, which means you don't need to brush it with oil. Serve this side dish hot or at room temperature.

1	aubergine (about 12 oz/350 g)	1
2	courgettes (about 7 inches/18 cm each)	2
2 tbsp	olive oil	30 ml
3	sweet peppers (red, green and yellow)	3
2 tbsp	balsamic vinegar	30 ml
2 tbsp	chopped fresh thyme (or ¼ tsp/1.25 ml dried)	30 ml
1 tbsp	water	15 ml
	salt and pepper	

1. Cut aubergine into ½-inch (1 cm) thick slices. Place in steamer in single layer; steam for 4 minutes.

2. Cut courgettes diagonally into ¼-inch (5 mm) thick slices; brush with 1 tsp (5 ml) of the oil.

3. Seed and cut peppers lengthways into 8 pieces.

4. Grill vegetables, in batches if necessary, under high heat for 4 to 6 minutes on each side or until tender but firm. Transfer to a serving bowl.

5. Whisk together remaining oil, vinegar, thyme, water, and salt and pepper to taste. Pour over hot vegetables and toss to coat. Makes 6 servings.

Make ahead

Vegetables can be covered and refrigerated for up to one day. Serve at room temperature.

PER SERVING	
calories	80
g protein	1
g total fat	5
g saturated fat	1
mg cholesterol	0
g carbohydrate	10
g dietary fibre	3
mg sodium	4
mg potassium	366

Good: Vitamin A
Excellent: Vitamin C

Barbecued Potato Packets

Just scrub tender new potatoes, leaving the skin on for texture and nutrients. Instead of dried herbs, you can use 1 tbsp (15 ml) of any fresh herbs such as rosemary, basil, thyme, dill and/or oregano.

4	new potatoes, thinly sliced	4
l	onion, thinly sliced	1
1	clove garlic, finely chopped	1
1 tbsp	olive oil	15 ml
¼ tsp	each dried thyme, rosemary	1.25 ml
	salt and pepper	

1. Toss potatoes with onion, garlic, oil, thyme, rosemary, salt and pepper.

2. Divide among 4 pieces of greased heavy-duty foil; wrap well to seal.

3. Barbecue over medium heat for 20 minutes or until tender. Makes 4 servings.

Make ahead
To end of step 2, refrigerate for up to four hours.

PER SERVING	
calories	165
g protein	3
g total fat	4
g saturated fat	0.5
mg cholesterol	0
g carbohydrate	31
g dietary fibre	3
mg sodium	153
mg potassium	515

Rosemary Garlic Roasted Potatoes

Cook these the same time you are roasting any meat or poultry. With these potatoes, the oven temperature can vary depending on what else is in the oven.

2 lb	potatoes, cut into wedges	900 g
1 tbsp	olive oil	15 ml
2 tsp	chopped fresh garlic	10 ml
2 tsp	chopped fresh or dried rosemary	10 ml
	salt and pepper	

1. In a large shallow baking dish, toss potatoes with oil, garlic, rosemary, and salt and pepper to taste.

2. Bake, uncovered, at 325°F (160°C) Gas Mark 3 for 1 hour or until fork-tender. Makes 6 servings.

PER SERVING	
calories	118
g protein	2
g total fat	2
g saturated fat	0.3
mg cholesterol	0
g carbohydrate	23
g dietary fibre	2
mg sodium	6
mg potassium	370

Oven-Baked Fries

Cut 4 (unpeeled) potatoes into wedges or ½ inch (1 cm) thick strips; toss with 1 tbsp (15 ml) vegetable oil, ½ tsp (2.5 ml) each paprika and chilli powder. Bake on baking sheet at 475°F (240°C) Gas Mark 9 for 25 to 30 minutes or until golden, turning occasionally. Toss with salt. Makes 4 servings. You can do this with peeled turnip, parsnips and sweet potatoes too.

New Potatoes with Herbs

Scrub 4 new potatoes; halve or quarter if large. Boil for 12 to 14 minutes or until tender. Drain and toss with 2 tbsp (30 ml) chopped fresh parsley or dill, 2 tsp (10 ml) olive oil, and salt and pepper to taste. Makes 4 servings.
Per Serving: about 160 calories, 3 g protein, 2 g fat, 32 g carbohydrate

Buttermilk Mashed Potatoes

These creamy potatoes are fabulous. I'm often asked what to do with leftover buttermilk: this is one of the best ways I know. Instead of mashing, a potato ricer or food mill also works well.

10	medium potatoes (about 3 lb/1.3 kg), peeled and quartered	10
¾ pt	buttermilk	425 ml
½ oz	soft margarine or butter	15 g
1	spring onion, chopped	1
Pinch	nutmeg	Pinch
	salt and pepper	

1. In a large saucepan, cover potatoes with cold water; bring to the boil and cook for 20 minutes or until fork-tender. Drain; return to low heat for 3 minutes to dry.

2. Mash potatoes to remove all lumps. Gradually beat in buttermilk and margarine. Stir in spring onion and nutmeg. Season with salt and pepper to taste. Makes 12 servings.

Make ahead

To end of step 2; spoon into lightly greased 3½ pint (2 L) baking dish. Let cool, cover and refrigerate for up to three days. Do not freeze. To serve: Let stand at room temperature for 30 minutes before reheating in the oven, covered, at 350°F (180°C) Gas Mark 4 for 50 minutes.

PER SERVING	
calories	97
g protein	3
g total fat	1
g saturated fat	0.4
mg cholesterol	1
g carbohydrate	19
g dietary fibre	1
mg sodium	60
mg potassium	339

Oven-Roasted Vegetables

Sunday night, I like to cook a chicken or joint. To go along with it, I usually roast onions (halved). and parsnips, carrots, potatoes, sweet potatoes and leeks cut in ½-inch (1 cm) thick pieces. I place them in a shallow pan and toss with enough meat-pan juices to keep them from sticking. Roast at 325°F (160°C) Gas Mark 3, or whatever temperature meat requires, for 60 to 90 minutes.

While the meat rests at room temperature for 15 minutes before carving, raise the oven temperature to 450°F (230°C) Gas Mark 8 if the vegetables are not yet cooked, and cook until tender.

To Toast Sunflower Seeds
Bake on baking sheet at 350°F
(180°C) Gas Mark 4 for 5
minutes or until golden.

Nutritional Note
Sweet potatoes are packed
with beta carotene, which the
body converts to Vitamin A.
They are also high in fibre and
Vitamin C. Try baking them in
the oven or microwave as you
would regular potatoes.

Sweet Potato and Apple Purée

This make-ahead dish goes well with roast chicken, turkey, ham or pork.

3 lb	sweet potatoes, peeled and cubed (about 6 medium)	1.3 kg
3	large cooking apples, peeled and chopped	3
4 tbsp	water	60 ml
1 oz	soft margarine or butter	25 g
	nutmeg, salt and pepper	
2 tbsp	toasted sunflower seeds (optional)	30 ml

1. In a saucepan of boiling water, cook potatoes for 15 minutes or until tender when pierced with fork. Drain and return to saucepan.

2. In a small saucepan, combine apples with water; cover and simmer for 5 to 6 minutes or until tender.

3. Using potato masher or in food processor, purée potatoes and apples until smooth. Stir in margarine, and nutmeg, salt and pepper to taste.

4. Transfer to serving dish; sprinkle sunflower seeds on top (if using). Makes 12 servings.

Make ahead
To end of step 3; transfer to 3½ pint (2 L) baking dish; cover and refrigerate for up to three days, or freeze for up to two weeks.
Let stand at room temperature for one hour, or thaw in refrigerator for 24 hours. Reheat, uncovered, in the oven at 350°F (180°C) Gas Mark 4 for 30 minutes or until heated through.

PER SERVING	
calories	150
g protein	2
g total fat	2
g saturated fat	0.4
mg cholesterol	0
g carbohydrate	32
g dietary fibre	4
mg sodium	38
mg potassium	235
Good: Vitamin C	
Excellent: Vitamin A	

Pasta

Pasta with Chick Peas, Tomatoes and Herbs

Pasta with Tomatoes, Cheese and Jalapeños

Spaghettini with Ham and Cheese

Macaroni and Cheese

Light Fettuccine Alfredo with Fresh Herbs

Linguine with Mushrooms and Green Peppers

Summer Prawn and Tomato Pasta

Linguine with Scallops and Leeks

Pasta Provençal with Tofu

Singapore Noodles with Pork

Jiffy Chinese Noodles

Make-Ahead Party Thai Noodles

Szechuan Beef with Noodles

Thai Noodles with Chicken and Broccoli

Singapore Noodle and Chicken Salad

Spicy Noodle Salad

Pasta Salad with Sun-Dried Tomatoes

Pasta and Ham Salad with Tomato Basil Dressing

Seafood Pasta Salad

Chick peas
Chick peas are high in fibre
and iron. They also contribute
calcium and protein.

Pasta with Chick Peas, Tomatoes and Herbs

Keep the makings for this easy, inexpensive yet tasty dinner on
your shelf for when the refrigerator is bare and you need to have
dinner ready in minutes.

8 oz	penne, twists or other pasta shape	225 g
1 tbsp	olive oil	15 ml
1	large clove garlic, crushed	1
1	can (19 oz/540 ml) tomatoes (undrained), chopped	1
1 tsp	each dried basil and oregano	5 ml
1	can (19 oz/540 ml) chick peas drained and rinsed	1
4 tbsp	chopped fresh basil or parsley	60 ml
4 tbsp	freshly grated Parmesan cheese	60 ml

1. In a large pan of boiling water, cook pasta until tender but firm,
7 to 10 minutes; drain and transfer to large bowl.

2. Meanwhile, in saucepan, heat oil over medium heat; cook
garlic for 30 seconds. Add tomatoes, dried basil, oregano and
chick peas; simmer for 5 minutes.

3. Add fresh basil; simmer for 5 minutes. Pour over hot pasta and
toss to mix. Sprinkle cheese over each serving. Makes 4 servings.

Make ahead
Sauce, to end of step 2, cover and refrigerate for up to two days.

PER SERVING	
calories	444
g protein	19
g total fat	8
g saturated fat	2
mg cholesterol	5
g carbohydrate	75
g dietary fibre	7
mg sodium	543
mg potassium	508

Good: Vitamin C, Calcium, Iron
Excellent: Folate

Leftovers

Any leftovers of this pasta dish can be covered and refrigerated; to reheat, add a spoonful or two of water, cover and microwave until hot.

Canned Tomatoes

Use 1 can (28 oz/ 796 ml) tomatoes, undrained (chopped), instead of fresh. Cook garlic mixture in oil for 1 minute; add tomatoes and simmer, uncovered, for 5 minutes. Toss with pasta and cheese.

Pasta with Tomatoes, Cheese and Jalapeños

Keep a jar of pickled jalapeños in your refrigerator to add zing to this easy pasta. Vary the amount or kind of hot pepper, depending upon your tastes. Serve with toasted wholemeal buns and a green salad.

1 lb	linguine or other pasta	450 g
2 tbsp	crushed fresh garlic	30 ml
2 oz	parsley, coarsely chopped	50 g
2 tbsp	chopped pickled jalapeño peppers	30 ml
2 tbsp	olive oil	30 ml
3	large beef tomatoes, chopped	3
4 oz	freshly grated Parmesan	115 g

1. In a large pan of boiling water, cook linguine until tender yet firm; drain.

2. Meanwhile, in food processor, chop garlic, parsley and peppers until fine.

3. In a nonstick frying pan, heat oil over high heat; cook garlic mixture and tomatoes for 1 minute or until hot. Toss with linguine. Add cheese and toss to mix. Makes 6 servings.

PER SERVING	
calories	424
g protein	18
g total fat	11
g saturated fat	4
mg cholesterol	13
g carbohydrate	63
g dietary fibre	5
mg sodium	326
mg potassium	355

Good: Vitamin A, Folate
Calcium, Iron
Excellent: Vitamin C

Nutritional Note
For a fat-restricted diet, use
2 oz (50 g) grated cheese.
The fat content will be 5 g per
serving.

Spaghettini with Ham and Cheese

Any shape or kind of pasta is fine in this recipe. Low-fat gouda-style cheese, mozzarella or reduced-fat Cheddar-type cheese work well here. Instead of courgettes, you can use a grated carrot, chopped spring onions or frozen peas.

8 oz	spaghettini	225 g
8 oz	low-fat cottage cheese	225 g
4 oz	low-fat cheese, grated	115 g
4 tbsp	skimmed milk	60 ml
¼ tsp	each salt and pepper	1.25 ml
Pinch	nutmeg	Pinch
2	small courgettes, halved lengthways and thinly sliced	2
4 oz	ham, cut in very fine strips	115 g
2 tbsp	chopped fresh parsley	30 ml

1. In a large pan of boiling water, cook pasta until tender yet firm; drain and return to saucepan.

2. Meanwhile, in food processor or pressing through sieve, purée cottage cheese. Combine with grated cheese, milk, salt, pepper and nutmeg; add to hot pasta.

3. Add courgettes and ham; cook over medium-low heat, stirring, for 1 minute or until heated through.

4. Sprinkle with parsley. Makes 4 servings.

PER SERVING	
calories	405
g protein	30
g total fat	9
g saturated fat	5
mg cholesterol	37
g carbohydrate	49
g dietary fibre	4
mg sodium	925
mg potassium	420
Good: Folate	
Excellent: Calcium	

Cooking Pasta
Cook pasta in a large pan of boiling water, uncovered. If there isn't enough water, the pasta could stick together. There is no need to add oil to the water to prevent the pasta from sticking.

I don't add salt to the cooking water. Rather, I taste the pasta after the sauce has been added to see if it needs salt. Usually the salt from cheese or canned tomatoes is enough.

Macaroni and Cheese

This creamy dish is made lower in fat by thickening the sauce with cornflour instead of the traditional butter-flour mixture and using lower-fat cheeses.

8 oz	macaroni	225 g
1	onion, coarsely chopped	1
¾ pt	skimmed milk	425 ml
2 tbsp	cornflour	30 ml
1 tsp	dry mustard	5 ml
4 oz	reduced-fat Cheddar-style cheese, grated	115 g
4 oz	gouda-style low-fat cheese, grated	115 g
	salt and pepper	
1	tomato, thinly sliced	1

Topping

1 oz	fresh breadcrumbs	25 g
2 tbsp	freshly grated Parmesan cheese	30 ml
½ oz	soft margarine or butter, melted	15 g

1. In a large pan of boiling water, cook macaroni for 5 minutes; add onion and cook for 5 minutes or until macaroni is tender but firm; drain.

2. In a separate large saucepan, combine milk, cornflour and mustard; cook, stirring, over medium heat until thickened.

3. Stir in Cheddar and gouda cheeses until melted. Stir in macaroni; season with salt and pepper to taste. Transfer to a large shallow baking dish. Top evenly with tomato slices.

4. Topping: Combine breadcrumbs, cheese and margarine; sprinkle over macaroni.

5. Bake, uncovered, at 350°F (180°C) Gas Mark 4 for 20 minutes or until pipping hot. Makes 5 servings.

Make ahead
To end of step 4, cover and refrigerate for up to four hours.

PER SERVING	
calories	406
g protein	24
g total fat	14
g saturated fat	8
mg cholesterol	36
g carbohydrate	46
g dietary fibre	3
mg sodium	442
mg potassium	310

Good: Vitamin A
Excellent: Calcium

Fettuccine Alfredo with Salmon
Stir in 1 can (7.5 oz/213 g) salmon, drained, before seasoning with salt and pepper only.

Nutritional Note
Traditional Fettuccine Alfredo recipes usually call for butter and whipping cream. This one has one-third of the fat yet is creamy and flavourful.

Light Fettuccine Alfredo with Fresh Herbs

This is the easiest and fastest way to make a creamy pasta dish – it's also delicious. Evaporated milk is creamier than semi-skimmed milk and works well in this dish.

8 oz	fettuccine	225 g
1 tbsp	olive oil	15 ml
1	clove garlic, crushed	1
8 fl oz	semi-skimmed evaporated milk	225 ml
2 oz	freshly grated Parmesan cheese	55 g
4 tbsp	chopped fresh parsley	60 ml
4 tbsp	chopped fresh basil (or 1 tsp/5 ml dried)	60 ml
	nutmeg, salt and pepper	

1. In a large pan of boiling water, cook fettuccine until tender but firm; drain and return to saucepan.

2. Meanwhile, in a small nonstick frying pan, heat oil over medium-high heat; cook garlic for 1 minute. (Alternatively, in microwaveable dish, microwave garlic and oil on Medium for 30 seconds.)

3. Add garlic mixture, evaporated milk, cheese, parsley and basil to drained pasta. Cook, stirring, over medium heat until sauce is heated through and thickened slightly, about 3 minutes. Season with nutmeg, salt and pepper to taste. Makes 3 servings.

PER SERVING	
calories	478
g protein	23
g total fat	13
g saturated fat	5
mg cholesterol	20
g carbohydrate	67
g dietary fibre	4
mg sodium	408
mg potassium	390

Good: Vitamin C, Folate
Excellent: Calcium

Linguine with Mushrooms and Green Peppers

I like to use a combination of different mushrooms – brown, flat or wild – in this pasta. If you use dried mushrooms, soak them first in hot water and add the soaking liquid to the pasta cooking water. I use evaporated milk because it is thick like cream, however you can also use ordinary whole milk.

1 lb	linguine	450 g
1 tbsp	olive oil	15 ml
1	large onion, chopped	1
2 tsp	chopped fresh garlic	10 ml
1 lb	mushrooms, sliced	450 g
1	sweet red, green or yellow pepper, thinly sliced	1
8 fl oz	semi-skimmed evaporated milk	225 ml
2 oz	chopped fresh parsley	55 g
2 oz	freshly grated Parmesan cheese	55 g
	salt and pepper	

1. In a large pan of boiling water, cook linguine until tender yet firm; drain.

2. Meanwhile, in a large nonstick frying pan, heat oil over medium heat; cook onion and garlic until softened.
Add mushrooms; cook, stirring often, for 5 minutes or until tender. Add sweet pepper; cook for 2 minutes.

3. Stir in milk; bring to the boil. Stir in parsley and cheese; toss with hot pasta. Season with salt and pepper to taste.
Makes 6 servings.

PER SERVING	
calories	411
g protein	18
g total fat	7
g saturated fat	3
mg cholesterol	10
g carbohydrate	69
g dietary fibre	6
mg sodium	210
mg potassium	516

Good: Vitamin A, Folate, Iron
Excellent: Vitamin C, Calcium

Nutritional Note
Someone on a cholesterol-
restricted diet should substitute
raw scallops or cooked mussels
for the prawns and cook for
2 to 4 minutes or until scallops
are opaque.

If using scallops instead of
prawns, cholesterol will be
42 mg per serving.

Summer Prawn and Tomato Pasta

This is one of my favourite meals during tomato season. It works fine with any kind or shape of pasta. (Pictured opposite page 192.)

1 lb	spaghetti or other pasta	450 g
1 tbsp	olive oil	15 ml
4 tsp	finely chopped fresh garlic	20 ml
3	large tomatoes, coarsely chopped	3
1 lb	cooked peeled large prawns	450 g
5 tbsp	each coarsely chopped fresh basil and parsley	75 ml
4 tbsp	freshly grated Parmesan cheese	60 ml
	salt and pepper	

1. In a large pan of boiling water, cook pasta until tender but firm; drain and return to pan.

2. Meanwhile, in a nonstick frying pan, heat oil over medium-high heat; cook garlic, stirring, for 1 minute.

3. Add tomatoes; cook, stirring, for 2 minutes. Add prawns; cook until heated through, about 2 minutes.

4. Add to hot pasta along with basil, parsley, Parmesan, and salt and pepper to taste; toss to mix. Makes 4 servings.

PER SERVING	
calories	677
g protein	50
g total fat	10
g saturated fat	3
mg cholesterol	241
g carbohydrate	94
g dietary fibre	7
mg sodium	363
mg potassium	624

Good: Vitamin C, Folate, Calcium
Excellent: Vitamin A, Iron

Linguine with Scallops and Leeks

For a really delicious dish, grate your own Parmesan cheese: it has much more flavour than if you buy it grated and is easy to grate in a food processor or with a ordinary grater. Serve with baby carrots, a tossed salad and garlic bread.

½ oz	soft margarine or butter	15 g
12 oz	leeks, chopped (white and light green parts only)	350 g
1 tbsp	plain flour	15 ml
12 oz	skimmed milk	350 ml
4 fl oz	dry white wine	125 ml
1 lb	scallops	450 g
4 tbsp	chopped Italian (flat leaf) parsley	60 ml
2 tbsp	chopped fresh chives or spring onions	30 ml
1 lb	linguine	450 g
2 oz	freshly grated Parmesan cheese	55 g

1. In a large nonstick frying pan, melt margarine over low heat; cook leeks, covered, for 10 minutes or until tender. (If mixture sticks to pan, add 1 tbsp/15 ml water, or more.)

2. Sprinkle flour over leeks; cook, stirring, for 1 minute. Gradually add milk, stirring constantly; bring to a simmer. Cook, stirring, for 2 to 3 minutes or until thickened. Gradually whisk in wine until smooth.

3. Add scallops to hot leek mixture; cook over low heat for 2 to 3 minutes or until scallops are opaque. Stir in parsley and chives.

4. Meanwhile, in a large pan of boiling water, cook linguine until tender but firm; drain and return to saucepan.

5. Pour leek mixture into hot pasta; add Parmesan cheese and toss gently. Makes 4 servings.

Make ahead
To end of step 2 for up to three hours.

PER SERVING	
calories	680
g protein	42
g total fat	11
g saturated fat	4
mg cholesterol	54
g carbohydrate	96
g dietary fibre	5
mg sodium	507
mg potassium	689

Good: Vitamin A, Folate, Iron
Excellent: Calcium

Herbs and Spices
I go easy on the amounts of spices, herbs and seasonings in these recipes, assuming that anyone who likes spicier tastes will add more. It's much easier to add spice than to take it away!

Pasta Provençal with Tofu

Use medium-sized pasta shells or penne. Courgette, grilled aubergine or black olives can also be added.

8 oz	penne	225 g
1 tbsp	olive oil	15 ml
1	large onion, chopped	1
1	sweet green pepper, chopped	1
4 tsp	finely chopped fresh garlic	20 ml
8 oz	mushrooms, sliced	225 g
1	can (28 oz/796 g) tomatoes, chopped	1
Pinch	red pepper flakes	Pinch
8 oz	extra-firm tofu, diced	225 g
5 tbsp	chopped fresh parsley	75 ml
5 tbsp	chopped fresh basil (or 1½ tsp/7 ml dried)	75 ml
4 tbsp	freshly grated Parmesan cheese	60 ml

1. In a large pan of boiling water, cook pasta for 7 to 10 minutes or until tender but firm; drain.

2. Meanwhile, in a large nonstick saucepan, heat oil over medium heat; cook onion, green pepper, garlic and mushrooms for 5 to 8 minutes or until tender. Add tomatoes and red pepper flakes; boil for 6 minutes or until thickened slightly.

3. Add tofu, parsley and basil. Toss with pasta; sprinkle with Parmesan. Makes 4 servings.

Make ahead
Sauce, to end of step 2, cover and refrigerate for up to one day.

PER SERVING	
calories	420
g protein	21
g total fat	11
g saturated fat	3
mg cholesterol	5
g carbohydrate	62
g dietary fibre	8
mg sodium	457
mg potassium	901

Good: Vitamin A
Excellent: Vitamin C, Folate, Calcium, Iron

Singapore Noodles with Pork

Prepare these spicy noodles in a variety of ways: use chicken or beef instead of pork; for a side dish, omit pork; for vegetarians, substitute diced firm tofu for the pork; for special occasions, add large prawns. Instead of red pepper, use two large carrots, cut in thin strips.

4 tbsp	rice wine vinegar or lemon juice	60 ml
4 tbsp	sodium-reduced soy sauce	60 ml
2 tbsp	brown sugar	30 ml
½ tsp	chilli paste or hot pepper sauce*	2.5 ml
8 oz	medium rice vermicelli noodles or very thin regular noodles	225 g
1 tbsp	vegetable oil	15 ml
1 tbsp	curry powder	15 ml
1 tbsp	finely chopped fresh garlic	15 ml
1 tbsp	grated root ginger	15 ml
1	sweet red pepper, thinly sliced	1
8 oz	lean pork, cut in thin strips	225 g
1 lb	bean sprouts	450 g
6 oz	frozen peas, thawed	175 g
4	spring onions, diagonally sliced	4
4 tbsp	chopped fresh coriander	60 ml

1. Combine vinegar, soy sauce, sugar and chilli paste; set aside.

2. Cook noodles according to package directions; drain.

3. Meanwhile, in a large nonstick frying pan, heat oil over medium-high heat; stir in curry powder, garlic and root ginger for 10 seconds. Add red pepper; stir-fry for 1 minute.

4. Add pork; stir-fry for 3 minutes or until no longer pink.

5. Add noodles, bean sprouts, peas and soy sauce mixture; cook, stirring, for 2 minutes or until heated through. Transfer to serving plate; sprinkle with onions and coriander. Makes 4 servings.

PER SERVING	
calories	432
g protein	20
g total fat	7
g saturated fat	1
mg cholesterol	32
g carbohydrate	76
g dietary fibre	5
mg sodium	585
mg potassium	693

Good: Vitamin A
Excellent: Vitamin C, Folate, Iron

* See Information on Ingredients, page 32.

Jiffy Chinese Noodles

My kids love these noodles. In fact, they heat any leftovers in the microwave to eat after school. I try to keep a package of oriental rice noodles or chow mein noodles so I can make this in 10 minutes. I often add whatever vegetables I have on hand. Sometimes I add strips of cooked chicken, pork, beef or prawns.

12 oz	Chinese noodles or thin fresh pasta	350 g
4 fl oz	Asian Sauce (page 99)	125 ml
8 oz	bean sprouts	225 g
2	carrots, grated	2
4	spring onions, diagonally sliced	4
4 tbsp	chopped fresh coriander or parsley	60 ml

1. In a saucepan of boiling water, cook noodles for 2 to 3 minutes or until tender but firm; drain and return to pan or serving bowl.

2. Add sauce, bean sprouts, carrots, green onions and coriander; toss to mix well. Makes 8 servings.

Make ahead
To end of step 2, cover and refrigerate for up to two days; microwave to reheat.

PER SERVING	
calories	173
g protein	7
g total fat	2
g saturated fat	0.2
mg cholesterol	32
g carbohydrate	34
g dietary fibre	3
mg sodium	246
mg potassium	156
Excellent: Vitamin A	

Make-Ahead Party Thai Noodles

These are particularly suitable for a buffet or when entertaining as
they can be made in advance and reheated.

8 oz	spaghetti	225 g
Half	each sweet red and yellow pepper, cut in thin strips	Half
1 oz	fresh coriander, chopped	25 g
3	spring onions, chopped	3
1 lb	bean sprouts	450 g
Sauce		
4 tbsp	rice vinegar or cider vinegar	60 ml
4 tbsp	hoisin sauce	60 ml
2½ tbsp	hot water	37.5 ml
1 tbsp	sesame oil	15 ml
1 tbsp	sodium-reduced soy sauce	15 ml
1 tbsp	grated root ginger	15 ml
1½ tsp	brown sugar	7.5 ml
1½ tsp	finely chopped fresh garlic	7.5 ml
½ tsp	dry mustard	2.5 ml
½ tsp	chilli paste or hot pepper sauce	2.5 ml

1. In a large pan of boiling water, cook pasta until tender but firm;
drain. Transfer to 5 pint (2.8 L) baking dish.

2. Sauce: Combine vinegar, hoisin sauce, water, sesame oil, soy
sauce, root ginger, sugar, garlic, mustard and chilli paste.
Set one-third of the sauce aside; stir remaining sauce into noodles.

3. Stir in red and yellow peppers, coriander, onion and bean
sprouts.

4. Add remaining sauce; bake, covered, at 350°F (180°C) Gas
Mark 4 for 20 to 30 minutes or until hot. Makes 8 servings.

Make ahead
To end of step 3, cover and refrigerate for up to 24 hours.
To reheat, let stand at room temperature for one hour; bake as in
step 4 for 30 to 40 minutes.

PER SERVING	
calories	168
g protein	6
g total fat	3
g saturated fat	0.3
mg cholesterol	0
g carbohydrate	30
g dietary fibre	2
mg sodium	238
mg potassium	179
Good: Vitamin C, Folate	

Szechuan Beef with Noodles

Chinese-style thin thread egg or rice noodles are fast and easy to prepare. They are the ones I like to use in this recipe.
If unavailable, use vermicelli or other thin noodles. Don't use the canned chow mein noodles because they are fried and high in fat.

1 tbsp	vegetable oil	15 ml
2	onions, sliced	2
4	cloves garlic, finely chopped	4
4 tsp	grated root ginger	20 ml
12 oz	lean beef, thinly sliced	350 g
3	tomatoes, cut in chunks	3
2	sweet green peppers, cut in strips	2
4 tbsp	oyster sauce*	60 ml
2 tbsp	sodium-reduced soy sauce	30 ml
1½ tsp	chilli paste	7.5 ml
1 lb	bean sprouts	450 g
12 oz	instant thread noodles or fresh vermicelli	350 g
2 tbsp	chopped peanuts	30 ml
6	spring onions, diagonally sliced	6

1. In a wok or large deep nonstick frying pan, heat oil over high heat; stir-fry onions for 2 minutes. Add garlic, ginger and beef; stir-fry for 2 minutes or until beef is browned.

2. Add tomatoes, green peppers, oyster sauce, soy sauce and chilli paste; stir-fry for 2 minutes. Stir in bean sprouts.

3. Meanwhile, in large pan of boiling water, cook noodles for 2 minutes or until heated through; drain. (If using vermicelli, cook for 6 to 8 minutes or until tender but firm; drain.)

4. Toss with beef mixture. Sprinkle with peanuts and spring onions. Makes 4 servings.

PER SERVING	
calories	535
g protein	37
g total fat	13
g saturated fat	3
mg cholesterol	103
g carbohydrate	72
g dietary fibre	10
mg sodium	809
mg potassium	1133

Good: Vitamin A
Excellent: Vitamin C, Folate, Iron

* See Information on Ingredients, page 32.

Thai Noodles with Chicken and Broccoli

Serve this dish as a main course, or omit the chicken and serve with fish, poultry or any grilled meats.

8 oz	spaghettini or thin noodles	225 g
1 lb	broccoli florets	450 g
2	carrots, cut in julienne strips	2
1 tbsp	vegetable oil	15 ml
1 tbsp	root ginger grated	15 ml
3	cloves garlic, finely chopped	3
12 oz	boneless skinless chicken breasts, cut in thin strips	350 g
4 tbsp	chopped fresh coriander	60 ml
Sauce		
4 fl oz	chicken stock	125 ml
3 tbsp	cider vinegar or rice wine vinegar	45 ml
3 tbsp	sodium-reduced soy sauce	45 ml
3 tbsp	peanut butter	45 ml
1 tbsp	granulated sugar	15 ml
1 tbsp	sesame oil	15 ml
1½ tsp	chilli paste or hot pepper sauce	7.5 ml

1. Sauce: Whisk together stock, vinegar, soy sauce, peanut butter, sugar, sesame oil and chilli paste. Set aside.

2. In a large pan of boiling water, cook noodles for 5 minutes. Add broccoli and carrots; cook for 2 to 3 minutes or until noodles are tender yet firm. Drain and set aside.

3. In a large nonstick frying pan, heat oil over high heat; stir-fry ginger and garlic for 30 seconds. Add chicken; stir-fry for 3 to 5 minutes or until no longer pink inside.

4. Stir sauce; add to frying pan and bring to the boil. Remove from heat; toss with noodles and vegetables. Sprinkle with coriander. Serve in large bowls. Makes 4 servings.

Make ahead
To end of step 1 for up to four hours.

PER SERVING	
calories	506
g protein	34
g total fat	15
g saturated fat	2
mg cholesterol	49
g carbohydrate	59
g dietary fibre	6
mg sodium	631
mg potassium	790

Good: Iron
Excellent: Vitamin A, Vitamin C, Folate

Singapore Noodle and Chicken Salad

Here's a delicious way to use up leftover barbecued chicken, roast chicken or turkey. Blanched asparagus and/or green beans are nice additions to the salad.

4 oz	thin noodles (capellini, spaghettini or rice vermicelli)	115 g
1 oz	unsalted peanuts	25 g
2	cloves garlic	2
2 tsp	chopped root ginger	10 ml
1 tsp	granulated sugar	5 ml
4 tbsp	water	60 ml
1 tbsp	sesame oil	15 ml
1 tbsp	sodium-reduced soy sauce	15 ml
1 tbsp	lime juice	15 ml
½ tsp	hot chilli paste or red pepper flakes	2.5 ml
2	spring onions, chopped	2
4 oz	cooked chicken, cut in thin strips	115 g
4 oz	carrots, cut into julienne strips and blanched	115 g
4 tbsp	chopped fresh coriander	60 ml

1. In a large pan of boiling water, cook noodles until tender but firm. Drain and rinse under cold water; drain well.

2. In food processor, coarsely chop peanuts; reserve 2 tbsp (30 ml). To food processor, add garlic, ginger and sugar; process for 30 seconds. Add water, sesame oil, soy sauce, lime juice and chilli paste; process to mix.

3. Toss sauce with noodles. Add spring onions, chicken and carrots; toss to mix.

4. Arrange on serving plate; sprinkle with coriander and reserved peanuts. Makes 6 servings.

Make ahead
To end of step 3, cover and refrigerate for up to one day.

PER SERVING	
calories	189
g protein	11
g total fat	8
g saturated fat	1
mg cholesterol	21
g carbohydrate	20
g dietary fibre	2
mg sodium	111
mg potassium	225
Excellent: Vitamin A	

Right:
Baked Breaded Fish Fillets with Almonds, made with Cod (page 112), Purple Vegetable Slaw (page 83)

Sodium-Reduced Soy Sauce
To make your own sodium-
reduced soy sauce, mix 1 tbsp
(15 ml) regular soy sauce with
1 tbsp (15 ml) water.

Easy Barbecue Supper
- Herb and Buttermilk
  Barbecued Chicken (page 93)
- Spicy Noodle Salad
- Sliced Tomatoes
- Focaccia or French Baguette
- Blueberries with Vanilla
  Cream (page 231)

Spicy Noodle Salad

This is a wonderful salad for a luncheon, buffet or summer supper.
Use any thin noodle or medium rice noodles. For a main course,
add prawns, sliced grilled chicken or a can of salmon.
Thinly sliced cabbage is a good addition.

8 oz	thin noodles (capellini, spaghettini or rice vermicelli)	225 g
4 oz	carrot, grated	115 g
4 oz	frozen peas, thawed	115 g
1	sweet red pepper, cut in thin strips	1
8 oz	bean sprouts	225 g
4 tbsp	chopped fresh coriander or parsley	60 ml
Dressing		
4 tbsp	rice vinegar or lemon juice	60 ml
4 tbsp	water	60 ml
2 tbsp	sodium-reduced soy sauce	30 ml
4 tsp	grated root ginger	20 ml
1 tbsp	sesame oil	15 ml
1	clove garlic, finely chopped	1
½ tsp	granulated sugar	2.5 ml
½ tsp	hot pepper sauce	2.5 ml

1. In a large pan of boiling water, cook noodles until tender but
firm; drain. Rinse thoroughly under cold water; drain.

2. In a salad bowl, combine vinegar, water, soy sauce, ginger,
oil, garlic, sugar and hot pepper sauce.

3. Add noodles and toss. Add carrot, peas, red pepper, bean
sprouts and coriander; toss. Makes 8 servings.

Make ahead
Salad can be covered and refrigerated for up to two hours; remove
from refrigerator 20 minutes before serving.

PER SERVING	
calories	158
g protein	6
g total fat	2
g saturated fat	0.3
mg cholesterol	0
g carbohydrate	29
g dietary fibre	3
mg sodium	151
mg potassium	194

Good: Folate
Excellent: Vitamin A,
Vitamin C

Left:
Potato, Bean and Tomato
Stew with Basil (page 179),
Muesli Soda Bread
(page 197)

Easy Summer Lunch
- Pasta Salad with Sun-Dried Tomatoes
- Whole Wheat Rolls
- Sliced Cucumbers
- Sliced Turkey Platter
- Melon with Berries

Pasta Salad with Sun-Dried Tomatoes

Sun-dried tomatoes add flavour, colour and a chewy texture to this salad. Use the dry-packed tomatoes because they are lower in fat than the ones packed in oil. For variety, add artichoke hearts, celery, carrots, cauliflower, cooked chicken or ham.

8 oz	penne, fusilli or macaroni	225 g
2 oz	dry-packed sun-dried tomatoes	55 g
8-10	spring onions, chopped	8-10
1 oz	fresh parsley, chopped	25 g
2 tbsp	freshly grated Parmesan cheese (optional)	30 ml
Vinaigrette		
4 tbsp	balsamic or cider vinegar	60 ml
4 tbsp	orange juice	60 ml
4 tbsp	olive oil	60 ml
1	clove garlic, finely chopped	1
2 tsp	Dijon mustard	10 ml
1 tsp	each dried basil and oregano	5 ml
	salt and pepper	

1. In a large pan of boiling water, cook pasta until tender but firm; drain and rinse under cold water. Drain thoroughly.

2. Pour hot water over tomatoes and let stand for 1 minute; drain, then coarsely chop. In a large bowl, combine pasta, tomatoes, onions, parsley, and cheese (if using).

3. Vinaigrette: Combine vinegar, orange juice, oil, garlic, mustard, basil and oregano; mix well. Pour over salad and toss to mix. Season with salt and pepper to taste. Makes 8 servings.

Make ahead
Salad can be covered and refrigerated for up to two days.

PER SERVING	
calories	197
g protein	5
g total fat	8
g saturated fat	1
mg cholesterol	0
g carbohydrate	28
g dietary fibre	3
mg sodium	189
mg potassium	382

Summer Sunday Lunch
- Pasta and Ham Salad
- Garlic Bread
- Roasted Sweet Peppers (page 174) drizzled with balsamic vinegar
- Berries with Orange Cream (page 228)
- Apricot Streusel Cake (page 203)

Nutritional Note
For a sodium-reduced diet, omit ham and olives.

Pasta and Ham Salad with Tomato Basil Dressing

Instead of ham, you can add any leftover cooked meats or chicken, or for a vegetarian meal, omit ham and add feta cheese.

8 oz	penne or other short pasta	225 g
4 oz	ham, cubed	115 g
10	black olives, pitted and sliced	10
5 tbsp	chopped fresh basil or parsley	75 ml
8 fl oz	Tomato Basil Dressing (page 86)	225 ml

1. In a large pan of boiling water, cook penne until tender but firm, 7 to 9 minutes; drain and cool under cold water. Drain.

2. In salad bowl, toss pasta, ham, olives and basil with dressing. Makes 4 servings.

Make ahead
Salad can be covered and refrigerated for up to 24 hours.

PER SERVING	
calories	348
g protein	14
g total fat	11
g saturated fat	2
mg cholesterol	16
g carbohydrate	47
g dietary fibre	4
mg sodium	641
mg potassium	301
Good: Iron	

Seafood Pasta Salad

Serve this at a special luncheon, at a buffet or for a summer supper. Use any short pasta twists or tubes. If fresh crab is available, I would use it instead of frozen or canned.

8 oz	penne or short pasta	225 g
8 oz	sea scallops (not queen scallops)	225 g
4 oz	mange tout, trimmed and strings removed	115 g
8 oz	cooked medium or small prawns	225 g
4 oz	cooked crabmeat, drained and broken into chunks	115 g
Half	sweet red pepper, diced	Half
5 tbsp	red or spring onions, chopped	75 ml
8 fl oz	Yogurt Herb Dressing (page 87)	225 ml
	salt and pepper	

1. In a large pan of boiling water, cook pasta until tender but firm, 7 to 10 minutes. Drain and rinse under cold water; drain.

2. In a pan of boiling water, cook scallops for about 3 minutes or until opaque in centre; drain.

3. In a pan of boiling water, cook mange tout for 1 minute; drain. Rinse under cold water; drain. Slice in half diagonally.

4. In a salad bowl, combine pasta, scallops, mange tout, prawns, crabmeat, red pepper, onion and dressing; toss gently. Add salt and pepper to taste. Makes 8 servings.

Make ahead
To end of step 4 except for adding mange tout, cover and refrigerate for up to one day. Wrap cooked mange tout in paper towels and refrigerate; add to salad up to one hour before serving (otherwise they will turn yellow).

PER SERVING	
calories	261
g protein	24
g total fat	5
g saturated fat	1
mg cholesterol	85
g carbohydrate	29
g dietary fibre	1
mg sodium	575
mg potassium	375
Good: Vitamin C, Folate	

Grains, Legumes and Meatless Main Dishes

Spinach Rice Casserole

Green Vegetable Risotto

Indian Rice with Lentils and Mushrooms

Spanish Rice with Coriander

Chinese Vegetable Fried Rice

Wild Rice Pilaf

Rice with Black Beans and Ginger

Lemon Parsley Rice Pilaf

Bulgur with Red Onion and Pimiento

Bulgur Pilaf with Prawns and Mange Tout

Quinoa-Stuffed Peppers

Barley and Corn Casserole

Bean and Sausage Casserole

Potato, Bean and Tomato Stew with Basil

Winter Vegetable Curry with Couscous

Quick and Easy Spiced Couscous

Crustless Vegetable Quiche

Marinated Baked Tofu

Vegetable Tofu Stir-Fry

Tomato, Aubergine and Courgette Gratin

Apricot-Raisin Muesli

When you substitute 4 oz (115 g) of grated 8% fat cheese for the same amount of 17% fat cheese in a recipe serving four, each person's fat intake is reduced by 3 g.

Fresh Herbs
Instead of dried basil and thyme in this recipe, you can use 2 tbsp (30 ml) chopped fresh basil and 1 tbsp (15 ml) chopped fresh thyme.

Spinach Rice Casserole

Avoid the pitfall of high-fat vegetarian dishes by using a flavourful lower-fat cheese. Serve with Tomato, Aubergine and Courgette Gratin (page 185) and toasted wholemeal bread.

7 oz	long grain brown or white rice	200 g
1 tbsp	olive oil	15 ml
1	medium onion, chopped	1
1	clove garlic, finely chopped	1
1 lb	spinach leaves	450 g
3	eggs, beaten	3
6 oz	low-fat Swiss-style cheese, grated	175 g
4 fl oz	skimmed milk	125 ml
5 tbsp	chopped fresh parsley	75 ml
¾ tsp	salt	3.75 ml
½ tsp	each dried basil and thyme	2.5 ml
Pinch	each cayenne and pepper	Pinch
1	toasted slivered almonds	25 g
2 tbsp	freshly grated Parmesan cheese	30 ml

1. In a pan of boiling water, cook rice 20 minutes for white, 40 minutes for brown; drain and rinse under cold water. Transfer to a large bowl.

2. Meanwhile, in a frying pan, heat oil over medium heat; cook onion and garlic until tender. In saucepan, cook spinach in small amount of water just until wilted; drain, squeeze dry and chop.

3. To rice, stir in onion mixture, spinach, eggs, cheese, milk, parsley, salt, basil, thyme, cayenne and pepper. Transfer to a greased 3½ pint (2 L) glass baking dish. Sprinkle with almonds and Parmesan cheese.

4. Bake, covered, at 350°F (180°C) Gas Mark 4 for 25 minutes. Uncover and bake for another 10 minutes or until golden. Makes 6 servings.

Make ahead
To end of step 3, cover and set aside for up to two hours.

PER SERVING	
calories	327
g protein	19
g total fat	15
g saturated fat	5
mg cholesterol	126
g carbohydrate	32
g dietary fibre	5
mg sodium	576
mg potassium	561

Excellent: Vitamin A, Folate
Calcium, Iron

Arborio
Arborio is an Italian rice mainly used in risotto.

About Risotto
Risotto is an Italian rice dish made by adding hot liquid to rice in small amounts, then stirring until all liquid has been absorbed before adding more liquid. The rice is creamy on the outside and al dente or firm on the inside. It takes about 25 minutes to make.

Some cooks recommend using a parboiled long grain rice, labelled as 'easy cook' if arborio isn't available.

Green Vegetable Risotto

Shannon Graham, who has worked with me on all my books, came up with this delicious rice dish, which has less fat than a traditional risotto. Serve as a vegetarian main dish or as a side dish with chicken, a green salad and whole granary bread.

1 oz	soft margarine or butter	25 g
4	spring onions, sliced	4
7 oz	Arborio rice or long grain white rice	200 g
1¾ pts	simmering chicken stock	1 L
6 oz	green beans, sliced	175 g
12	mange tout	12
5 oz	courgettes, coarsely chopped	140 g
4 tbsp	chopped fresh parsley	60 ml
4 tbsp	freshly grated Parmesan cheese	60 ml
	pepper	

1. In a large nonstick frying pan, melt half of the margarine over medium heat; cook spring onions until softened, about 3 minutes.

2. Add rice and stir to coat.

3. Add about half of the chicken stock, 2 fl oz (50 ml) at a time, cooking and stirring until each addition is absorbed before adding next, about 8 minutes in total.

4. Stir in green beans; cook for 2 minutes. Stir in mange tout and courgette.

5. Stir in remaining stock, 2 fl oz (50 ml) at a time, cooking and stirring until each addition is absorbed before adding next, 10 to 15 minutes in total or until rice is creamy and firm.

6. Stir in parsley, Parmesan, remaining margarine, and pepper to taste. Serve immediately. Makes 4 main-course servings, 8 side-dish servings.

Make ahead
Risotto should always be eaten as soon as it's cooked, but leftovers are delicious reheated the next day.

PER SERVING	(SIDE DISH)
calories	162
g protein	6
g total fat	5
g saturated fat	1
mg cholesterol	2
g carbohydrate	23
g dietary fibre	1
mg sodium	487
mg potassium	251

Whole Grain Rice
Whole grain brown rice takes longer to cook but has more fibre than white. Combined with fibre- and iron-rich lentils, rice makes a complete source of protein.

Basmati
Basmati is an aromatic rice, mainly imported from India or Pakistan. Rinse in cold water before using.

Any long grain rice (white or brown) can be used in this recipe.

Indian Rice with Lentils and Mushrooms

Easy to make, this rice dish is delicious.

½ oz	soft margarine or butter	15 g
1 lb	onions, sliced	450 g
1¼ pts	vegetable or chicken stock	700 ml
5 oz	mushrooms, quartered	140 g
7 oz	whole grain or basmati rice	200 g
3½ oz	green lentils	100 g
1 tbsp	grated root ginger	15 ml
1 tsp	curry powder	5 ml
¼ tsp	cinnamon	1.25 ml
2	cloves garlic, crushed	2
1 oz	fresh parsley, chopped	25 g
	salt and pepper	

1. In a heavy nonstick frying pan, melt margarine over low heat; cook onions, stirring occasionally, for 25 minutes or until very tender and lightly browned.

2. Meanwhile, in a saucepan, combine stock, mushrooms, rice, lentils, ginger, curry powder, cinnamon and garlic; bring to the boil. Reduce heat, cover and simmer for 25 minutes or until rice and lentils are tender and most of the liquid is absorbed.

3. Stir in parsley, and salt and pepper to taste. Top each serving with some fried onions. Makes 4 main-course servings, 8 side-dish servings.

Make ahead
Best when just made but can be covered and refrigerated for up to one day.

PER SERVING	(SIDE DISH)
calories	180
g protein	8
g total fat	3
g saturated fat	1
mg cholesterol	0
g carbohydrate	31
g dietary fibre	4
mg sodium	318
mg potassium	388

Good: Iron
Excellent: Folate

Variation
For colour and variety, use half a sweet green pepper and half a yellow pepper in this Spanish rice.

Canned Tomatoes
Drained canned tomatoes, chopped, can also be used in this recipe instead of the fresh.

Spanish Rice with Coriander

Fresh coriander gives this traditional recipe an updated flavour. If it's unavailable, add 2 tsp (10 ml) ground cumin or curry powder along with the tomatoes.

1¼ pts	water or vegetable stock	700 ml
10 oz	long grain rice	280 g
2 tsp	olive oil	10 ml
1	medium onion, chopped	1
2	cloves garlic, finely chopped	2
3	medium tomatoes, chopped	3
1	sweet green pepper, chopped	1
¼ tsp	red pepper flakes	1.25 ml
6 oz	frozen green peas	175 g
4 tbsp	each chopped fresh coriander and parsley	60 ml
	salt and pepper	

1. In a large saucepan, bring water to the boil; add rice. Reduce heat, cover and simmer for 20 minutes or until rice is tender and liquid absorbed.

2. In a large nonstick frying pan, heat oil over medium heat; cook onion for 3 minutes or until tender.

3. Add garlic, tomatoes, green pepper and red pepper flakes; cook, stirring occasionally, for 5 minutes.

4. Stir in cooked rice, peas, coriander, parsley, and salt and pepper to taste; cook, stirring, for 1 minute. Makes 6 servings.

Make ahead
Spanish Rice can be covered and refrigerated for up to one day or frozen for up to one month.

PER SERVING	
calories	228
g protein	6
g total fat	2
g saturated fat	0.4
mg cholesterol	0
g carbohydrate	46
g dietary fibre	3
mg sodium	34
mg potassium	308

Good: Folate
Excellent: Vitamin C

What's in a Serving?

As a general guide to healthy eating we should have 5 to 12 servings of grain products and 5 to 10 servings of fruits and vegetables per day. 6 oz (175 g) of cooked rice equals two servings of grain.

One of my servings of Chinese Vegetable Fried Rice is what I think an adult would eat for a main course, and would equal two servings of grains, three servings of vegetables and one serving of meat.

Nutritional Note

To reduce sodium, omit ham (which adds 393 mg sodium per serving) and oyster sauce (which adds 643 mg sodium per serving).

Chinese Vegetable Fried Rice

This is such a great way to use up leftover rice that I try to have leftovers. Oyster sauce adds extra flavour; sesame oil and soy sauce could be added instead. For a vegetarian dish, omit ham. Add tofu if desired.

1 tbsp	vegetable oil	15 ml
10 oz	courgettes, diced	280 g
4 oz	celery, sliced	115 g
1½ lb	cold cooked rice*	675 g
4 oz	diced cooked ham	115 g
1	sweet red pepper, diced	1
2	eggs, lightly beaten	2
4 oz	bean sprouts	115 g
5 tbsp	oyster sauce	75 ml
4	spring onions, chopped	4

1. In a large nonstick frying pan or wok, heat oil over high heat; stir-fry courgette and celery for 2 minutes.

2. Add rice; stir-fry for 1 minute.

3. Add ham and red pepper; stir-fry for 1 minute.

4. Make a well in centre; stir in eggs for 30 seconds.

5. Add bean sprouts; stir-fry for 1 minute or until eggs are set. Stir in oyster sauce. Sprinkle with green onions. Makes 4 servings.

Make ahead

Fried rice can be covered and set aside for up to one hour.

PER SERVING	
calories	362
g protein	17
g total fat	9
g saturated fat	2
mg cholesterol	124
g carbohydrate	54
g dietary fibre	3
mg sodium	1103
mg potassium	590

Good: Vitamin A, Iron
Excellent: Vitamin C, Folate

* About 8 oz (225 g) uncooked 'easy cook' long grain rice makes 1½ lb (675 g) cooked.

Wild Rice Pilaf with Lemon and Raisins
Omit fresh basil. Add 2½ oz (70 g) raisins and 1 tsp (5 ml) grated lemon rind; stir in with parsley.

Wild Rice Pilaf

A combination of wild, brown and white rice looks attractive. Smoked bacon adds extra flavour to this entertaining dish. If you don't have brown rice, use half wild and half white.

2	rashers bacon, diced	2
1	onion, diced	1
3 oz	wild rice	85 g
1¼ pts	water or chicken stock	700 ml
3 oz	brown rice	85 g
3 oz	long grain white rice	85 g
4 tbsp	chopped fresh parsley	60 ml
2 tbsp	chopped fresh basil	30 ml
	salt and pepper	

1. In a saucepan, cook bacon over medium heat for 3 minutes; add onion and cook, stirring, until tender, about 5 minutes.

2. Rinse wild rice under cold running water; drain. Add water to bacon and onion in saucepan; stir in wild rice and bring to boil. Add brown rice; cover and simmer for 15 minutes.

3. Add white rice; cover and simmer for 25 minutes or until tender.

4. Stir in parsley, basil, and salt and pepper to taste. Makes 8 servings.

Make ahead
To end of step 3, but reduce cooking time from 25 minutes to 10 minutes; remove from heat and let cool. Refrigerate for up to one day. Reheat in the oven at 325°F (160°C) Gas Mark 3 covered, for 25 to 30 minutes or until hot.

PER SERVING	
calories	135
g protein	4
g total fat	1
g saturated fat	0.4
mg cholesterol	1
g carbohydrate	27
g dietary fibre	2
mg sodium	30
mg potassium	105

Rice with Black Beans and Ginger

This absolutely delicious recipe is a favourite of my husband.
Use Chinese fermented black beans (not black kidney beans).
I use Chinese bottled black bean sauce made with whole beans.
Serve with fish, chicken or meats.

1 tbsp	vegetable oil	15 ml
1 tbsp	crushed fresh garlic	15 ml
1 tbsp	chopped onion or shallots	15 ml
1 tbsp	grated root ginger	15 ml
6 oz	long grain rice	175 g
¾ pt	boiling water	425 ml
4 tbsp	black bean sauce (made with whole beans)	60 ml
1	spring onion, chopped	1

1. In a heavy or nonstick saucepan, heat oil over medium heat; cook garlic, onion and ginger for 1 minute, stirring.

2. Add rice and water; simmer, covered, for 20 minutes or until rice is tender. Stir in black bean sauce and spring onion.
Makes 4 servings.

Make ahead
Rice can be covered and refrigerated for up to two days.

PER SERVING	
calories	220
g protein	5
g total fat	4
g saturated fat	0.4
mg cholesterol	0
g carbohydrate	41
g dietary fibre	1
mg sodium	31
mg potassium	126

Fast-Cooking Carbohydrates

Cooking these is as easy as boiling water.

Grain Products	Minutes cooking time
Rice noodles	2
Pasta (fresh)	3
Couscous (instant)	3
Rice, microwave	2
Rolled oats, quick-cooking	5
Pasta (dried)	3-17

For up to 25 minutes of cooking time, consider bulgur, rice, barley, kasha and quinoa.

Lemon Parsley Rice Pilaf

This is a favourite dish of mine. Grated lemon rind adds a delicious flavour to this rice. Serve with fish, chicken or meat. (Pictured opposite page 129.)

1 tsp	vegetable oil	5 ml
1	onion, chopped	1
10 oz	long grain white or brown rice	280 g
1½ pts	chicken or vegetable stock	700 ml
	grated rind of 1 lemon	
1 tbsp	lemon juice	15 ml
1 oz	fresh parsley, coarsely chopped	25 g
	pepper	

1. In a heavy saucepan, heat oil over medium heat; cook onion for 5 minutes or until softened.

2. Stir in rice, then stock; bring to the boil. Reduce heat, cover and simmer for 20 minutes for white, 40 minutes for brown, or until rice is tender.

3. Stir in lemon rind and juice, parsley, and pepper to taste. Makes 8 servings.

Make ahead
Pilaf can be covered and refrigerated for up to three days; reheat gently.

PER SERVING	
calories	154
g protein	5
g total fat	1
g saturated fat	0.3
mg cholesterol	0
g carbohydrate	30
g dietary fibre	1
mg sodium	295
mg potassium	168

Compare

High-carbohydrate, low-fat, low-sodium grains and pulses

6–7 oz (175–200 g)	Calories	Protein (g)	Fibre (g)
Macaroni	198	7	2
Bulgur	151	6	8
Couscous	201	7	2
Rice, white, easy cook	200	4	1
Rice, brown, long grain	217	5	3
Barley	192	4	9
Lentils	230	18	9
Kidney beans (red)	224	15	17
Quinoa	159	6	2

Roasted Red Peppers
Bake sweet red peppers in the oven at 400°F (200°C) Gas Mark 6 for 20 to 30 minutes, turning once or twice, or until blackened and blistered. Scrape skin from peppers; discard seeds and coarsely chop.

Bulgur and Cracked Wheat
Both are made from wheat berries. Bulgur is cooked first, then dried, then cracked. Cracked wheat is made from wheat berries that are cracked then milled. They are available from health food stores and provide very high amounts of fibre. Use in salads or as you would rice and pasta.

Bulgur with Red Onion and Pimiento

Pimientos or sweet red peppers are a colourful and flavourful addition to rice, pasta and grain dishes. In the autumn when sweet red peppers are not too expensive, roast them and freeze them to capture some sunshine flavours for the winter. Ordinary cooking onions can also be used instead of red onions. (Pictured opposite page 96.)

1 tbsp	olive oil	15 ml
1	red onion, thinly sliced	1
6 oz	bulgur or cracked wheat	175 g
16 fl oz	boiling water	450 ml
1 tbsp	lemon juice	15 ml
3 oz	roasted red peppers, chopped	75 g
1 oz	fresh parsley or basil, chopped	25 g
½ tsp	dried basil	2.5 ml
	salt and pepper	

1. In a small frying pan, heat oil over medium heat; cook onion, stirring often, for 10 minutes or until tender.

2. Meanwhile, in saucepan, combine bulgur and water; simmer, covered, for 20 minutes or until liquid is absorbed.

3. Add onions, lemon juice, pimientos, parsley, dried basil and salt and pepper to taste. Makes 4 servings.

Make ahead
Bulgur can be covered and refrigerated for up to two days.

PER SERVING	
calories	171
g protein	5
g total fat	4
g saturated fat	1
mg cholesterol	0
g carbohydrate	32
g dietary fibre	7
mg sodium	14
mg potassium	225
Good: Vitamin C, Folate, Iron	

Rice Pilaf with Prawns and Mange Tout

If bulgur or cracked wheat is not available, substitute 7 oz (200 g) long grain rice and reduce stock to 16 fl oz (450 ml); cook for 20 minutes.

Nutritional Note

For someone on a cholesterol-restricted diet, substitute cubes of cooked boneless chicken breast or Marinated Baked Tofu (recipe page 183) for the prawns.

Bulgur Pilaf with Prawns and Mange Tout

Quick and easy to make, this pilaf is golden yellow like paella – a perfect choice for a special Friday night supper. Serve with a tossed salad and fresh bread.

1 tsp	vegetable oil	5 ml
1	onion, chopped	1
¼ tsp	each turmeric and pepper	1.25 ml
Pinch	cayenne pepper	Pinch
9 oz	bulgur or cracked wheat	250 g
1½ pts	hot vegetable stock	850 ml
½ tsp	saffron threads	2.5 ml
8 oz	mange tout, trimmed	225 g
8 oz	cooked peeled prawns	225 g
1 oz	chopped fresh parsley	25 g
2	medium tomatoes, chopped	2
	salt	
	lemon wedges	

1. In a large nonstick frying pan, heat oil over medium heat; cook onion, turmeric, pepper and cayenne, stirring occasionally, for 5 minutes or until onion is softened.

2. Add bulgur, vegetable stock and saffron; bring to the boil. Reduce heat to low; simmer, covered, for 15 minutes or until liquid is absorbed.

3. Meanwhile, in a pot of boiling water, cook mange tout for 1 minute. Drain and rinse under cold water; drain again.

4. To bulgur mixture, add mange tout, prawns, parsley and tomatoes; cook over medium heat, tossing gently, for about 3 minutes or until hot. Season with salt to taste. Garnish each plate with lemon wedge. Makes 4 servings.

Make ahead

Pilaf can be covered and refrigerated for up to four hours; reheat gently.

PER SERVING	
calories	334
g protein	26
g total fat	4
g saturated fat	1
mg cholesterol	118
g carbohydrate	52
g dietary fibre	13
mg sodium	675
mg potassium	625

Good: Vitamin A
Excellent: Vitamin C, Folate, Iron

Quinoa Pilaf
Prepare quinoa mixture, but omit bread crumbs and green peppers.

Quinoa
Quinoa (pronounced keen-wah) is available at health food stores. It is higher in iron than most other grains and has high-quality protein. Cooked, it puffs up to four times its dry volume.

Quinoa-Stuffed Peppers

This quinoa mixture is delicious as a stuffing for sweet peppers – red, green or purple – or on its own. I keep dried sliced Chinese mushrooms on hand and often use them when I don't have fresh ones.

3½ oz	quinoa	100 g
4	sweet green peppers	4
1 tsp	vegetable oil	5 ml
1	medium onion, chopped	1
8	mushrooms, quartered (or dried mushrooms*)	8
6 oz	sweetcorn kernels	175 g
2 tbsp	chopped fresh coriander or parsley	30 ml
1 tbsp	sodium-reduced soy sauce	15 ml
2 tsp	sesame oil	10 ml
2 tsp	chopped fresh garlic	10 ml
Pinch	red pepper flakes	Pinch
½ oz	fresh wholemeal breadcrumbs (see page 185)	15 g

1. Rinse quinoa under cold water; drain. In a saucepan, bring 8 fl oz (225 ml) water to the boil; stir in quinoa. Reduce heat, cover and simmer for 15 minutes or until water is absorbed and quinoa is transluscent.

2. Cut off ½ inch (1 cm) from tops of green peppers; remove seeds. In large saucepan of boiling water, cook peppers for 5 minutes or until tender-crisp. Remove and drain upside down.

3. In a frying pan, heat oil over medium heat; cook onion until tender. Stir in mushrooms, quinoa, sweetcorn, half the coriander, soy sauce, sesame oil, garlic and red pepper flakes; stuff into peppers.

4. Sprinkle with breadcrumbs and remaining coriander. Bake in greased 8-inch (20 cm) square baking dish at 350°F (180°C) Gas Mark 4 for 30 minutes or until heated through. Makes 4 servings.

Make ahead
To end of step 3, cover and refrigerate for up to four hours.

* If using dried mushrooms, soak in hot water for 5 minutes; drain, discard tough stems and slice.

PER SERVING	
calories	202
g protein	7
g total fat	5
g saturated fat	1
mg cholesterol	0
g carbohydrate	36
g dietary fibre	5
mg sodium	148
mg potassium	560

Good: Folate, Iron
Excellent: Vitamin C

Barley
Barley is a good source of soluble fibre – the same kind that is in oat bran and kidney beans and may help to reduce blood cholesterol.

Cooking Tip
Thaw frozen corn kernels under hot water, then drain well before using in this recipe.

Barley and Corn Casserole

This recipe is the result of a conversation I had with editor Kirsten Hanson, who told me that corn and barley is a nice combination. This dish goes well with any meats, fish or poultry or as part of a meatless meal.

1 tbsp	vegetable oil	15 ml
1	onion, chopped	1
1 tbsp	garlic, finely chopped	15 ml
6 oz	carrots, finely chopped	175 g
7 oz	pearl barley	200 g
1¼ pt	vegetable or chicken stock	700 ml
12 oz	sweetcorn kernels	350 g
1 oz	fresh parsley, chopped	25 g
	salt and pepper	

1. In a heavy flameproof casserole, heat oil over medium-high heat; cook onion, garlic and carrots for 4 minutes or until onion is softened. Stir in barley; pour in stock. Cover and bake in the oven at 350°F (180°C) Gas Mark 4 for 1 hour.

2. Stir in corn, parsley, and salt and pepper to taste. Bake for another 5 minutes or until heated through and barley is tender. Makes 8 servings.

Make ahead
Casserole can be covered and refrigerated for up to two days. To reheat, add 4 fl oz (125 ml) stock or water and warm in microwave or oven.

PER SERVING	
calories	155
g protein	4
g total fat	2
g saturated fat	0.2
mg cholesterol	0
g carbohydrate	32
g dietary fibre	6
mg sodium	250
mg potassium	216
Excellent: Vitamin A	

Compare	
Sweetcorn (6 oz/175 g)	**Sodium (mg)**
frozen	29
canned	559

Bean Casserole
Making this dish without sausage reduces the fat to 9 g per serving.

Recipe made with cooked dried beans instead of canned reduces sodium to 372 mg per serving.

Dried Beans
Instead of using canned beans, you can cook dried beans.

One pound (450 g) dried beans equals 2-2½ lb (900 g-1.2 kg) of cooked beans. Cooked beans freeze up to 6 months.

Bean and Sausage Casserole

A bit of Chorizo sausage adds a lot of flavour to this nutrient-packed dish. Serve with a green salad or coleslaw and fresh bread.

1 tsp	olive oil	5 ml
1 lb	onions, coarsely chopped or leeks (white parts only)	450 g
3	cloves garlic, finely chopped	3
14 oz	cooked or canned haricot beans	400 g
4 oz	low-fat Cheddar-style cheese, grated	115 g
2 oz	Chorizo sausage, chopped	55 g
2	tomatoes, chopped*	2
¼ tsp	dried rosemary	1.25 ml
Topping		
2 oz	fresh wholemeal breadcrumbs (see page 185)	55 g
2 tbsp	chopped fresh parsley	30 ml
2 tsp	olive oil	10 ml
1	clove garlic, crushed	1

1. In a nonstick frying pan, heat oil over medium heat; cook onions and garlic, stirring occasionally, for about 5 minutes or until tender, adding water if necessary to prevent scorching.

2. Remove from heat; stir in beans, cheese, sausage, tomatoes and rosemary. Spoon into gratin dish.

3. Topping: Combine breadcrumbs, parsley, oil and garlic; sprinkle over bean mixture.

4. Bake at 350°F (180°C) Gas Mark 4 for 20 minutes or until heated through. Makes 4 servings.

Make ahead
To end of step 3, cover and refrigerate for up to three hours.

PER SERVING	
calories	341
g protein	21
g total fat	13
g saturated fat	5
mg cholesterol	25
g carbohydrate	38
g dietary fibre	9
mg sodium	802
mg potassium	560

Good: Iron
Excellent: Folate, Calcium

* If you don't have any fresh tomatoes, substitute drained chopped canned tomatoes.

Legumes or Pulses
Legumes are dried beans, peas and lentils. They have more protein than any other vegetable and are an alternative to meat. Served with a grain product such as bread, they form a complete protein.

Legumes are low in fat, high in fibre, iron and calcium. Dried beans are a good source of Vitamin E.

Potato, Bean and Tomato Stew with Basil

This fast and easy main dish is gentle on the budget, full of flavour and packed with nutrients. It is also delicious with fresh rosemary instead of basil. (Pictured opposite page 161.)

1 tbsp	olive oil	15 ml
1	medium onion, chopped	1
2	large cloves garlic, finely chopped	2
½ tsp	paprika	2.5 ml
3	large tomatoes, coarsely chopped*	3
4 tbsp	chopped fresh basil (or ½ tsp/2.5 ml dried)	60 ml
½ tsp	dried oregano	2.5 ml
2	medium potatoes, peeled and diced	2
8 fl oz	water or vegetable stock	225 ml
14 oz	cooked or canned chick peas	400 g
	salt and pepper	
1 oz	fresh parsley, chopped	25 g

1. In a large heavy saucepan, heat oil over medium heat; cook onion until tender, about 5 minutes.

2. Add garlic, paprika, 2 of the tomatoes, basil (if using dried) and oregano; simmer, stirring often, for 5 minutes.

3. Add potatoes and water; cover and boil for 5 minutes, stirring occasionally. Add chick peas; reduce heat and simmer for 5 minutes or until potatoes are tender.

4. Add remaining tomato, basil (if using fresh), and salt and pepper to taste; heat for 1 minute. Serve garnished with parsley in large shallow bowls. Makes 3 main-course servings.

Make ahead
To end of step 3, cover and refrigerate for up to two days. Reheat gently before step 4.

PER SERVING	
calories	334
g protein	13
g total fat	7
g saturated fat	1
mg cholesterol	0
g carbohydrate	58
g dietary fibre	8
mg sodium	293
mg potassium	906

Good: Vitamin A, Iron
Excellent: Vitamin C, Folate

* Instead of fresh tomatoes, you can use canned tomatoes, undrained.

Nutritional Note
A delicious and painless way to
increase fibre in your diet is to
add cooked lentils or beans to
salads, soups, casseroles,
stews or tacos. Both are low in
fat and very high in fibre.

Couscous
I think of couscous as a grain
but it is actually a very fine
(grain-like) pasta made from
Durum wheat semolina.
   Most couscous sold is the
quick-cooking, or instant, type
and is the fastest of all the
grains to prepare. You can buy
it at most supermarkets and at
health food stores. If you can't
find it, use rice or bulgur.

Winter Vegetable Curry with Couscous

This is one of my favourite winter meals. I like to make a lot
and can quite happily eat it for a few days.

1 tbsp	olive or vegetable oil	15 ml
1	red or cooking onion, cut into wedges	1
1 tbsp	curry powder	15 ml
1 tsp	ground cumin	5 ml
¼ tsp	cinnamon	1.25 ml
2 tbsp	grated root ginger	30 ml
1 tsp	finely chopped fresh garlic	5 ml
¼ tsp	red pepper flakes (optional)	1.25 ml
12 fl oz	vegetable stock or water	350 ml
2 tbsp	lemon juice	30 ml
2	carrots, sliced	2
12 oz	sweet potato, cubed (about 1-inch/2.5 cm)	350 g
7 oz	cauliflower florets	200 g
1	courgette (8-inch/20 cm), cut into chunks	1
14 oz	cooked or canned chick peas	400 g
4 tbsp	chopped fresh coriander or parsley	60 ml
	salt and pepper	
Couscous		
12 fl oz	water	350 ml
1 tbsp	olive or vegetable oil	15 ml
10 oz	couscous	280 g
	salt and pepper	

1. In a large saucepan, heat oil over medium heat; cook onion
for about 3 minutes or until softened. Add curry powder, cumin,
cinnamon, ginger, garlic, and red pepper flakes (if using); cook,
stirring often, for 1 minute.

PER SERVING

calories	386
g protein	13
g total fat	7
g saturated fat	1
mg cholesterol	0
g carbohydrate	70
g dietary fibre	7
mg sodium	331
mg potassium	561

Good: Iron
Excellent: Vitamin A, Folate
Vitamin C, Folate

2. Add stock, lemon juice, carrots and sweet potato; bring to boil. Reduce heat, cover and simmer for 8 minutes. Add cauliflower and courgette; cook for 5 minutes or until vegetables are tender.

3. Stir in chick peas, coriander, and salt and pepper to taste.

4. Couscous: Meanwhile, in saucepan, bring water and oil to boil; stir in couscous. Cover and remove from heat; let stand for 5 minutes. Fluff with fork; season with salt and pepper to taste. Serve vegetable curry over hot couscous. Makes 6 servings.

Make ahead
To end of step 3; cover and refrigerate for up to two days.

Quick and Easy Spiced Couscous

A hint of cinnamon and allspice is delicious in couscous. This is nice with curries, chicken, lamb or pork.

16 fl oz	chicken stock	450 ml
10 oz	couscous	280 g
¼ tsp	each pepper, allspice and cinnamon	1.25 ml
Pinch	salt	Pinch
½ oz	soft margarine or butter	15 g

1. In a saucepan, bring chicken stock to boil; stir in couscous, pepper, allspice, cinnamon and salt. Remove from heat; cover and let stand for 5 minutes.

2. Using two forks, fluff couscous. Stir in butter. Makes 6 servings.

Make ahead
Couscous can be covered and refrigerated for up to one day; reheat, covered, in oven or microwave.

Couscous with Tomato and Basil
Prepare Spiced Couscous. Stir in 1 small finely chopped tomato and 4 tbsp (60 ml) chopped fresh basil along with butter.

PER SERVING

calories	203
g protein	8
g total fat	3
g saturated fat	1
mg cholesterol	0
g carbohydrate	36
g dietary fibre	2
mg sodium	292
mg potassium	162

Sunday Brunch
- Crustless Vegetable Quiche
- Asparagus and Mushroom Salad (page 78)
- Rhubarb Bran Muffins (page 195)
  or
  Lemon Poppyseed Muffins (page 194)
- Apricot Orange and Fig Compote (page 227)
- Gingerbread Cake (page 204)

Nutritional Note
Compare:

1 serving	Fat (g)
Traditional Quiche Lorraine	48
This recipe	9

Crustless Vegetable Quiche

Not only is this lighter in fat and calories than a traditional quiche, it is much faster and easier to make.

½ oz	soft margarine or butter	15 g
1 oz	fine fresh breadcrumbs	25 g
2 oz	mushrooms, sliced	55 g
6 oz	courgette, chopped	175 g
6 oz	fresh spinach leaves, chopped	175 g
2	eggs	2
2	egg whites	2
8 fl oz	skimmed milk	225 ml
2	spring onions, chopped	2
1 oz	feta cheese, crumbled	25 g
4 tbsp	chopped fresh parsley	60 ml
2 tbsp	chopped fresh basil (or 1 tsp/5 ml dried)	30 ml
Dash	hot pepper sauce	Dash
2	medium tomatoes, sliced	2

1. Spread 1 tsp (5 ml) of the margarine in 10-inch (25 cm) quiche dish or glass pie plate; sprinkle bottom and sides evenly with breadcrumbs.

2. In a large nonstick frying pan, melt remaining margarine over medium heat; cook mushrooms and courgette, stirring, for 5 to 7 minutes or until tender and liquid has evaporated. Add spinach; cook, stirring, for 2 minutes or until wilted.

3. In a large bowl, beat together eggs and egg whites; add milk. Stir in onions, cheese, parsley, basil, hot pepper sauce and spinach mixture.

4. Spoon into prepared dish; top evenly with tomato slices.

5. Bake at 350°F (180°C) Gas Mark 4 for 40 to 50 minutes or until firm to the touch and knife inserted in centre comes out clean. Makes 4 servings.

Make ahead
To end of step 3, cover and refrigerate for up to two hours.

PER SERVING	
calories	170
g protein	11
g total fat	9
g saturated fat	3
mg cholesterol	120
g carbohydrate	13
g dietary fibre	3
mg sodium	279
mg potassium	636

Good: Vitamin C, Calcium, Iron
Excellent: Vitamin A, Folate

Marinated Baked Tofu

This is one of the very best ways to cook tofu. It's really delicious baked in this mixture of ginger and soy sauce.

10 oz	extra-firm tofu	280 g
2 tbsp	sodium-reduced soy sauce	30 ml
1 tbsp	dark sesame oil	15 ml
1 tbsp	grated root ginger	15 ml

1. Cut tofu into slices slightly larger than ½ inch (1 cm) thick.

2. In an 8-inch (20 cm) square glass baking dish just large enough to hold tofu in single layer, combine soy sauce, sesame oil and ginger with 1 tbsp (15 ml) water. Arrange tofu in dish, turning to coat both sides with mixture. Let marinate for 15 to 30 minutes.

3. Bake at 375°F (190°C) Gas Mark 5 for 20 minutes, turning after 10 minutes. Makes 4 servings.

Make ahead
To end of step 2, cover and refrigerate for up to 24 hours. Or to end of step 3, cover and refrigerate for one day; reheat or eat cold.

PER SERVING	
calories	139
g protein	12
g total fat	10
g saturated fat	1
mg cholesterol	0
g carbohydrate	4
g dietary fibre	2
mg sodium	252
mg potassium	193
Excellent: Calcium, Iron	

Tofu

Tofu is made from soya beans, and is rich in protein, iron and calcium, although tofus vary: some have three times as much calcium as others. For calcium-packed tofu, choose one that contains calcium sulphate or calcium chloride (those made wtih magnesium sulphate have less calcium). To top off its nutritional benefits, tofu is low in saturated fats and calories. And because it's made from a vegetable (not animal) product, it's cholesterol-free. If you're lactose intolerant, don't use dairy products or don't mix dairy and meat, consider tofu's versatility.

Torfu
Tofu, made from soya beans, is an excellent source of vegetable protein, and most kinds are also an excellent source of calcium. If firm-style tofu is unavailable, place regular tofu in sieve over bowl, weight down and drain for one hour or overnight.

Nutritional Note
To reduce the fat to 14 g per serving, use only 1 tbsp (15 ml) each of vegetable oil and sesame oil. In any case, the amount of saturated fat is low.

Garnish
Top with 4 tbsp (60 ml) chopped unsalted roasted peanuts if desired.

Vegetable Tofu Stir-Fry

Serve this flavourful dish over rice, noodles, bulgur or couscous.

12 oz	firm-style tofu	350 g
4 tsp	cornflour	20 ml
2 tbsp	vegetable oil	30 ml
1	medium onion, chopped	1
1	carrot, thinly sliced	1
2	stalks celery, sliced	2
1	sweet red or yellow pepper, cut into chunks	1
6 oz	frozen peas	175 g
6 oz	courgette, diced	175 g
4	spring onions, chopped	4
3	cloves garlic, finely chopped	3

Tofu Marinade

5 tbsp	rice or cider vinegar	75 ml
2 tbsp	sodium-reduced soy sauce	30 ml
2 tbsp	sesame oil	30 ml
1½ tsp	granulated sugar	7.5 ml
¼ tsp	red pepper flakes	1.25 ml

1. Tofu Marinade: In bowl, combine vinegar, soy sauce, sesame oil, sugar and red pepper flakes with 1 tbsp (15 ml) water.
Cut tofu into ½-inch (1 cm) cubes; add to marinade. Cover and marinate in refrigerator for 1 hour, stirring occasionally.

2. Drain tofu marinade into small dish; stir in cornflour, mixing well.

3. In a large nonstick frying pan, heat oil over high heat; stir-fry onion, carrot and celery for 3 minutes. Add red pepper, peas, courgette, spring onions and garlic; stir-fry for 3 minutes or until tender-crisp. Add tofu; stir-fry for 1 minute.

4. Whisk cornflour mixture; add to pan and cook for 1 minute or until thickened. Makes 4 servings.

Make ahead
To end of step 1 for up to 24 hours.

PER SERVING	
calories	334
g protein	17
g total fat	21
g saturated fat	3
mg cholesterol	0
g carbohydrate	24
g dietary fibre	6
mg sodium	316
mg potassium	591

Excellent: Vitamin A
Vitamin C, Folate, Calcium, Iron

Breadcrumbs

Make fresh breadcrumbs by crumbling 2 slices of day-old bread in a food processor. Or rub bread over a grater.

Make your own dry breadcrumbs by letting bread dry completely before processing into fine crumbs. Packaged dried breadcrumbs are very fine and not as nice as fresh breadcrumbs for a topping.

Fresh Herbs

If fresh herbs are available, use 2 tbsp (30 ml) chopped fresh marjoram and 1 tbsp (15 ml) chopped fresh thyme in the Gratin.

Autumn Dinner

- Italian Chick Pea and Pasta Soup (page 67)
- Tomato, Aubergine and Courgette Gratin
- Tossed Salad Leaves with Yogurt Herb Dressing (page 87)
- Baked Pear Bread Pudding (page 216)

PER SERVING	
calories	167
g protein	8
g total fat	7
g saturated fat	2
mg cholesterol	7
g carbohydrate	22
g dietary fibre	5
mg sodium	226
mg potassium	704

Good: Vitamin A, Vitamin C, Folate, Iron

Tomato, Aubergine and Courgette Gratin

Try to use long, narrow aubergines or very small. In this type of Mediterranean dish, all the vegetables traditionally would be first sautéed in oil. This method is faster to prepare and much lower in fat.

1 tbsp	olive oil	15 ml
1	onion, sliced	1
8 oz	mushrooms, sliced	225 g
2	cloves garlic, finely chopped	2
4	medium tomatoes, chopped	4
½ tsp	dried marjoram	2.5 ml
¼ tsp	dried thyme	1.25 ml
	salt and pepper	
2	courgettes, green or yellow (4 oz/115 g each)	2
2	small aubergines (4 oz/115 g each)	2
2 oz	fresh breadcrumbs	55 g
5 tbsp	freshly grated Parmesan cheese	75 ml

1. In a nonstick frying pan, heat 1 tsp (5 ml) of the oil over medium-high heat; cook onion, mushrooms, garlic and 2 tbsp (30 ml) water, stirring, for 3 minutes or until softened.

2. Add tomatoes, marjoram, thyme, and salt and pepper to taste; cook for 20 minutes or until thickened, stirring often.

3. Slice courgettes and aubergines diagonally into ¼-inch (5 mm) thick slices. Toss aubergine with remaining oil.

4. Spread 4 fl oz (125 ml) of the tomato sauce in a 13- x 9-inch (33 x 23 cm) glass baking dish. Layer with half of the courgette, aubergine and sauce; repeat layers.

5. Mix breadcrumbs with cheese; sprinkle over top. Bake, uncovered, at 400°F (200°C) Gas Mark 6 for 35 minutes or until bubbling. Makes 4 main-course servings.

Make ahead

To end of step 4 for up to one hour.

Fibre
Adults need 25 to 35 grams of fibre a day. One of the best ways to get this much fibre is to start the day by eating whole grain cereals. Read cereal boxes and choose ones with at least four grams of fibre per serving. Then for lunch, choose whole wheat pasta, and for supper, have whole grain or brown rice.

Vitamin E
Wheat germ is an excellent source of Vitamin E, an important antioxidant which may help to reduce heart disease. There is some concern that people on a very low-fat diet may not have an adequate amount of Vitamin E in their diet.

To Toast Nuts
Spread on baking sheet and bake at 350°F (180°C) Gas Mark 4 for 5 minutes or until golden.

Apricot-Raisin Muesli

You can save money by making your own muesli cereal. Use any combination of your favourite dried fruits and nuts. Sometimes I toast the rolled oats, and occasionally I use toasted oat bran. Serve with fresh fruit and milk or yogurt.

7 oz	rolled oats (not instant)	200 g
2 oz	toasted wheat germ	55 g
1 oz	oat or wheat bran	25 g
2½ oz	dried apricots, chopped	70 g
1½ oz	raisins or chopped figs	40 g
1¼ oz	brazil nuts or almonds, toasted and chopped	35 g
1 tsp	cinnamon	5 ml

1. Spread rolled oats on baking sheet; toast in the oven at 400°F (200°C) Gas Mark 6 for 5 minutes. Let cool.

2. In a large jar or airtight container, combine oats, wheat germ, bran, apricots, raisins, nuts and cinnamon; mix well. Makes 8 servings, 2 oz (55 g) each.

Make ahead
Store at room temperature for up to one month.

PER SERVING	
calories	178
g protein	8
g total fat	5
g saturated fat	1
mg cholesterol	0
g carbohydrate	31
g dietary fibre	5
mg sodium	3
mg potassium	353
Good: Folate, Iron	

Breads, Muffins, Cakes and Cookies

Cornmeal Pancakes with Jalapeño Peppers and Ginger

Apple Cinnamon Wholemeal Pancakes

Upside-Down Apple Pancake

Banana Blender Pancakes

Citrus Double-Bran Muffins

Jalapeño Cornmeal Muffins

Lemon Poppy Seed Muffins

Rhubarb Bran Muffins

High-Fibre Carrot Bran Muffins

Muesli Soda Bread

Raspberry Pecan Tea Bread

Fruit and Fibre Squares

Light Lemon Squares

Orange Hazelnut Biscotti

Apple Cinnamon Cookies

Apricot Streusel Cake

Gingerbread Cake

Pumpkin Spice Cake

Elizabeth Baird's Chocolate Angel Food Cake

Double Corn Pancakes
Before turning pancakes, top
each one with 1 tbsp (15 ml)
kernel sweetcorn.

Cornmeal Pancakes with Jalapeño Peppers and Ginger

This unlikely combination is surprisingly delightful. Serve for
lunch or a light supper and top the pancakes with salsa and
yogurt.

4 oz	cornmeal	115 g
4 oz	plain flour	115 g
2 tbsp	granulated sugar	30 ml
1 tbsp	baking powder	15 ml
½ tsp	bicarbonate of soda	2.5 ml
2	eggs, lightly beaten	2
16 fl oz	skimmed milk	450 ml
2 tbsp	vegetable oil	30 ml
2 tbsp	grated root ginger	30 ml
2 tbsp	chopped pickled jalapeño peppers	30 ml
½ tsp	soft margarine or butter	2.5 ml

1. In a large bowl, mix cornmeal, flour, sugar, baking powder and
baking soda.

2. Combine eggs, milk, oil, root ginger and jalapeño peppers;
pour into flour mixture, stirring just until combined.

3. Heat a nonstick frying pan over medium heat until hot; add
margarine to lightly grease. Pour in batter, 2 fl oz (50 ml) for each
pancake; cook until bubbles form on surface and underside is
golden brown. Turn and cook just until bottom is lightly browned.
Makes 6 servings of 3 pancakes each.

Make ahead
To end of step 1 for up to one day.

PER SERVING	
calories	291
g protein	9
g total fat	9
g saturated fat	2
mg cholesterol	78
g carbohydrate	44
g dietary fibre	2
mg sodium	366
mg potassium	233
Good: Calcium	

Apple Cinnamon Pancakes
You can substitute plain flour for the wholemeal, but pancakes won't be as high in fibre.

Lower-Fat Baking
Try to use the minimum of high-fat ingredients such as butter, margarine, oil or cream. When possible, I use a liquid vegetable oil instead of butter, margarine, vegetable oil or lard, because it is lower in saturated fats and is not hydrogenated.

Apple Cinnamon Wholemeal Pancakes

Top these tasty pancakes with yogurt mixed with brown sugar or maple syrup.

2 oz	plain flour	55 g
2 oz	wholemeal flour	55 g
1 tbsp	granulated sugar	15 ml
1½ tsp	baking powder	7.5 ml
1 tsp	cinnamon	5 ml
¼ tsp	bicarbinate of soda	1.25 ml
1	egg, lightly beaten	1
8 fl oz	skimmed milk	225 ml
2 oz	apple, peeled	55 g
1 tbsp	vegetable oil	15 ml
½ tsp	soft margarine or butter	2.5 ml

1. In a bowl, combine flours, sugar, baking powder, cinnamon and bicarbonate of soda.

2. Combine egg, milk, apple and oil; pour into flour mixture, stirring just until combined.

3. Heat a nonstick frying pan over medium heat until hot; add margarine to lightly grease. Pour in batter, 2 fl oz (50 ml) for each pancake; cook until bubbles form on surface and underside is golden brown. Turn and cook just until bottom is lightly browned. Makes 3 servings of 3 pancakes each.

Make ahead
To end of step 1 for up to one day.

PER SERVING	
calories	288
g protein	10
g total fat	9
g saturated fat	2
mg cholesterol	78
g carbohydrate	43
g dietary fibre	4
mg sodium	299
mg potassium	281
Good: Calcium, Iron	

Upside-Down Apple Cake
This pancake can just as easily
be called a cake and served for
dessert.

Upside-Down Apple Pancake

Make this fabulous-tasting pancake at the weekend for brunch or
breakfast. If you make it in two pie plates, it's easy to turn upside
down onto serving plates and looks great. Top with yogurt mixed
with a little honey or maple syrup.

1 oz	soft margarine or butter	25 g
2 oz	granulated sugar	55 g
2 tsp	cinnamon	10 ml
3	medium apples, peeled and sliced	3
Batter		
1½ oz	plain flour	40 g
½ tsp	baking powder	2.5 ml
2	egg yolks	2
5 tbsp	skimmed milk	75 ml
4	egg whites	4
2½ oz	granulated sugar	70 g

1. In two 9-inch (23 cm) pie plates or one 13- x 9-inch (33- x
23-cm) baking dish, melt margarine in the oven at 400°F (200°C)
Gas Mark 6, about 2 minutes.

2. Combine sugar and cinnamon; sprinkle evenly over margarine.
Bake for 2 minutes or until melted.

3. Arrange apple slices in overlapping circles over the top; bake
for 10 minutes.

4. Batter: Meanwhile, in a bowl, combine flour and baking
powder; blend in egg yolks and milk.

5. In a large bowl, beat egg whites until white and frothy;
gradually beat in sugar until soft peaks form. Fold into milk
mixture.

6. Spread evenly over apples. Bake for 15 to 20 minutes or until
lightly browned.

7. Loosen edges with knife; turn out on to serving plate.
Makes 6 servings.

Make ahead
Best served immediately, but fine prepared a few hours in advance
and served at room temperature.

PER SERVING	
calories	210
g protein	5
g total fat	6
g saturated fat	1
mg cholesterol	75
g carbohydrate	36
g dietary fibre	2
mg sodium	118
mg potassium	137

Nutritional Note
For extra fibre and maximum nutrients, have whole fruit rather than juice at breakfast.

Banana Blender Pancakes

These take two minutes to prepare and taste absolutely delicious. Try topping the pancakes with low-fat yogurt mixed with brown sugar, fresh fruit or traditional maple syrup instead of high-fat butter or margarine.

2 oz	plain flour	55 g
1 oz	cornmeal*	25 g
1 oz	wholemeal flour	25 g
1 tbsp	granulated sugar	15 ml
1½ tsp	baking powder	7.5 ml
1	egg	1
8 fl oz	skimmed milk	225 ml
1 tbsp	vegetable oil	15 ml
1	banana, diced	1
1 tsp	soft margarine or butter	5 ml

1. In a blender or food processor, blend together flour, cornmeal, wholemeal flour, sugar and baking powder.

2. Add egg, milk and oil; process until mixed. Stir in banana.

3. Heat a nonstick frying pan over medium heat until hot; add margarine to lightly grease.

4. Pour in batter, 2 fl oz (50 ml) for each pancake; cook for about 1 minute or until bubbles form on surface and underside is golden. Turn and cook just until bottom is browned. Makes eight 5-inch (13 cm) pancakes.

Make ahead
To end of step 1 for up to one day.

PER PANCAKE	
calories	121
g protein	4
g total fat	4
g saturated fat	1
mg cholesterol	29
g carbohydrate	19
g dietary fibre	1
mg sodium	78
mg potassium	144

* Instead of using cornmeal, you can substitute wholemeal flour if desired. The pancakes are also fine made with 4 oz (115 g) plain flour but won't be as nutritious.

Muffin Exposé
All muffins are not created
equal, and it's not only the size
that varies. A muffin can be as
nutritious as a slice of bread or
as frivolous as a piece of cake,
with as little as 2 g of fat or as
much as 20 g.

When buying muffins, the
best bet nutritionally is a low-
fat muffin made with whole
grains or bran. When you
make your own muffins, use
whole grains and as little fat as
possible.

PER MUFFIN	
calories	163
g protein	4
g total fat	6
g saturated fat	1
mg cholesterol	19
g carbohydrate	24
g dietary fibre	3
mg sodium	218
mg potassium	133

Right:
Summer Prawn and Tomato
Pasta (page 152)

Citrus Double-Bran Muffins

Chopped prunes add flavour and keep these delicious muffins
moist.

4 oz	plain flour	115 g
1 oz	wheat bran	25 g
1 oz	oat bran	25 g
4 oz	granulated sugar	115 g
1 tsp	baking powder	5 ml
1 tsp	baking soda	5 ml
¼ tsp	salt	1.25 ml
3½ oz	prunes, chopped	100 g
1	egg, lightly beaten	1
8 fl oz	buttermilk or soured milk*	225 ml
4 tbsp	vegetable oil	60 ml
	grated rind of 1 lemon and 1 orange	
1 tbsp	sesame seeds	15 ml

1. In a large bowl, combine flour, wheat bran, oat bran, sugar,
baking powder, bicarbonate of soda and salt. Stir in prunes.

2. In a separate bowl, mix egg, buttermilk, oil, and lemon and
orange rinds. Pour into flour mixture and stir just enough to
moisten, being careful not to overmix.

3. Spoon into greased nonstick muffin tins. Sprinkle with sesame
seeds. Bake at 375°F (190°C) Gas Mark 5 for 20 minutes or until
tops are firm to the touch. Makes 12 muffins.

Make ahead
Muffins can be stored in airtight container for up to three days or
frozen for up to two weeks.

* To sour milk, add 1 tbsp (15 ml) lemon juice or vinegar to 8 fl oz
(225 ml) milk and let stand for 10 minutes.

Jalapeño Cornmeal Muffins

Creamed corn makes these muffins very moist, and jalapeño
peppers add a zing of flavour. Serve with a main course of chicken
or ham or as part of a brunch menu.

4 oz	cornmeal	115 g
4 oz	plain flour	115 g
1 tsp	baking powder	5 ml
1 tsp	bicarbonate of soda	5 ml
¼ tsp	salt	1.25 ml
2 tbsp	chopped pickled jalapeño peppers	30 ml
1	egg, lightly beaten	1
1	can (10 oz/284 ml) creamed corn	1
8 fl oz	buttermilk or soured milk*	225 ml
4 tbsp	vegetable oil	60 ml

1. In a large bowl, combine cornmeal, flour, baking powder,
bicarbonate of soda and salt. Stir in jalapeño peppers.

2. In a separate bowl, mix egg, corn, buttermilk and oil. Pour into
flour mixture and stir just enough to moisten, being careful not to
overmix.

3. Spoon into greased nonstick muffin tins. Bake at 375°F (190°C)
Gas Mark 5 for 25 to 30 minutes or until tops are firm to the touch.
Makes 12 muffins.

Make ahead
Muffins can be stored in airtight container for up to three days or
frozen for up to two weeks.

PER MUFFIN	
calories	154
g protein	4
g total fat	6
g saturated fat	1
mg cholesterol	19
g carbohydrate	23
g dietary fibre	1
mg sodium	303
mg potassium	104

Left:
Meringues with Lemon Cream
(page 222)

* To sour milk, add 1 tbsp (15 ml) lemon juice or vinegar to 8 fl oz
(225 ml) milk and let stand for 10 minutes.

Wholemeal Flour
Wholemeal flour is much higher in fibre than white flour. In many recipes, you can substitute half the amount of white flour with wholemeal flour. Vitamin E, an important antioxidant vitamin, is found in whole grain cereals and wheat germ.

Lemon Poppy Seed Muffins

If you like a strong lemon flavour, use the rind, or zest, of two lemons in these light muffins.

4 oz	plain flour	115 g
4 oz	wholemeal flour	115 g
4 oz	granulated sugar	115 g
4 tbsp	poppy seeds	60 ml
1 tsp	baking powder	5 ml
1 tsp	bicarbonate of soda	5 ml
¼ tsp	salt	1.25 ml
1	egg, lightly beaten	1
6 fl oz	milk	175 ml
4 tbsp	vegetable oil	60 ml
	grated rind of 1 or 2 lemons	
4 tbsp	lemon juice	60 ml

1. In a large bowl, combine flours, sugar, poppy seeds, baking powder, bicarbonate of soda and salt.

2. In a separate bowl, mix egg, milk, oil, lemon rind and juice. Pour into flour mixture and stir just enough to moisten, being careful not to overmix.

3. Spoon into greased nonstick muffin tins. Bake at 375°F (190°C) Gas Mark 5 for 25 to 30 minutes or until tops are firm to the touch. Makes 12 muffins.

Make ahead
Muffins can be stored in airtight container for up to two days or frozen for up to two weeks.

PER MUFFIN	
calories	175
g protein	4
g total fat	7
g saturated fat	1
mg cholesterol	19
g carbohydrate	26
g dietary fibre	2
mg sodium	182
mg potassium	108

Pumpkin Muffins
Substitute 8 oz (225 g) canned or cooked puréed pumpkin for rhubarb.

Apple Bran Muffins
Substitute 8 oz (½ kg) stewed apple for rhubarb.

Rhubarb Bran Muffins

In this recipe, use Stewed Rhubarb (page 225) or rhubarb stewed with a minimum amount of liquid: just a spoonful or two.

1½ oz	wheat bran	40 g
4 oz	wholemeal flour	115 g
4 oz	granulated sugar	115 g
2 tsp	cinnamon	10 ml
1 tsp	baking powder	5 ml
1 tsp	bicarbonate of soda	5 ml
2½ oz	raisins	70 g
8 oz	stewed rhubarb	225 g
1	egg, lightly beaten	1
4 fl oz	buttermilk or low-fat yogurt	125 ml
4 tbsp	vegetable oil	60 ml

1. In a bowl, combine bran, flour, sugar, cinnamon, baking powder and bicarbonate of soda; stir in raisins.

2. Combine stewed rhubarb, egg, buttermilk and oil; pour into flour mixture and stir just until combined.

3. Spoon into greased nonstick muffin tins. Bake at 400°F (200°C) Gas Mark 6 for 25 minutes or until tops are firm to the touch. Makes 12 muffins.

Make ahead
Muffins can be stored in airtight container for up to two days or frozen for up to two weeks.

PER MUFFIN	
calories	169
g protein	3
g total fat	6
g saturated fat	1
mg cholesterol	18
g carbohydrate	30
g dietary fibre	4
mg sodium	137
mg potassium	202

Preparing Muffin Tins
Use nonstick tins; spray lightly over entire pan with nonstick vegetable coating spray.

Filling Muffin Tins
Fill muffin tins to the top. Depending on the size of your tins, you could get 14 muffins from this recipe.

High-Fibre Carrot Bran Muffins

These easy-to-make muffins are great for breakfast, snacks or lunch. Grated apple could be substituted for carrot.

6 oz	wholemeal flour	175 g
4 oz	high-fibre ready-to-eat bran cereal (not flakes)	115 g
4 oz	brown sugar	115 g
1 tbsp	cinnamon	15 ml
1 tsp	baking powder	5 ml
1 tsp	bicarbonate of soda	5 ml
¼ tsp	salt	1.25 ml
5 oz	raisins or chopped dates	140 g
4 oz	carrots, grated	115 g
14 fl oz	buttermilk or soured milk*	400 ml
4 tbsp	vegetable oil	60 ml
1	egg, lightly beaten	1
	grated rind of 1 lemon or orange	

1. In a large bowl, stir together flour, cereal, sugar, cinnamon, baking powder, soda, salt, raisins and carrots.

2. Add buttermilk, oil, egg and lemon rind, stirring just until combined.

3. Spoon into greased nonstick muffin tins. Bake at 400°F (200°C) Gas Mark 6 for 20 minutes or until tops are firm to the touch. Makes 12 muffins.

Make ahead
Muffins will keep, wrapped in cling film and refrigerated, for up to two days, or frozen for up to one month.

PER MUFFIN	
calories	213
g protein	5
g total fat	6
g saturated fat	1
mg cholesterol	19
g carbohydrate	40
g dietary fibre	6
mg sodium	291
mg potassium	368
Good: Vitamin A, Iron	

* Instead of buttermilk, you can substitute 13 fl oz (375 ml) milk mixed with 2 tbsp (30 ml) lemon juice. Let stand for 10 minutes.

Wholemeal Versus White

All white and brown flour sold in this country is enriched with thiamine, niacin, iron and calcium. All baked goods are therefore made with these enriched flours. If a bread is to be labelled 'enriched,' it must also have added nutrients and these must be listed. Wholemeal flour is not enriched with anything.

The best choices are usually breads made from whole grains: they have more nutrients, flavour, fibre and texture.

Muesli Soda Bread

This wholemeal, raisin quick bread warm from the oven is a nice treat. You can substitute an equal amount of dried fruit mixture for the raisins. (Pictured opposite page 161.)

8 oz	wholemeal flour	225 g
4 oz	plain flour	115 g
1½ oz	rolled oats	40 g
3 tbsp	granulated sugar	45 ml
1 tbsp	baking powder	15 ml
1 tsp	bicarbonate of soda	5 ml
1 tsp	salt	5 ml
4 oz	raisins	115 g
2 tbsp	vegetable oil	30 ml
14 fl oz	buttermilk	400 ml

Muesli Topping

1	egg white	1
1 tbsp	each rolled oats, wheat germ, oat bran, sunflower seeds and sesame seeds	15 ml

1. In a bowl, combine wholemeal and plain flours, rolled oats, sugar, baking powder, soda and salt; stir in raisins.

2. Add oil to buttermilk; pour into flour mixture. Stir to make soft dough.

3. Turn out on to lightly floured surface and knead about 10 times or until smooth. Place on greased baking sheet; shape into circle about 2½ inches (6 cm) thick. Cut large shallow X on top.

4. Muesli Topping: Brush egg white over top of loaf. Combine rolled oats, wheat germ, oat bran, sunflower seeds and sesame seeds; sprinkle over loaf.

5. Bake at 350°F (180°C) Gas Mark 4 for 65 to 70 minutes or until skewer inserted in centre comes out clean. Makes 1 loaf, about 20 slices.

Make ahead

Best eaten warm from oven, but keeps well for two days.

PER SLICE	
calories	128
g protein	4
g total fat	3
g saturated fat	0.4
mg cholesterol	1
g carbohydrate	24
g dietary fibre	2
mg sodium	239
mg potassium	156

Baking Note
Soft reduced-fat spreads and
low-fat tub margarines contain
more water than ordinary soft
margarines and are not
recommended for baking.

Raspberry Pecan Tea Bread

Frozen raspberries make this easy to prepare all year round.
Buy the individually frozen raspberries.

8 oz	granulated sugar	225 g
2 oz	soft margarine	55 g
1	egg	1
¼ pt	milk	150 ml
6 oz	plain flour	175 g
1 tsp	baking powder	5 ml
½ tsp	cinnamon	2.5 ml
2 oz	pecans, chopped	55 g
4 oz	raspberries (fresh or frozen, unthawed)	115 g

1. Line 8- x 4-inch (20- x 10-cm) loaf tin with foil; grease lightly.

2. In a large bowl, cream sugar with margarine. Beat in egg, then milk.

3. Mix flour, baking powder and cinnamon; beat into egg mixture until blended. Stir in pecans and raspberries.

4. Spoon into tin; bake at 350°F (180°C) Gas Mark 4 for 60 to 70 minutes or until skewer inserted in centre comes out clean. Let stand in tin for 3 minutes.

5. Transfer foil and tea bread to rack; loosen foil and let cool completely before cutting. Makes 16 slices.

Make ahead
Tea bread can be wrapped in foil and stored for up to four days or frozen for up to one month.

PER SLICE	
calories	154
g protein	2
g total fat	6
g saturated fat	1
mg cholesterol	14
g carbohydrate	24
g dietary fibre	1
mg sodium	64
mg potassium	59

Apricots
Dried apricots and dates are
high in fibre and iron.
   For a softer, moister bar,
soak apricots in hot water for
10 minutes, then drain.

Nutritional Note
Instead of spending a large part
of your budget and calorie
allowance (1,900 a day for an
average active woman) on
foods such as crisps and
biscuits, spend it on
wholesome foods. When
buying bread, remember that
wholemeal has the same
calories as white yet more
vitamins and three times the
fibre. When baking, add fibre
and nutrients by using
wholemeal flour (or a half-and-
half mixture of wholemeal and
white flour).

Fruit and Fibre Squares

Packed with fruit and fibre, these are perfect for a breakfast-on-
the-run, lunch-box treat or a quick snack.

3 oz	bran flakes	85 g
4 oz	wholemeal flour	115 g
5 oz	brown sugar	140 g
2 tsp	bicarbonate of soda	10 ml
½ tsp	salt	2.5 ml
8 fl oz	buttermilk	225 ml
2 tbsp	vegetable oil	30 ml
2	eggs	2
	grated rind of 1 orange	
5 oz	dried apricots, chopped	140 g
6 oz	chopped dates	175 g
2 oz	almonds, chopped	55 g

1. In a food processor, combine bran flakes, flour, sugar, soda and
salt; process for 1 second.

2. Add buttermilk, oil, eggs and orange rind; process until
blended.

3. Stir in apricots, dates and almonds.

4. Spread in greased 13- x 9-inch (33 x 23-cm) baking dish.
Bake at 375°F (190°C) Gas Mark 5 for 25 minutes or until skewer
inserted in centre comes out clean. Let cool before cutting into
squares. Makes 16 squares.

Make ahead
Wrap individual squares in cling film and store in biscuit tin
for up to two days, or freeze for up to one month.

PER SQUARE	
calories	173
g protein	4
g total fat	4
g saturated fat	1
mg cholesterol	28
g carbohydrate	33
g dietary fibre	4
mg sodium	301
mg potassium	320

Nutritional Note
The traditional lemon square recipe uses 4 oz (115 g) butter in the base and 2 whole eggs in the topping. Instead, I cut the fat in half.

Light Lemon Squares

This is a light version of a favourite square.

4 oz	plain flour	115 g
2 oz	granulated sugar	55 g
2 oz	soft margarine	55 g
2 tbsp	low-fat yogurt	30 ml
Topping		
6 oz	granulated sugar	175 g
2 tbsp	plain flour	30 ml
½ tsp	baking powder	2.5 ml
¼ tsp	salt	1.25 ml
1	egg	1
1	egg white	1
	grated rind of 1 large lemon	
4 tbsp	lemon juice	60 ml
2 tsp	icing sugar	10 ml

1. In a food processor or bowl, mix together flour, sugar, margarine and yogurt until just combined.

2. Press into an 8-inch (20 cm) square cake tin lightly coated with cooking spray or greased. Bake at 325°F (160°C) Gas Mark 3 for 25 minutes or until golden.

3. Topping: In a food processor or bowl, combine sugar, flour, baking powder, salt, egg, egg white and lemon rind and juice; mix well.

4. Pour over base. Bake for 30 minutes or until top is set.

5. Let cool in tin. Sift icing sugar over top. Cut into squares. Makes 16 squares.

Make ahead
Squares can be stored in an airtight container for up to one week or frozen for up to two weeks.

PER SQUARE	
calories	115
g protein	2
g total fat	3
g saturated fat	1
mg cholesterol	14
g carbohydrate	20
g dietary fibre	0.3
mg sodium	92
mg potassium	27

Almond Ginger Biscotti
Omit hazelnuts, vanilla and orange rind. Substitute 3 oz (85 g) coarsely chopped unblanched almonds, 1½ tsp (7.5 ml) ground ginger and 3 tbsp (45 ml) finely chopped crystallized ginger.

Orange Hazelnut Biscotti

These crunchy Italian biscuits are meant to be dunked in your tea, coffee or hot chocolate.

4 oz	(unskinned) hazelnuts, coarsely chopped	115 g
6 oz	plain flour	175 g
2 tsp	baking powder	10 ml
2	eggs	2
4 oz	brown sugar	115 g
2 tsp	vanilla essence	10 ml
	grated rind of 1 orange	
1	egg white	1

1. In a large bowl, combine nuts, flour and baking powder.

2. In a separate bowl, beat eggs, sugar, vanilla and orange rind; stir into flour mixture, mixing well to form stiff dough.

3. Shape dough into 2 logs about 1-inch (2.5 cm) in diameter. Transfer to ungreased baking sheet.

4. Brush tops with egg white. Bake at 350°F (180°C) Gas Mark 4 for 25 minutes. Let cool for 5 minutes.

5. Slice diagonally into ½-inch (1 cm) thick slices. Arrange on a baking sheet. Reduce temperature to 300°F (150°C) Gas Mark 2 and bake for 25 minutes or until crisp and golden.
Makes 36 biscuits.

Make ahead
Biscotti can be stored in an airtight container for up to two weeks.

PER BISCUIT	
calories	52
g protein	1
g total fat	2
g saturated fat	0.2
mg cholesterol	12
g carbohydrate	8
g dietary fibre	0.4
mg sodium	21
mg potassium	33

Baking Note
Grated apple adds moistness
and flavour to this low-fat
cookie.

Apple Cinnamon Cookies

These old-fashioned cookies are favourites in our house.

4 oz	soft margarine or butter	115 g
12 oz	brown sugar	350 g
1	egg	1
6 oz	apple, grated	175 g
5 oz	raisins	140 g
1½ oz	almonds, chopped	40 g
4 tbsp	apple juice	60 ml
8 oz	wholemeal flour	225 g
2 tsp	cinnamon	10 ml
1 tsp	bicarbonate of soda	5 ml
½ tsp	salt	2.5 ml
¼ tsp	ground cloves	1.25 ml
Glaze (Optional)		
4 oz	icing sugar	115 g
2 tbsp	lemon juice	30 ml

1. In a large bowl, cream margarine with sugar until fluffy; beat in egg. Add apple, raisins, almonds and apple juice; mix well.

2. In a separate bowl, combine flour, cinnamon, soda, salt and cloves. Stir into apple mixture; mix well.

3. Drop by tablespoonfuls (15 ml) about 2 inches (5 cm) apart on to lightly greased baking sheets. Bake at 375°F (190°C) Gas Mark 5 for 10 to 12 minutes or until evenly browned. Let stand on baking sheets for 1 to 2 minutes before removing to racks to let cool.

4. Glaze: In a small bowl, combine icing sugar and lemon juice until smooth. Spread over each cookie. Makes 60 cookies.

Make ahead
Cookies can be stored in an airtight container for up to one week or frozen for up to one month.

PER COOKIE (WITHOUT GLAZE)	
calories	60
g protein	1
g total fat	2
g saturated fat	0.3
mg cholesterol	4
g carbohydrate	11
g dietary fibre	1
mg sodium	62
mg potassium	65

Apricot Streusel Cake

This amazingly delicious moist cake has no fat except from the semi-skimmed evaporated milk. It's a lovely dessert accompanied by any fresh fruit, or serve as a treat with morning coffee.

4 oz	plain flour	115 g
8 oz	granulated sugar	225 g
1 tsp	bicarbonate of soda	5 ml
½ tsp	salt	2.5 ml
1	egg, lightly beaten	1
6 fl oz	semi-skimmed evaporated milk	175 ml
8	fresh apricots (1 lb/450 g), coarsely chopped, or 1 can (14 oz/400 g) apricots, drained and coarsely chopped	8

Topping

2 oz	brown sugar	55 g
1 tsp	cinnamon	5 ml

1. In a large bowl, combine flour, sugar, soda and salt.

2. Add egg and evaporated milk; mix well. Stir in apricots.

3. Spread in an 8-inch (20-cm) square cake tin lightly coated with cooking spray or greased.

4. Topping: Combine brown sugar and cinnamon; sprinkle over top. Bake an 350°F (180°C) Gas Mark 4 for 60 to 70 minutes or until skewer inserted in centre comes out clean.
Makes 12 servings.

Make ahead
Cake can be covered with foil and stored for three days or frozen for up to two weeks.

PER SERVING	
calories	157
g protein	3
g total fat	1
g saturated fat	0.3
mg cholesterol	19
g carbohydrate	35
g dietary fibre	1
mg sodium	218
mg potassium	188

Baking Note
Instead of using fresh ginger, you can add 2 tsp (10 ml) ground ginger and 1 tsp (5 ml) ground cinnamon to the dry ingredients for this cake.

Gingerbread Cake

Grated fresh root ginger adds an extra flavour dimension to this moist cake, but ground ginger also works well. This cake is delicious topped with stewed sliced apples (see Apple Filling in Apple-Pecan Fillo Crisps, page 217), or serve with fresh fruit, Microwave Rhubarb Sauce with Ginger (page 225) or ice cream.

4 oz	brown sugar	115 g
2 oz	soft margarine or butter	55 g
	grated rind of 1 orange	
1	egg	1
1	egg white	1
8 oz	apple purée or stewed apples	225 g
4 oz	treacle	115 g
4 tbsp	grated root ginger	60 ml
6 oz	plain flour, sifted	175 g
1 tsp	bicarbonate of soda	5 ml
1 tsp	baking powder	5 ml
½ tsp	salt	2.5 ml

1. In a bowl and using an electric mixer, beat brown sugar, margarine and orange rind until smooth.

2. Beat in egg and egg white, beating well after each addition. Mix in apple purée, treacle and ginger until smooth.

3. Combine flour, soda, baking powder and salt; gradually beat into sugar mixture, beating for 2 to 3 minutes.

4. Transfer to an 8-inch (20-cm) square cake tin. Bake at 350°F (180°C) Gas Mark 4 for 40 minutes or until cake pulls away from sides of tin and skewer inserted in centre comes out clean. Serve warm or cold. Makes 12 servings.

Make ahead
Cake can be covered with foil and refrigerated for up to four days or frozen for up to two weeks.

PER SERVING	
calories	170
g protein	2
g total fat	4
g saturated fat	1
mg cholesterol	18
g carbohydrate	31
g dietary fibre	1
mg sodium	281
mg potassium	202

Pumpkin Spice Cake

Serve this flavourful, moist cake with coffee or for dessert with fruit. Buttermilk and pumpkin purée take the place of fat in this dark, spicy, raisin-studded cake.

14 oz	granulated sugar	400 g
2 oz	soft margarine or butter	55 g
1	egg	1
4 fl oz	buttermilk	125 ml
1	can (14 oz/398 g) pumpkin purée	1
	grated rind of 1 orange	
1 tsp	vanilla	5 ml
6 oz	plain flour	175 g
6 oz	wholemeal flour	175 g
2 tsp	each cinnamon and bicarbonate of soda	10 ml
5 oz	raisins	140 g
Glaze		
1 oz	icing sugar	25 g
1½ tsp	orange juice	7.5 ml

1. Grease and flour a 10-inch (25 cm) Bundt or Kugelhopf* pan.

2. In a bowl, beat sugar with margarine; beat in egg until light.

3. Beat in buttermilk, pumpkin, orange rind and vanilla.

4. Combine flours, cinnamon, soda and raisins; stir into pumpkin mixture just until combined.

5. Pour into tin; bake at 325°F (160°C) Gas Mark 3 for 60 to 65 minutes or until skewer inserted in centre comes out clean. Let cool on rack for 20 minutes; remove from pan.

6. Glaze: Blend icing sugar with orange juice; drizzle over cooled cake. Makes 16 servings.

Make ahead
Cake can be stored in airtight container for up to two days or frozen for up to one month.

PER SERVING	
calories	247
g protein	4
g total fat	4
g saturated fat	1
mg cholesterol	14
g carbohydrate	52
g dietary fibre	3
mg sodium	200
mg potassium	210
Excellent: Vitamin A	

* If neither is available, use a ring mould.

Elizabeth Baird's Chocolate Angel Food Cake

My friend Elizabeth Baird, food director of *Canadian Living* magazine, made this fabulous cake for my birthday. More flavourful than ordinary angel food cake, it is still nearly fat-free. Serve with Vanilla Cream (page 231) and fresh berries.

3 oz	sifted self-raising flour	85 g
12 oz	granulated sugar	350 g
1 oz	unsweetened cocoa powder	25 g
12 fl oz	egg whites (about 11 large eggs), at room temperature	350 ml
1 tbsp	lemon juice	15 ml
1 tsp	cream of tartar	5 ml
½ tsp	salt	2.5 ml
1 tsp	vanilla	5 ml
½ tsp	almond extract	2.5 ml
	icing sugar	

1. On to a piece of greaseproof paper, sift together flour, half of the sugar and the cocoa. Sift again; set aside.

2. In a large nonplastic bowl, beat egg whites until foamy. Add lemon juice, cream of tartar and salt; beat until soft peaks form. Gradually add remaining sugar, 2 tbsp (30 ml) at a time, beating until glossy and stiff peaks form.

3. Sprinkle with vanilla and almond extract. Sift one-quarter of the cocoa mixture at a time over egg whites, folding in each with a rubber spatula.

4. Scrape into an ungreased 10-inch (25 cm) very deep ring tin or angel food tube pan. Run spatula through mixture to eliminate large air pockets; smooth top. Bake at 350°F (180°C) Gas Mark 4 for 40 to 45 minutes or until cake springs back when lightly touched.

5. Invert pan on to neck of large bottle unless pan has legs attached; let cake hang until cool. Loosen edges with a knife; remove cake from pan. Place on plate; place doily over top and dust with icing sugar. Remove doily. Makes 12 servings.

Make ahead
Cake can be stored at room temperature for up to two days or frozen for up to one month.

PER SERVING	
calories	143
g protein	4
g total fat	1
g saturated fat	0.3
mg cholesterol	0
g carbohydrate	32
g dietary fibre	1
mg sodium	160
mg potassium	65

Desserts

Chocolate Crêpes with Banana Cream Filling and Chocolate Sauce

Chocolate Mocha Ice Cream Pie with Gingersnap Crust

Chocolate Marbled Cheesecake

Orange Chocolate Refrigerator Cake

Lemon Mousse with Raspberry Sauce

Easy Berry Flan

Fresh Plum Flan

Baked Pear Bread Pudding with Honey-Almond Sauce

Apple-Pecan Fillo Crisps

Pumpkin Pie with Orange Cream

Light Pastry

Deep-Dish Pear Pie with Apricots and Ginger

Winter Berry Trifle

Meringues with Lemon Cream

Kiwi Fool

Microwave Rhubarb Sauce with Ginger

Nectarine and Orange Compote

Apricot, Orange and Fig Compote

Berries with Orange Cream

Orange or Lemon Yogurt Cream

Amaretto Custard Sauce

Vanilla Cream

Butterscotch Sauce

Chocolate Crêpes with Banana Cream Filling and Chocolate Sauce

This is a fabulous, light dessert. Even though it has a little whipped cream, this fancy dessert is relatively low in fat. It has two egg whites instead of a whole egg and cocoa powder instead of higher-fat chocolate.

4 fl oz	Chocolate Sauce (recipe follows)	125 ml
Chocolate Crêpes		
1½ oz	plain flour	40 g
2 tbsp	unsweetened cocoa powder	30 ml
1 tbsp	granulated sugar	15 ml
Pinch	salt	Pinch
2	egg whites, lightly beaten	2
5 tbsp	skimmed milk	75 ml
4 tbsp	water	60 ml
1 tsp	soft margarine or butter	5 ml
Banana Cream Filling		
5 tbsp	whipping cream	75 ml
5 tbsp	plain yogurt or extra-thick yogurt	75 ml
2 tbsp	granulated sugar	30 ml
½ tsp	vanilla	2.5 ml
3	bananas, sliced	3

1. Chocolate Crêpes: In a bowl, combine flour, cocoa, sugar and salt; make a well in centre. Add egg whites and whisk lightly to combine. Gradually whisk in milk and water until smooth.

2. Heat small nonstick crêpe pan over medium heat; brush with some of the margarine. For each crêpe, pour in 2 tbsp (30 ml) batter, swirling to cover bottom of pan; pour off any excess. Cook until edges begin to curl and crêpe no longer sticks; turn and cook for 30 seconds. Remove and set aside. Repeat with remaining batter, brushing pan with margarine as necessary.

3. Banana Cream Filling: Whip cream; stir in yogurt, sugar and vanilla.

PER SERVING (INCLUDING SAUCE)	
calories	357
g protein	7
g total fat	11
g saturated fat	6
mg cholesterol	28
g carbohydrate	63
g dietary fibre	5
mg sodium	83
mg potassium	605
Good: Iron	

4. Assembly: Spread about 2 tbsp (30 ml) filling over one half of each crêpe. Arrange overlapping banana slices over half of filling. Fold uncovered crêpe in half over filling; fold in half again. Arrange on dessert plates; drizzle with chocolate sauce. Makes 4 servings, 2 crêpes each.

Make ahead
To end of step 2: crêpes can be stacked between greaseproof paper, wrapped and refrigerated for up to one day or frozen for up to one month.

Nutritional Note
Cocoa is made from roasted cocoa beans with most of the fat (cocoa butter) removed; it is much lower in fat than chocolate but still has all the chocolate flavour.

Chocolate Sauce

Chocolate can be part of a healthy diet when you use this low-fat sauce. Drizzle over ice cream, frozen yogurt, or the Chocolate Crêpes.

2 oz	unsweetened cocoa powder	55 g
2½ oz	granulated sugar	70 g
5 tbsp	water	75 ml
5 tbsp	corn syrup or golden syrup	75 ml
½ tsp	vanilla essence	2.5 ml

1. In a saucepan, combine cocoa and sugar. Whisk in water and corn syrup.

2. Bring to boil over medium-high heat; boil for 2 minutes, stirring constantly.

3. Remove from heat and stir in vanilla. Let cool (sauce will thicken upon cooling). Makes about 8 fl oz (225 ml).

Make ahead
Sauce can be refrigerated for up to two weeks.

PER SERVING 2 tbsp/30 ml	
calories	90
g protein	1
g total fat	1
g saturated fat	1
mg cholesterol	0
g carbohydrate	21
g dietary fibre	2
mg sodium	10
mg potassium	89

Lower-Fat Variations
Although ice cream is called for in the recipe, they are not all the same. Read the nutrition labels carefully.

Recipe made with:	Fat (g)/ serving
Wall's Too Good to be True	6.6
Weightwatchers	9.0
Haagen-Dazs	17.5

To Toast Almonds
Bake on a baking sheet in the oven at 350°F (180°C) Gas Mark 4 for 5 to 10 minutes or until lightly browned.

Chocolate Mocha Ice Cream Pie with Gingersnap Crust

This easy-to-make dessert tastes delicious and will keep for a few weeks in the freezer.

20	gingersnap biscuits	20
1½ oz	soft margarine, melted	40 g
¾ pt	low-fat coffee ice cream*	425 ml
¾ pt	low-fat vanilla ice cream	425 ml
¾ pt	low-fat chocolate ice cream	425 ml
1 oz	flaked almonds, toasted	25 g

1. In food processor, process biscuits into crumbs. Mix with margarine; press on to bottom and slightly up sides of a 9-inch 23-cm round loose-bottomed tin.

2. Bake at 350°F (180°C) Gas Mark 4 for 10 minutes or until crisp and brown. Let cool completely; freeze for 10 minutes.

3. Soften coffee ice cream; spoon into pie crust, spreading evenly. Cover and freeze for 30 minutes or until firm.

4. Soften vanilla ice cream; spread over coffee ice cream. Cover and freeze until firm.

5. Repeat with chocolate ice cream; cover and freeze.

6. Sprinkle with almonds. Makes 12 servings.

Make ahead
To end of step 5, cover and freeze for up to two weeks.

PER SERVING (USING VIRTUALLY-FAT-FREE ICE CREAM)	
calories	209
g protein	5
g total fat	7
g saturated fat	1
mg cholesterol	9
g carbohydrate	33
g dietary fibre	0.3
mg sodium	149
mg potassium	108

* If low-fat coffee ice cream is unavailable, soften ¾ pt (425 ml) vanilla ice cream. Dissolve 1 tbsp (15 ml) instant coffee granules in 2 tsp (10 ml) hot water; stir into softened ice cream. Return to freezer for 10 minutes before using.

Chocolate Marbled Cheesecake

The secret to the rich taste of this cheesecake is low-fat yogurt, light cream cheese and cocoa.

1¾ pts	low-fat yogurt (not set)	1 L
2 tbsp	digestive biscuit crumbs	30 ml
8 oz	light cream cheese	225 g
1½ tsp	vanilla essence	7.5 ml
6 oz	granulated sugar	175 g
1 tbsp	cornflour	15 ml
2	eggs	2
2	egg whites	2
1 oz	unsweetened cocoa powder	25 g

1. In a cheesecloth-lined sieve set over bowl, drain yogurt in refrigerator for 4 hours or until yogurt is 18 fl oz (500 ml). Discard liquid.

2. Sprinkle biscuit crumbs evenly in lightly greased 8-inch (20 cm) round loose-bottomed cake tin.

3. In a bowl, beat together drained yogurt, cream cheese and vanilla. Combine sugar and cornflour; beat into yogurt mixture.

4. Beat in eggs and egg whites one at a time, beating well after each addition. Remove 1 pint (600 ml) to separate bowl; blend in cocoa.

5. Spoon half of the white mixture into prepared tin. Spoon in chocolate mixture, then remaining white mixture.

6. Without going completely through to bottom of tin, draw knife through mixture to make marbled effect.

7. Bake at 325°F (160°C) Gas Mark 3 for 55 minutes or until edge is set. Remove from oven; immediately run knife around edge of cake to loosen from tin. Let cool completely; remove side of tin. Cover and refrigerate for 4 hours before serving. Makes 8 servings.

Make ahead
Cheesecake can be refrigerated for up to two days.

PER SERVING	
calories	271
g protein	12
g total fat	11
g saturated fat	6
mg cholesterol	83
g carbohydrate	34
g dietary fibre	1
mg sodium	286
mg potassium	370

Good: Calcium

If you are in a hurry, buy the extra-thick or Greek-style drained yogurt, or use quark instead of drained yogurt in this recipe.

Orange Chocolate Refrigerator Cake

A little whipped cream added to drained yogurt makes a tasty lower-fat topping.

18 fl oz	low-fat yogurt	500 ml
2½ oz	granulated sugar	70 g
	grated rind of 1½ oranges	
4 fl oz	whipping cream, whipped	125 ml
40	round chocolate wafers*	40
2	oranges, sectioned, or 1 can (10 oz/284 g) mandarin oranges	2

1. In a cheesecloth-lined sieve set over bowl, drain yogurt in refrigerator for 4 hours or until yogurt is 9 fl oz (250 ml). Discard liquid.

2. In a bowl, mix together drained yogurt, sugar, orange rind; fold in whipped cream.

3. Sandwich about half of the mixture between wafers to make bar; ice with remaining mixture. Stand cocktails sticks on top (so cover won't touch cream); cover and refrigerate for 4 hours.

4. Decorate with oranges on top and around cake. Slice diagonally to serve. Makes 8 servings.

Make ahead
Cake can be refrigerated for up to one day.

PER SERVING	
calories	236
g protein	6
g total fat	9
g saturated fat	4
mg cholesterol	23
g carbohydrate	34
g dietary fibre	1
mg sodium	212
mg potassium	276
Good: Vitamin C	

* Any thin round chocolate biscuits can be used.

Strawberry Sauce
Substitute strawberries for
raspberries. Do not strain.

Lemon Mousse with Raspberry Sauce

This long-time favourite dessert is lightened by using only half the usual amount of whipping cream and no eggs.

1	envelope unflavoured gelatine	1
4 tbsp	cold water	60 ml
8 oz	granulated sugar	225 g
4 fl oz	lemon juice (approx 2½ large lemons)	125 ml
1 tbsp	grated lemon rind	15 ml
8 fl oz	low-fat yogurt	250 ml
4 fl oz	whipping cream, whipped	125 ml
	Raspberry Sauce (recipe follows)	

1. In a small saucepan, sprinkle gelatine over water; let stand for 1 minute or until softened. Stir over low heat until dissolved.

2. In a bowl, whisk together sugar, lemon juice, rind and yogurt; whisk in gelatine. Refrigerate until slightly thickened.

3. Fold in whipped cream. Spoon into a 2½ pint (1.4 L) serving bowl or individual sundae glasses. Chill for 2 hours.

4. Spoon Raspberry Sauce on to plates; top with scoop of mousse. (Or, spoon sauce over mousse in sundae glasses.)
Makes 6 servings.

Make ahead
To end of step 3 for up to one day.

PER SERVING (NO SAUCE)	
calories	227
g protein	4
g total fat	8
g saturated fat	5
mg cholesterol	28
g carbohydrate	38
g dietary fibre	0.2
mg sodium	42
mg potassium	135

Raspberry Sauce

10 oz	frozen unsweetened raspberries (partially thawed)	280 g
3 tbsp	icing sugar	45 ml
1 tbsp	lemon juice and/or Grand Marnier	15 ml

1. In a blender, purée raspberries, sugar and lemon juice. Strain through sieve to remove seeds. Makes 8 fl oz (225 ml).

Make ahead
Sauce can be refrigerated for up to three days.

PER SERVING 2 tbsp/30 ml	
calories	28
g protein	0.3
g total fat	0.2
g saturated fat	0
mg cholesterol	0
g carbohydrate	7
g dietary fibre	2
mg sodium	0
mg potassium	59

Raspberry and Blueberry Flan
Substitute fresh or individually quick-frozen (unthawed) raspberries for strawberries.

Bumbleberry Flan
Use at least 3 kinds of berries to make a total of 1¼–1½ lb (550–675 g) berries in the filling: strawberries, raspberries, blueberries, loganberries and/or blackberries.

Easy Berry Flan

This spectacular dessert is one of my all-time favourites. I make it with any combination of fresh or frozen (unthawed) berries. Making the base is much easier than rolling out pastry.

6 oz	plain flour	175 g
4 oz	granulated sugar	115 g
1½ tsp	baking powder	7.5 ml
2½ oz	soft margarine or butter	70 g
2	egg whites	2
1 tsp	vanilla	5 ml
Filling		
4 oz	granulated sugar	115 g
2 tbsp	plain flour	30 ml
1 lb	fresh strawberries, sliced	450 g
5 oz	fresh blueberries	140 g
Topping		
5–6 oz	halved fresh strawberries and/or blueberries	140–175 g
2 tsp	icing sugar	10 ml

1. In a food processor or bowl, combine flour, sugar, baking powder, margarine, egg whites and vanilla; mix well. Press on to bottom of 11-inch (28 cm) flan tin.

2. Filling: In a bowl, combine sugar and flour; toss with strawberries and blueberries. Spoon over base. Bake at 350°F (180°C) Gas Mark 4 for 60 to 70 minutes or until top is bubbling. Let cool.

3. Topping: Arrange berries decoratively over flan. Sift icing sugar over top. Makes 10 servings.

Make ahead
To end of step 2, cover and refrigerate for up to 24 hours. Complete step 3 up to one hour before serving.

PER SERVING	
calories	237
g protein	3
g total fat	7
g saturated fat	1
mg cholesterol	0
g carbohydrate	42
g dietary fibre	2
mg sodium	133
mg potassium	148
Good: Vitamin C	

Fresh Pear Flan
Instead of plums, substitute 2 fresh ripe pears, peeled, cored and cut into ¼-inch (5 mm) thick slices. Arrange slightly overlapping slices in circles on top, lightly pushing into mixtures.

Fresh Apple Flan
Instead of plums, use 2 large apples, peeled, cored and cut into ¼-inch (5 mm) thick slices. Arrange slightly overlapping slices in circles on top, lightly pushing into mixture.

Fresh Plum Flan

This is a lovely autumn dessert when plums are in season. In the winter, use a large can of plums, thoroughly drained. (Pictured opposite page 224.)

6 oz	granulated sugar	175 g
2 oz	soft margarine or butter	55 g
2	eggs	2
4 oz	plain flour	115 g
1 tsp	baking powder	5 ml
1 tsp	grated orange or lemon rind	5 ml
4 tbsp	skimmed milk	60 ml
1 lb	plums stoned and halved	450 g
4 oz	brown sugar	115 g
1 tsp	cinnamon	5 ml

1. In a large bowl and using electric mixer, cream together granulated sugar and margarine; beat in eggs one at a time, beating well after each addition.

2. Combine flour, baking powder and orange rind; beat into egg mixture alternately with milk, making three additions of flour and two of milk.

3. Turn into greased 10-inch (25 cm) loose-bottomed round cake tin. Arrange plums, cut side down, in circles on top, lightly pushing into mixture.

4. Combine brown sugar and cinnamon; sprinkle over plums. Bake at 350°F (180°C) Gas Mark 4 for 45 to 55 minutes or until top is golden and skewer inserted into flan comes out clean. Makes 10 servings.

PER SERVING	
calories	222
g protein	3
g total fat	6
g saturated fat	1
mg cholesterol	44
g carbohydrate	40
g dietary fibre	1
mg sodium	106
mg potassium	129

Toppings
Compare
2 tbsp (30 ml):   Fat (g)

Whipping
cream 11.0

Whipped
cream 5.5

Vanilla Cream
(page 231) 1.0

Honey-Almond
Sauce 0.5

PER SERVING	
calories	326
g protein	8
g total fat	6
g saturated fat	2
mg cholesterol	77
g carbohydrate	60
g dietary fibre	3
mg sodium	281
mg potassium	285

PER SERVING	2 tbsp/30 ml
calories	41
g protein	2
g total fat	0.5
g saturated fat	0.3
mg cholesterol	2
g carbohydrate	8
g dietary fibre	0
mg sodium	22
mg potassium	76

Baked Pear Bread Pudding with Honey-Almond Sauce

This recipe is for my friend Alister Spiers, who every autumn generously keeps me supplied with pears from his tree. It is also good served with Vanilla Cream (page 231).

Half	large loaf French bread	Half
12 fl oz	skimmed milk	350 ml
4 oz	granulated sugar	115 g
1 tsp	almond essence	5 ml
1 lb	pears, peeled and chopped	450 g
2	eggs, beaten	2
1 tsp	soft margarine or butter	5 ml
3 tbsp	brown sugar	45 ml
2 tbsp	flaked almonds	30 ml

1. Remove crusts from bread; tear bread into 1-inch (2.5 cm) pieces. Combine milk, sugar and almond; stir in bread cubes and let stand for 10 minutes. Stir in pears and eggs.

2. Spread margarine in an 8-inch (20 cm) square baking dish; pour in mixture, levelling top with spoon. Bake at 350°F (180°C) Gas Mark 4 for 40 minutes or until firm to the touch. Sprinkle with brown sugar and almonds; grill for 1 minute or until sugar melts. Serve warm with sauce or topping. Makes 6 servings.

Make ahead
To end of step 2 for up to four hours.

Honey-Almond Sauce

6 fl oz	low-fat yogurt	175 ml
2 tbsp	liquid honey	30 ml
½ tsp	almond extract	2.5 ml

1. In a small bowl, combine yogurt, honey and almond essence. Makes 6 fl oz (175 ml).

Make ahead
Sauce can be refrigerated for up to two days.

About Fillo Pastry

- Packs of Fillo pastry containing about 20 paperthin sheets are available at most supermarkets.

- Thaw before using.

- Unwrap package just before using. Cover Fillo with damp tea towel. Use sheets as you need them and recover stack right away to keep from drying out.

- Extra sheets should be thoroughly wrapped and frozen as quickly as possible.

Apple-Pecan Fillo Crisps

Once you are familiar with using Fillo pastry, this is a very easy and delicious dessert to make. (Pictured opposite page 225.)

2	sheets Fillo pastry	2
2 tsp	soft margarine or butter, melted	10 ml
2 tbsp	chopped pecans, toasted*	30 ml
1½ tsp	icing sugar	7.5 ml

Apple Filling

3 oz	brown sugar	85 g
	grated rind of half a lemon	
1 tbsp	lemon juice	15 ml
½ tsp	cinnamon	2.5 ml
1 lb	apples, peeled and sliced	450 g

1. Lay single sheet of Fillo on counter; brush with half of the margarine. Using scissors, cut crossways into three 5-inch (12 cm) wide strips; fold each strip into thirds to form square shape.

2. Using scissors, round off corners and gently mold into bun tins. Repeat with remaining Fillo to make 6 shells. Bake at 400°F (200°C) Gas Mark 6 for 5 minutes or until golden.

3. Apple Filling: In a heavy frying pan, combine sugar, lemon rind, lemon juice and cinnamon; cook over medium heat until bubbly.

4. Add apples and cook, stirring often, for 5 minutes or until tender; let cool slightly.

5. Spoon into prepared shells. Sprinkle with pecans; sift icing sugar over top. Serve warm or at room temperature.
Makes 6 servings.

Make ahead
To end of step 2; Fillo crisps can be stored in airtight container for up to three days. To end of step 4 for up to six hours.

PER SERVING	
calories	132
g protein	1
g total fat	3
g saturated fat	0.4
mg cholesterol	0
g carbohydrate	26
g dietary fibre	2
mg sodium	71
mg potassium	123

* Toast pecans in a small frying pan over medium-low heat for 1 to 2 minutes, stirring.

Pumpkin Pie with Orange Cream

This traditional pie is lightened by using whole milk instead of cream, a minimum of pastry and an orange cream topping instead of whipped cream.

2	eggs, lightly beaten	2
1 lb	cooked mashed pumpkin	450 g
½ pt	whole milk or semi-skimmed evaporated milk	300 ml
6 oz	brown sugar	175 g
½ tsp	each ginger, cinnamon, nutmeg and allspice	2.5 ml
Pinch	salt	Pinch
1	unbaked 9-inch (23 cm) pastry case (Flaky Pastry, page 219)	1
	Orange Yogurt Cream (page 229)	

1. In a bowl, beat together eggs, pumpkin, milk, sugar, ginger, cinnamon, nutmeg, allspice and salt. Pour into pastry case.

2. Bake at 425°F (220°C) Gas Mark 7 for 15 minutes. Reduce heat to 350°F (180°C) Gas Mark 4; bake for 45 minutes or until firm to the touch and knife inserted in centre comes out clean. Serve warm or cold with Orange Yogurt Cream. Makes 8 servings.

Make ahead
Pie can be covered and refrigerated for up to three days.

PER SERVING (NO SAUCE)	
calories	226
g protein	5
g total fat	7
g saturated fat	4
mg cholesterol	71
g carbohydrate	37
g dietary fibre	2
mg sodium	160
mg potassium	269
Good: Iron	
Excellent: Vitamin A	

Food Processor Pastry
When making pastry in a food processor, it's very important that the butter and water be very cold.

In food processor, combine flour and salt. Add butter and process with on/off motion until mixture resembles coarse crumbs. With processor running, add water all at once through feed tube. Process just until dough starts to clump together. Remove from processor and proceed as with bowl method.

Flaky Pastry

This is a tender pastry using a minimum amount of fat. I tried to make a pastry using vegetable oil, which is lower in saturated fat than butter or margarine, but the pastry was too tough.

4 oz	plain flour	115 g
¼ tsp	salt	1.25 ml
1½ oz	hard butter, cut in chunks	40 g
3 tbsp	(approx) cold water	45 ml

1. In a bowl, combine flour and salt. With pastry blender or fingers, cut or rub in butter until mixture is crumbly.

2. Sprinkle with cold water, tossing with fork to mix. Gather dough together and form into ball. Wrap in cling film and refrigerate for 30 minutes.

3. Roll out on lightly floured surface and fit into 9-inch (23 cm) pie plate. Makes 1 pastry case enough for 8 servings.

Make ahead
To end of step 3, cover and refrigerate for up to one day.

PER SERVING	(⅛ CASE)
calories	87
g protein	1
g total fat	4
g saturated fat	3
mg cholesterol	12
g carbohydrate	11
g dietary fibre	0.4
mg sodium	116
mg potassium	16

Pastry Case Notes
Enjoy just as much flavour but
half the fat in a one-crust pie.
For a sugar crust, brush top of
pastry with milk, then sprinkle
with granulated sugar before
baking.

Tip
Use scissors to cut apricots into
thin strips.

Deep-Dish Pear Pie with Apricots and Ginger

Ginger goes well with pears, but you could substitute one or two teaspoons (5 or 10 ml) of cinnamon instead. Choose ripe yet firm pears as they will keep their shape.

2 lb	pears, peeled and sliced	900 g
4 oz	dried apricots, cut in strips	115 g
	grated rind of 1 lemon	
2 tbsp	lemon juice	30 ml
1 tbsp	grated root ginger (or 1 tsp/5 ml ground)	15 ml
4 oz	granulated sugar	115 g
1 oz	plain flour	25 g
	Flaky Pastry (page 219)	

1. In a bowl, combine pears, apricots, lemon rind, lemon juice and ginger. Mix sugar with flour; stir into fruit. Pour into a deep 9- or 10-inch (23 or 25 cm) pie plate.

2. On a lightly floured surface, roll out pastry and fit over top. (If pastry isn't large enough, place in centre with fruit showing around edge.) With knife, cut slits in pastry.

3. Bake at 425°F (220°C) Gas Mark 7 for 15 minutes; reduce heat to 350°F (180°C) Gas Mark 4 and bake for 45 minutes longer or until pastry is golden and filling is bubbling. Makes 8 servings.

Make ahead
Pie can be set aside for up to six hours; serve hot or cold.
To reheat, warm in the oven at 350°F (180°C) Gas Mark 4 for 10 to 15 minutes.

PER SERVING	
calories	254
g protein	3
g total fat	5
g saturated fat	3
mg cholesterol	12
g carbohydrate	53
g dietary fibre	4
mg sodium	119
mg potassium	339

Decoration
Just before serving the trifle, decorate with an array of colourful fruit. Strawberrries, thawed raspberries, peeled sliced kiwi fruit and mint leaves would add a festive touch.

Winter Berry Trifle

This light version of a Christmas favourite uses low-fat trifle sponges, a custard with half the egg yolks and no whipping cream. No one will notice the difference. In fact, after a large meal, they'll like this version better.

8	trifle sponges	8
4 fl oz	brandy, dry sherry or raspberry juice	125 ml
10 oz	each frozen unsweetened blueberries and raspberries, thawed and drained*	280 g

Custard Sauce

6 oz	granulated sugar	175 g
5 tbsp	cornflour	75 ml
Pinch	salt	Pinch
1½ pts	semi-skimmed milk	850 ml
4	egg yolks, lightly beaten	4
2 tsp	vanilla essence	10 ml
¼ tsp	cinnamon	1.25 ml

1. Custard Sauce: In a heavy non-aluminum saucepan, combine sugar, cornflour and salt; stir in milk. Bring to the boil over medium heat; simmer for 2 minutes or until slightly thickened, stirring constantly.

2. Whisk about ¼ pint (150 ml) into egg yolks; whisk yolks back into saucepan. Cook, stirring, over low heat for about 1 minute or until thickened; strain into bowl. Stir in vanilla and cinnamon. Place greaseproof paper directly on surface; refrigerate for at least 2 hours.

3. Line bottom of 4½ pint (2.5 L) glass bowl with 4 trifle spinges; sprinkle with half of the brandy and all of the blueberries. Spoon half of the custard over top. Repeat layers, using raspberries. Cover and refrigerate for 2 hours. Makes 8 servings.

Make ahead
To end of step 2 for up to two days. To end of step 3 for up to four hours.

PER SERVING	
calories	372
g protein	10
g total fat	6
g saturated fat	2
mg cholesterol	120
g carbohydrate	69
g dietary fibre	3
mg sodium	207
mg potassium	319
Good: Folate, Calcium	

* To use fresh berries, substitute 8 oz (225 g) each fresh blueberries and raspberries.

Meringues with Lemon Cream

I like to serve these for buffets – they taste scrumptious, and are easy to serve and eat. Arrange meringues on large platters and let guests help themselves. (Pictured opposite page 193.)

Meringues

6	egg whites	6
¼ tsp	cream of tartar	1.25 ml
12 oz	granulated sugar	350 g
1 tbsp	cornflour	15 ml
	grated rind of 1 lemon	
1 tsp	vanilla essence	5 ml

Lemon Cream

16 fl oz	low-fat yogurt	450 ml
5½ oz	granulated sugar	150 g
4 tbsp	cornflour	60 ml
4 fl oz	lemon juice	125 ml
4 fl oz	water	125 ml
2	egg yolks, lightly beaten	2
	grated rind of 2 lemons	
4 fl oz	whipping cream, whipped	125 ml

Garnish

10 oz	strawberries and/or raspberries	280 g

1. Meringues: In a large bowl, beat egg whites with cream of tartar until soft peaks form. Beat in half the sugar, 1 tbsp (15 ml) at a time, until stiff glossy peaks form. Combine remaining sugar, cornflour and lemon rind; gradually beat into whites. Beat in vanilla essence.

2. On nonstick baking parchment-lined baking sheets, spoon meringue into twelve 4- to 5-inch (10 to 13 cm) rounds and twelve 1½-inch (4 cm) rounds. Using back of spoon, press down on larger rounds to indent and form shells. Bake at 225°F (110°C) Gas Mark ¼ for 2½ to 3 hours or until firm to the touch and paper peels away easily from meringue. (The smaller rounds will take less time.) Remove paper; let cool on rack.

3. Lemon Cream: In a cheesecloth-lined sieve set over bowl, drain yogurt in refrigerator for 4 hours or until yogurt is 8 fl oz (225 ml). Discard liquid.

4. In non-aluminum saucepan, mix sugar and cornflour. Add lemon juice and water; bring to the boil, stirring constantly. Reduce heat and simmer gently for 3 minutes or until thickened.

5. Whisk a little hot mixture into yolks; gradually stir back into saucepan. Cook over low heat, stirring, for 2 minutes; stir in lemon rind.

6. Let cool to room temperature (if in a hurry, stir over a bowl of ice). Stir in drained yogurt. Gently fold in whipped cream.

7. Spoon into meringues; top each with small meringue round. Garnish with fruit. Makes 12 servings.

Make ahead
To end of step 2; meringues can be stored in airtight container for up to one week. Steps 3 to end of 6; cover Lemon Cream with cling film and refrigerate for up to one day. Assemble meringues up to two hours before serving.

PER SERVING	
calories	239
g protein	5
g total fat	5
g saturated fat	3
mg cholesterol	52
g carbohydrate	45
g dietary fibre	0.8
mg sodium	64
mg potassium	185
Good: Vitamin C	

Cherry Fool
Instead of kiwi fruit, substitute 10 oz (280 g) sweet dark cherries, stoned and puréed. Reduce sugar to 2 tbsp (30 ml) and add 1 tbsp (15 ml) lemon juice. Decorate with cherries.

Rhubarb Fool
Instead of kiwi fruit, substitute 1 recipe Microwave Rhubarb Sauce with Ginger or Stewed Rhubarb (see page 233); drain well and purée. Increase whipping cream to 4 fl oz (125 ml). Decorate with raspberries, strawberries and/ or blueberries. Makes 6 servings.

Kiwi for Breakfast
Serve kiwi fruit halves in egg cups for an easy-to-eat and different presentation.

PER SERVING	
calories	237
g protein	5
g total fat	8
g saturated fat	5
mg cholesterol	29
g carbohydrate	38
g dietary fibre	4
mg sodium	55
mg potassium	572
Good: Vitamin A	
Excellent: Vitamin C	

Kiwi Fool

Serve this creamy dessert garnished with sliced kiwi fruit and any other fruit such as strawberries or mandarin oranges. Because there is no other fat, this dessert has room for a little whipping cream and it still fits into a healthy diet.

8 fl oz	low-fat yogurt (not set)	225 ml
4	ripe kiwi fruit	4
2 oz	granulated sugar	55 g
2½ fl oz	whipping cream	75 ml
Garnish		
1	kiwi fruit, sliced	1
6 oz	mandarin orange segments or small strawberries	175 g

1. In a cheesecloth-lined sieve set over bowl, drain yogurt in refrigerator for 3 to 4 hours or until yogurt is 4 fl oz (125 ml). Discard liquid.

2. Cut kiwi fruit in half; scoop out fruit and purée in food processor to make about ½ pint (300 ml). Stir in sugar and yogurt.

3. Whip cream; fold into kiwi mixture.

4. Decorate: Serve in stemmed glasses or on dessert plates and top or surround with sliced kiwi and orange segments. Makes 4 servings.

Make ahead
To end of step 3, cover and refrigerate for up to four hours.

Right:
Fresh Plum Flan (page 215)

Stewed Rhubarb

Follow Microwave Rhubarb Sauce (root ginger is optional): In saucepan, combine rhubarb, sugar, water, and root ginger (if using); cook over medium heat, stirring, until sugar dissolves. Simmer, uncovered and stirring occasionally, for 10 to 15 minutes or until rhubarb is tender.

Tip

Don't peel the rhubarb, just wash. The skin provides colour and I'm sure must have fibre and vitamins. (Discard leaves.)

PER SERVING	
calories	137
g protein	1
g total fat	0.2
g saturated fat	0
mg cholesterol	0
g carbohydrate	34
g dietary fibre	2
mg sodium	5
mg potassium	260

Left:
Apple-Pecan Fillo Crisps
(page 217)

Microwave Rhubarb Sauce with Ginger

Fresh ginger adds a pleasing flavour to rhubarb sauce. Serve with Gingerbread Cake (page 204) or over frozen vanilla yogurt or strawberries.

1¼ lb	rhubarb, chopped	550 g
6 oz	granulated sugar	175 g
1 tbsp	water	15 ml
4 tsp	grated root ginger	20 ml

1. In a microwaveable dish, combine rhubarb, sugar, water and root ginger; cover with lid or vented microwaveable cling film.

2. Microwave at High for 4 minutes; stir. Microwave for another 3 minutes or until rhubarb is tender. Makes 5 servings.

Peach and Orange Compote
Substitute peaches for
nectarines.

Nutritional Note
Government guide-lines to
Healthy Eating recommends
we have at least 5 pieces of
fruit or vegetables per day.
Choose dark green and orange
vegetables and orange fruit
more often.

These foods are higher than
other vegetables and fruits in
certain key nutrients such as
Vitamin A and folate. Go for
cantaloupes, oranges,
mangoes, peaches and
papayas.

Nectarine and Orange Compote

Poached nectarines spiked with rum and finished with orange
slices makes a beautiful summer dessert. Add fresh berries or
sliced yellow plums to taste.

1¾ pts	water	1 L
6 oz	granulated sugar	175 g
6	nectarines	6
2	oranges	2
2 tbsp	lemon or lime juice	30 ml
4 tbsp	white rum (optional)	60 ml

1. In a saucepan, bring water and sugar to the boil, stirring until
sugar dissolves.

2. Meanwhile, blanch nectarines in boiling water for 30 to 60
seconds; plunge into cold water to cool. Peel, halve and remove
the stones.

3. Using zester or vegetable peeler, cut thin strips of rind from one
of the oranges; squeeze juice into hot syrup. Add orange rind and
lemon juice. Add nectarines (syrup should cover fruit; if necessary
cook in batches); simmer for 5 to 8 minutes or until fruit is tender
when pierced. Place nectarines in bowl and pour hot syrup over
top; let cool.

4. Slice remaining orange; halve each slice and add to bowl.
Add rum (if using). Makes 8 servings.

Make ahead
Compote can be covered and refrigerated for up to one day; serve
at room temperature.

PER SERVING	
calories	138
g protein	1
g total fat	0.5
g saturated fat	0
mg cholesterol	0
g carbohydrate	35
g dietary fibre	2
mg sodium	5
mg potassium	280

Nutritional Note
Orange juice is a good source
of folate as well as Vitamin C.
Folate is required for growth
and is especially important
during pregnancy, particularly
in the first month.

Apricot, Orange and Fig Compote

I love to have this in the refrigerator on hand for breakfast or dessert. I often add fresh fruit such as grapes, kiwi, banana or berries.

6 oz	dried figs	175 g
16 fl oz	water	450 ml
6 oz	dried apricot halves	175 g
6	whole allspice	6
	grated rind and juice of 1 lemon	
1 tbsp	liquid honey	15 ml
2	oranges, peeled and sliced	2

1. Trim off tough ends of figs.

2. In a saucepan, combine water, figs, apricots, allspice and grated rind and juice of lemon; bring to the boil. Cover and reduce heat; simmer for 20 minutes or until fruit is tender. Let cool.

3. Stir in honey and oranges. Serve at room temperature or cold. Makes 8 servings.

Make ahead
Compote can be stored in refrigerator for up to five days.

PER SERVING	
calories	127
g protein	2
g total fat	0.4
g saturated fat	0.1
mg cholesterol	0
g carbohydrate	33
g dietary fibre	4
mg sodium	6
mg potassium	470
Good: Vitamin C	

Berries with Orange Cream

Spoon this low-fat creamy sauce over juicy fresh strawberries. You'll enjoy it so much you'll want to try it over other fresh berries or sliced fruit or combinations of both. I love this made with Grand Marnier; it's also good with rum or concentrated frozen orange juice.

1 lb	small strawberries	450 g
Orange Cream		
4 fl oz	virtually-fat-free fromage frais	125 ml
3 tbsp	granulated sugar	45 ml
1 tbsp	orange liqueur or rum or concentrated frozen orange juice	15 ml
1 tbsp	low-fat yogurt	15 ml
½ tsp	grated orange rind	2.5 ml

1. Orange Cream: Combine fromage frais, sugar, orange liqueur, yogurt and orange rind; mix well.

2. Spoon sauce over individual bowls of berries. Makes 4 servings.

Make ahead
Sauce can be refrigerated for up to four days.

PER SERVING	
calories	119
g protein	4
g total fat	1
g saturated fat	0.3
mg cholesterol	2
g carbohydrate	24
g dietary fibre	3
mg sodium	30
mg potassium	273
Good: Vitamin C	

Compare	
Ice Cream:	**Fat (g)**
Haagen-Dazs Vanilla	14.6
Wall's Blue Ribbon Vanilla	7.2
Wall's Too Good to be True	0.4

To Make Your Own Extra-Thick Yogurt

In a cheesecloth-lined sieve set over bowl, drain 16 fl oz (450 ml) low-fat (no gelatine) yogurt in refrigerator for 4 hours or until yogurt is 6 fl oz (225 ml). Discard liquid.

Orange or Lemon Yogurt Cream

This is delicious over fresh fruit, or as a dessert topping instead of whipped cream. There is a new product on the market called extra-thick yogurt. Use it in this recipe, or, if it isn't available, drain yogurt as described, left.

8 fl oz	extra-thick yogurt	225 ml
2 oz	granulated sugar	55 g
1 tsp	grated orange or lemon rind	5 ml
1 tbsp	frozen orange juice concentrate or lemon juice (optional)	15 ml

1. Stir together yogurt, sugar, rind and juice (if using). Makes 8 fl oz (225 ml).

Make ahead
Cream can be covered and refrigerated for up to one week.

PER SERVING	2 tbsp / 30 ml
calories	52
g protein	2
g total fat	1
g saturated fat	1
mg cholesterol	4
g carbohydrate	10
g dietary fibre	0
mg sodium	22
mg potassium	74

About Yogurt

• Low-fat plain yogurt is very useful in low-fat cooking and often can be substituted for higher-fat ingredients such as sour cream or whipping cream.

• Because yogurt is more acidic than other dairy products, reduce other acidic ingredients such as lemon juice or vinegar when substituting yogurt.

• When heating yogurt, to prevent it from separating, mix 1 tbsp (15 ml) cornflour or plain flour into 8 fl oz (225 ml) of yogurt.

• When buying yogurt to drain, be sure to get the kind without any gelatine. You want the kind that has a little liquid on top.

Almond Custard Sauce
Prepare Amaretto Custard
Sauce, substituting 1 tsp (5 ml)
almond essence for the
amaretto.

Amaretto Custard Sauce

Serve this light sauce over berries or fresh fruit and top with
toasted slivered almonds. Or, for a super-fast sauce, stir amaretto
(almond liqueur) into slightly softened vanilla ice cream.

1 tbsp	granulated sugar	15 ml
2 tsp	cornflour	10 ml
8 fl oz	semi-skimmed milk	225 ml
1	egg yolk, whisked	1
2 tbsp	amaretto or coffee liqueur	30 ml

1. In a small non-aluminium saucepan, combine sugar and
cornflour; stir in milk. Bring to simmer over medium heat, stirring
constantly; reduce heat to low and cook, stirring, for 5 minutes
or until thickened slightly.

2. Whisk about half of the hot mixture into yolk; whisk back into
hot milk mixture. Cook, stirring, over low heat for 2 minutes or
until thickened. Remove from heat and stir in amaretto. Let cool.
Makes about ½ pint (300 ml).

Make ahead
Sauce can be covered and refrigerated for up to two days.

PER SERVING	2 tbsp / 30 ml
calories	33
g protein	1
g total fat	1
g saturated fat	1
mg cholesterol	24
g carbohydrate	5
g dietary fibre	0
mg sodium	13
mg potassium	40

Vanilla Cream

Thanks go to my friend and fabulous cook Mary Holmes for this low-cal, lower-fat, crème-fraîche sauce. It's delicious over fresh berries or any fresh fruit along with Gingerbread Cake (page 204), or with Baked Pear Bread Pudding (page 216) or with any dessert instead of whipped cream. If possible, make it a day in advance because the sauce thickens considerably upon standing.

4 fl oz	crème fraîche	125 ml
4 fl oz	semi-skimmed milk	125 ml
4 fl oz	low-fat or extra-thick yogurt	125 ml
4 oz	granulated sugar	55 g
½ tsp	vanilla essence	2.5 ml

1. Combine crème fraîche, milk, yogurt, sugar and vanilla; stir to dissolve sugar. Cover and refrigerate for at least 1 hour.
Makes 12 fl oz (350 ml).

Make ahead
Sauce can be covered and refrigerated for up to three days.

PER SERVING	2 tbsp/30 ml
calories	40
g protein	1
g total fat	1
g saturated fat	1
mg cholesterol	3
g carbohydrate	6
g dietary fibre	0
mg sodium	21
mg potassium	65

Butterscotch Sauce

Serve this sauce hot or cold over frozen yogurt, or vanilla, chocolate or coffee ice cream, or with gingerbread, baked apples, poached pears or peaches.

8 oz	light brown sugar	225 g
4 fl oz	semi-skimmed evaporated milk	125 ml
½ oz	soft margarine or butter	15 g
2 tbsp	light corn syrup or golden syrup	30 ml

1. In a heavy saucepan, combine sugar, milk, margarine and corn syrup; over medium heat, stirring often, bring to a simmer. Immediately remove from heat. Makes 8 fl oz (225 ml).

Make ahead
Sauce can be covered and refrigerated for up to one week.

PER SERVING	2 tbsp/30 ml
calories	145
g protein	1
g total fat	2
g saturated fat	0.4
mg cholesterol	1
g carbohydrate	32
g dietary fibre	0.1
mg sodium	48
mg potassium	146

Index

A

Alcohol consumption, 12
Almond(s):
  custard sauce, 230
  ginger biscotti, 201
  to toast, 210
Amaretto custard sauce, 230
Angel food cake, 206
Antioxidants, 22
Apple:
  cider, 54
  cookies, 202
  flan, 215
  pancakes, 190
    cinnamon, 189
  and sausage stuffing, 105
  and sweet potato purée, 144
Apple-pecan Fillo crisps, 217
Apple bran muffins, 195
Apricot-raisin muesli, 186
Apricot(s):
  about, 199
  fruit squares, 199
  orange and fig compote, 227
  pear pie with, 220
  sauce, 41
  streusel cake, 203
Arborio rice, about, 167
Artichoke hearts:
  Greek salad, 50
  and mushroom stuffing, 116
Arugula, and scallop salad, 73
Asian:
  chicken, 98
  sauce, 99
  vinaigrette, 85
Asparagus:
  and mushroom salad, 78
  and tortilla pizza, 47
  and turkey sandwich, 51
Aubergine:
  dip, 37
  grilled, 141
  tomato and courgette gratin, 185
Avocado, salmon fajitas, 120

B

Baked:
  chicken
    breasts, 96
    in buttermilk, 93

  spicy, 100
  fish fillets with almonds, 112
  potato fries, 143
  salmon, whole stuffed, 116
  trout, 114
Baking, low-fat, 191
Balsamic vinegar, about, 75
Banana:
  cream filling, 208
  pancakes, 191
  and tofu drink, 54
Barbecue:
  light and lean, 99
  safety, 93
  syndrome, 127
Barbecued:
  Asian chicken, 98
  chicken in buttermilk, 93
  curried chicken breast, 100
  lamb leg, 129
  potato packets, 142
  salmon fillets, 115
  trout, 114
  See also Grilled
Barley:
  about, 177
  and corn casserole, 177
  and vegetable soup, 65
Basil, about, 86
Basmati, about, 168
Bean sprouts:
  and Asian chicken, 98
  beef with noodles, 158
  Chinese
    fried rice, 170
    noodles, 156
  coleslaw, 82
  noodle salad, 161
  and noodles with pork, 155
  and shrimp salad, 43
  Thai noodles, 157
Bean(s):
  dried, 178
  and sausage casserole, 178
  See also names of specific beans
Beef:
  and chick pea curry, 125
  with noodles, 158
Beetroot(s):
  how to cook, 80
  salad, 80
Berry(ies):
  flan, 214

  with orange cream, 228
  trifle, 221
Beta carotene:
  about, 134
  sources of, 22
Biscotti, orange hazelnut, 201
Blueberry trifle, 201
Body Mass Index (BMI), 23-4
Bran:
  cereal
    fruit squares, 199
    muffins, 196
  muesli, 196
  muffins, 192
    carrot, 196
    with rhubarb, 195
Bread:
  crumbs, to make, 185
  muesli soda, 197
  pudding, 216
  raspberry pecan, 198
Broccoli:
  about, 60
  and noodles with chicken, 159
  sesame, 134
  soup, 60
Bruschetta, 50
Bulgur:
  about, 174
  buying, 76
  pilaf with prawns and mange
    tout, 175
  with red onion, 174
  salad, 76
  and vegetable soup, 65
Bumbleberry flan, 214
Burgers:
  chicken, 90, 91
  tuna fillet, 113
Butter vs margarine, 19
Buttermilk:
  about, 93
  bran muffins, 195, 196
  chicken, 93
  cornmeal muffins, 193
  dill dressing, 79, 87
  fruit and fibre squares, 199
  marinade, 93
  mashed potatoes, 143
  muesli soda bread, 197
  pumpkin spice cake, 205
Butternut squash, and curry, 125
Butterscotch sauce, 232

C

Cabbage:
  coleslaw, 82
  Scotch broth, 70
  and vegetable soup, 65
Caffeine, 12
Cajun chicken fingers, 40
Cakes:
  apple upside-down, 190
  apricot streusel, 203
  chocolate
    angel food, 206
    cheesecake, 211
    orange, 212
  gingerbread, 204
Calcium-rich foods, 14
Calvados, and spiced cider, 54
Cantaloupe and smoked turkey, 42
Carrot(s):
  bran muffins, 196
  and corn chowder, 68
  noodle salad, 161
    with chicken, 160
  sesame, 134
  tagine, 132
Casseroles:
  barley and corn, 177
  bean and sausage, 178
  spinach rice, 166
  turkey vegetable, 102
Cauliflower, 138
  soup, 58
  vegetable curry, 180
Chalupas:
  about, 124
  pork, 124
Cheddar cheese:
  bean and sausage casserole, 178
  macaroni and, 149
Cheese:
  herbed with mushrooms, 38
  pasta and ham, 148
  and tomato quesadillas, 52
  See also names of specific
    cheeses
Cheesecake, chocolate marbled,
  211
Cherry fool, 224
Chèvre. *See* Goat cheese
Chick pea(s):
  about, 146
  how to cook, 74
  and pasta

soup, 67
  with tomatoes, 146
and pork curry, 125
potato and tomato stew, 179
salad, 80
and sweet pepper salad, 74
vegetable curry, 180
Chicken:
  barbecued with buttermilk, 93
  breasts
    Asian, 98
    baked, 100
    burgers, 91
    curried, 100
    fingers, 40
    hoisin sesame platter, 96
    and mange tout, 97
    and noodles with broccoli, 159
    and prawn jambalaya, 118-19
    sandwich, 51
    spicy, 100
    stuffed, 94
  burgers, 90
    with onions and sun-dried
      tomatoes, 91
  buying, 63, 95
  and chick-pea curry, 125
  cooked, with noodle salad, 160
  fingers, 40
  Jamaican jerk, 92
  and noodle soup, 63
  salad, 100
  skewers, 49
  stew with dumplings, 101
  tagine, 132
Chilli:
  sauce, about, 32
  paste, about, 32
  peppers, about, 32
Chinese:
  chicken balls, 41
  chicken burgers, 90
  noodles, 156
  vegetable fried rice, 170
Chocolate:
  angel food cake, 206
  crêpes, 208
  marbled cheesecake, 211
  mocha ice cream pie, 210
  orange cake, 212
  sauce, 209
Cholesterol and fat, 16
  kinds of, 17

children and infants, fat in diet,
  17
Chorizo:
  and bean casserole, 178
  paella, 126
Chowder:
  carrot and corn, 68
  mariners', 69
Christmas Eve punch, 56
Chutney-glazed ham, 128
Cider, 54
  party quantities, 54
Citrus double-bran muffins, 192
Clam dip, with herbs, 35
Cocoa, chocolate crêpes, 208,
  209
Cod:
  steamed, 110
  vegetable chowder, 69
Coleslaw, Oriental, 82
Compote:
  apricot, orange and fig, 227
  nectarine and orange, 226
Cookies, almond cinnamon, 202
Coriander:
  about, 32, 83
  sauce, 41
Corn:
  and barley casserole, 177
  and carrot chowder, 68
  creamed, muffins, 193
  double corn pancakes, 188
  fish chowder, 69
  quinoa-stuffed peppers, 176
Cornmeal:
  muffins, 193
  pancakes, 188
Cottage cheese:
  clam dip, 35
  with pasta and ham, 148
Courgette:
  aubergine and tomato gratin, 185
  Chinese fried rice, 170
  fish chowder, 69
  grilled, 141
  and pasta, 148
  quiche, 182
  stir-fry, 139
    tofu, 184
  stuffing for chicken breasts, 94
Couscous, 180-1
  about, 180
  spiced, 181

with tomato and basil, 181
vegetable salad, 77
Crabmeat, pasta salad, 164
Cracked wheat, about, 174
Cranberry lime punch, 56
Cream cheese, chocolate
cheesecake, 211
Crêpes, chocolate, 208
Crostini, 39
Cucumber:
about, 58
and Asian chicken, 98
and bulgur salad, 76
mint soup, 58
salad, 81
Curry(ied):
cauliflower soup, 58
chick pea and pork, 125
chicken breasts, 100
Custard sauce, 221
almond, 220
amaretto, 220

D
Dates, fruit squares, 199
Dessert sauces:
butterscotch, 232
chocolate, 209
custard, 221, 230
honey-almond, 216
orange cream, 228
raspberry, 213
rhubarb, 225
strawberry, 213
vanilla cream, 231
yogurt cream, 229
Dieting, 23-4
Dill, sauce, 117
Dinner menu. See Menus
Dips:
aubergine, 37
bases for, 34
clam, 35
salsa, 34
sweet red pepper and basil, 36
Dressing. See Salad dressing
Drink(s):
cider, 54
cranberry lime punch, 56
fruit spritzers, 55
non-alcoholic, 55
for parties, 54, 55, 56
sangria punch, 56

tofu, 54
Dumplings, with chicken stew, 101

E
Eating out:
fast food, 39
and food choices, 24-5
Egg(s):
adding to soup, 62
Chinese fried rice, 170
chocolate angel food cake, 206
cornmeal pancakes, 188
vegetable quiche, 182
Elizabeth Baird's chocolate angel
food cake, 206
Escalopes:
about, 108
turkey, 108

F
Fajitas and salmon salad, 120
Fast-cooking carbohydrates, 172
Fat:
content
and cheese, 148, 166
and chicken, 101
in food, 16
and pasta, 148
and turkey, 106
control of, 17
cooking with, 97
and health, 16-20
kinds, 13, 17
menus compared, 18
tips about, 19
Feta cheese:
Greek salad, 50
and lamb stuffing, 131
Fettuccine Alfredo, 150
Fibre:
content chart, 21
in diet, 20-1, 26, 180, 186
Fig, apricot and orange compote,
227
Fillo, about, 217
Fish:
buying, 110
cooking, 116
fillets, baked, 112
frozen, about, 110
how to cook, 113
Mediterranean, 110-11
Mariners' chowder, 69

sauce, about, 32
See also names of specific fish
Flaky pastry, 219
Flan:
berry, 214
fruit, 215
Flour tortillas. See Tortillas
Flour, wholemeal, 199
Folate, 22, 227
Food processor pastry, 219
Fools, fruit, 224
Free radicals, 22
Fruit:
and fibre squares, 199
food group, 11
spritzers, 55

G
Garlic, about, 32
Giblet gravy, 106
Ginger, about, 32
Gingerbread cake, 204
Gingersnap crust, 210
Glazed ham, 128
Goat cheese:
bruschetta, 50
dip, 36
and pesto tortilla pizzas, 47
Gouda cheese
macaroni and, 149
tomato quesadillas, 52
Grain products:
compared, 173
food group, 11
Grape juice punch, 56
Gravy, giblet, 106
Greek salad, 50
Green bean(s), 136, 137
salad, 78, 79
Green salad, 85
Green vegetable risotto, 167
Greens, and scallop salad, 73
Grilled:
chicken
breasts, 96
burgers, 90
field mushrooms, 140
salmon, 48
sweet peppers, 141
tuna fillet burgers, 113
vegetables, 141
See also Barbecued

H

Haddock:
baked, 112
vegetable chowder, 69
Halibut, steamed, 110
Ham:
Chinese fried rice, 170
glazed, 128
pasta
with cheese, 148
salad, 163
Hazelnut biscotti, 201
Healthy eating, 10-13
Herbed cheese spread, 38
Herb(s):
about, 67, 137, 166, 185
and buttermilk chicken, 93
cream sauce, 102-3
High Fibre Carrot Bran Muffins, 196
Hoisin sauce, about, 32
Hoisin sesame chicken platter, 96
Honey garlic roast pork, 127
Honey-almond sauce, 216
Hors d'oeuvres:
goat cheese and pesto tortilla
pizza, 47
melon balls, 42
Thai prawn salad, 43
Hot and sour soup, 62

I

Ice cream, chocolate mocha pie,
210
Indian rice with lentils, 168
Iron-rich foods, 14
Italian chick pea and pasta soup, 67

J

Jalapeño peppers:
cornmeal
muffins, 193
pancakes, 188
and pasta with tomatoes and
cheese, 147
Jamaican jerk chicken, 92
Jambalaya, prawn and chicken,
118-19
Jerk, definition of, 92
Juices, about, 55

K

Kidney bean and rice soup, 66
Kiwi fool, 224

L

Labels, claims, 25
Lamb:
about, 70, 129
and feta pitta pockets, 131
leg, 129
marinade for, 129
Scotch broth, 70
stuffing for onions, 130
tenderloin, 129
Leek(s):
how to wash, 61
and linguine with scallops, 153
and mushroom soup, 61
stuffing for chicken breasts, 94
Leftovers, 147, 151
Legumes:
about, 179
compared, 173
Lemon:
cream, 222-3
cumin vinaigrette, 77
mousse, 213
parsley rice pilaf, 173
pepper turkey loaf, 107
poppy seed muffins, 194
sesame tuna fillets, 113
squares, 208
tarragon sole fillets, 111
yogurt cream, 229
Lemon grass:
about, 32, 63
marinated leg of lamb, 129
Lemon-soy marinade, 113
Lentil(s):
and bean salad, 75
Indian rice, 168
and vegetable soup, 65
Lettuce:
and Asian chicken, 98
wrapped pork, 123
Linguine:
with mushrooms, 151
with scallops and leeks, 153
with tomatoes and cheese, 147
Low-fat:
baking, 189
cheese, 9
choices, 13
dips, 34
ice cream, 210
snacks, 52
Lunch menu. *See* Menus

M

Macaroni and cheese, 148
Make-ahead party Thai noodles,
157
Mange tout:
bulgar pilaf with prawns, 175
and chicken breasts, 97
seafood pasta salad, 164
Mango salsa, 51
Margarine:
baking with, 198
choosing, 19
vs butter, 19
Marinade:
buttermilk, 93
curried chicken breast, 100
for lamb, 129
lemon-soy, 113
pork loin, 127
tofu, 184
Meat, buying minced, 95
Meatballs, chicken, 41
Meat products, 12
Mediterranean:
fish, 110-11
lentil and bean salad, 75
Melon balls, with turkey, 42
Menus, 27-31
barbecue supper, 161
brunch, 182
buffet
dinner, 102
for 50, 128
party, 118
dinner
autumn, 185
buffet, 102, 128
Oriental, 98
for six, 95
fat comparison in, 13, 18
lunch
bridge party, 50
Sunday summer, 162, 163
Meringues, 222
Microwave:
fish, 113
rhubarb sauce, 225
sauce for green beans, 136
Milk products, 11-12
Minted coriander sauce, 41
Miso:
about, 64
soup, 64

Mocha, chocolate ice cream pie, 210
Monounsaturated fats, 17
Moroccan rabbit tagine, 132
Mousse, lemon, 213
Mozzarella cheese:
  pizza, 45
  and tortilla pizza, 47
  and tortillas, 46
Muesli:
  apricot-raisin, 186
  soda bread, 197
Muffins, about, 192
Muffins:
  bran, 192
    apple, 195
    high-fibre carrot, 196
    rhubarb, 195
  cornmeal, 193
  lemon poppy seed, 194
  preparing tins for, 196
  pumpkin, 195
Mushroom(s):
  and artichoke stuffing, 115
  and asparagus salad, 78
  fish chowder, 69
  and leek soup, 61
  with linguine, 151
  pasta Provençal, 154
  quiche, 182
  quinoa-stuffed peppers, 176
  stuffed with cheese, 36
  stuffing for chicken breasts, 94
  with sugar-snap peas, 135
  with sweet peppers, 140
  tomato, aubergine and courgette gratin, 185
Mussels, pasta with tomatoes, 152
Mustard garlic vinaigrette, 88

N
Nectarine and orange compote, 226
Non-alcoholic drinks, 55
Noodles:
  and chicken salad, 160
  Chinese, 156
  salad, 161
  Singapore, with pork, 155
  Szechuan beef, 158
  Thai, 157
    with chicken and broccoli, 159

Nutritional information, in recipes, 26
Nutritional notes:
  cake mixes, 205
  cheese, 166
  cholesterol
    and prawns, 152, 175
  cocoa, 209
  cooking vegetables, 139
  fettuccine Alfredo, 150
  fibre, 180
  fish, 116
  folate, 227
  fruit, 226
  rice, 126
  scallops, 111
  sweet potato, 144
  wholemeal flour, 199
Nuts, to toast, 186

O
Oats, muesli, 186
Oil, how to choose, 20
  kinds, 17
Olives, about, 111
Omega-3 fatty acids, 117
Onion(s):
  sautéed, and chicken burgers, 91
  stuffed with lamb, 130
  and sun-dried tomato toasts, 44
Orange:
  apricot and fig compote, 227
  chocolate refrigerator cake, 212
  cream, 228
  hazelnut biscotti, 201
  and nectarine compote, 226
  and peach compote, 226
  yogurt cream, 229
Orange juice and tofu drink, 54
Oriental:
  coleslaw, 82
  dinner menu, 123
  lettuce wrapped pork, 123
  noodle and chicken soup, 63
Oven-roasted vegetables, 143
Overeating and parties, 42
Oyster sauce, about, 32

P
Paella, sausage, 126
Pancakes:
  apple, 190
    cinnamon, 189

banana, 191
cornmeal, 188
Parmesan cheese, and pasta with tomatoes, 147
Parsnips:
  oven-baked fries, 143
  tagine, 132
Parties, and overeating, 42
Pasta:
  and chick pea soup, 67
  with chick peas, 146
  fettuccine Alfredo, 150
  and ham salad, 163
  how to cook, 149
  salad with sun-dried tomatoes, 162
  with tomatoes, cheese and jalapeños, 147
  See also names of specific pastas: fettuccine, linguine, macaroni, noodles
Pastry, 219
Peach, and orange compote, 226
Pear:
  bread pudding, 216
  flan, 215
  pie with apricots, 220
Peas:
  noodle salad, 161
  noodles with pork, 155
  Spanish rice, 169
  tofu stir-fry, 184
Penne:
  with chick peas, 146
  seafood salad, 164
  with tofu, 154
Pie:
  chocolate mocha ice cream, 210
  pumpkin, 218
Pie crust, 220
Pilaf:
  bulgur with prawns and mange tout, 175
  lemon parsley, 173
  wild rice, 171
Pimiento. See Sweet red pepper
Pine nuts, with green beans, 137
Pinto beans, chalupas, 124
Pitta bread, lamb and feta with, 131
Pizza:
  appetizer, tortilla, 46, 47
  frozen store-bought, 45
  goat cheese and pesto, 47

tomato, 45
toppers, 45
Plum:
    flan, 215
    sauce, 41
Polyunsaturated fats, 17
Popcorn, 53
    candied, 53
    spicy, 53
Poppy seed muffins, 194
Pork:
    about, 127
    buying, 49
    and chick pea curry, 125
    loin, chalupas, 124
    marinade for, 127
    noodles with, 155
    Oriental, 123
    skewers, 49
    tenderloin teriyaki, 122
Potassium, in diet, 26
Potato(es):
    bean and tomato stew, 179
    fish chowder, 69
    how to cook, 80, 84
    mashed, 143
    new, 142, 143
    packets, barbecued, 142
    roasted, 142
    salad, 80, 87
    and tuna salad, 84
Poultry, buying minced, 95
Prawns:
    about, 43
    bulgar pilaf with mange tout,
        175
    and chicken jambalaya, 118-19
    how to cook, 164
    pasta salad, 164
    Thai salad, 43
    and tomato pasta, 152
Provençal pasta with tofu, 154
Prunes, tagine, 132
Pumpkin:
    muffins, 195
    pie, 218
    spice cake, 205
Punch:
    cranberry lime, 56
    sangria, 56
Purée, sweet potato and apple,
    144
Purple vegetable slaw, 83

Q
Quark:
    about, 38
    dill sauce, 117
    herbed cheese spread, 38
Quesadillas:
    about, 52
    cheese and tomato, 52
Quiche, vegetable, 182
Quinoa, about, 176
Quinoa-stuffed peppers, 176

R
Rabbit tagine, 132
Rainbow trout, barbecued, 114
Raisins:
    carrot bran muffins, 196
    muesli, 186
Raspberry:
    flan, 214
    pecan tea bread, 198
    sauce, 213
    trifle, 221
Recipe analysis, about, 26
Red bean and rice soup, 66
Red cabbage slaw, 83
Red snapper, Mediterranean, 110-11
Rhubarb:
    about, 225
    bran muffins, 195
    fool, 224
    sauce, 225
    stewed, 225
Rice:
    about, 65
    basmati, about, 168
    with black beans and ginger, 172
    brown, 168
    Chinese fried, 170
    and kidney bean soup, 66
    pilaf, 171, 173
        with prawns and mange tout,
        175
    risotto, green vegetable, 167
    and sausage paella, 126
    prawn and chicken jambalaya,
        118-19
    Spanish, 169
    and spinach casserole, 166
    vegetable salad, 77
    whole grain, about, 168
Rice vermicelli:
    and Asian chicken, 98

chicken soup, 63
    with pork, 155
Rice, wild. See Wild rice
Ricotta cheese, dip, 36
Risotto:
    about, 167
    green vegetable, 167
Roast(ed):
    pork
        loin, 127
        tenderloin, 122
    potatoes, 142
    sweet red peppers, 36, 47, 174
    turkey, 104
    vegetables, 143
Rocket, scallop salad, 73
Rosemary garlic roasted potatoes,
    142

S
Salad dressing, 76
    Asian vinaigrette, 85
    coleslaw, 82
    and fat content, 85
    for noodle salad, 161
    mustard garlic vinaigrette, 88
    tomato basil, 86
    yogurt herb, 87
    See also vinaigrette
Salade composée, 80
Salad(s):
    asparagus and mushroom, 78
    bulgur with cucumber and feta,
        76
    chick pea, sweet pepper and
        basil, 74
    composée, 80
    couscous vegetable, easy, 77
    Greek, 50
    green bean with buttermilk
        dressing, 79
    lentil and bean, 75
    meal, 75
    noodle, 161
        and chicken, 160
    Oriental coleslaw, 82
    pasta
        and ham, 163
        seafood, 164
        with sun-dried tomatoes, 162
    prawn, 43
    purple vegetable slaw, 83
    scallop, warm, 73

Thai cucumber, 81
tossed green, with Asian
    vinaigrette, 85
tuna, 72
    warm potato and, 84
Salmon:
    canned, salad fajitas, 120
    fettuccine, 150
    fillets, 115
    skewers, 48
    whole stuffed, 116
Salsa, mango, 51
Salt. See Sodium
Sandwiches:
    open-face, 50
    smoked turkey, 51
Sangria, 56
Saturated fats, 17
Sauce:
    Asian, 99
    dessert. See Dessert sauces
    dill, 117
    dipping, 41
    herb cream, 102-3
    lettuce wrapped pork, 123
    Mediterranean fish, 110-11
    microwave, for green beans, 136
    for scallops, 119
    tartare, 114
    for Thai noodles, 157, 159
Sausage:
    apple and herb stuffing, 105
    and bean casserole, 178
    and rice paella, 126
Scallop(s), 119
    linguine with leeks, 153
    pasta
        salad, 164
        and tomatoes, 152
    salad, 73
    spicy, 119
Scotch broth, 70
Seafood:
    pasta salad, 164
    vegetable chowder, 69
Sesame:
    broccoli and carrots, 134
    carrots, 134
    oil, about, 32
    vinaigrette, 78
Sherry(ied):
    chicken breasts stuffed, 94
    green beans, 136

Shopping, and food choices,
    24-5
Singapore:
    noodle and chicken salad, 160
    noodles with pork, 155
Skewers:
    meat, 49
    salmon, 48
Snacks, low-fat, 52
Sodium, in diet, 26
Sodium-reduced:
    beans, 124
    chicken stew, 101
    diet, 66, 84, 92
    soup stock, 67
Sole:
    baked, 112
    fillets, 111, 112
    Mediterranean, 110-11
    vegetable chowder, 69
Soup(s):
    broccoli, 60
    chicken noodle, 63
    cucumber mint, 58
    curried cauliflower, 58
    hot and sour, 62
    leek and mushroom, 61
    miso, 64
    Scotch broth, 70
    tomato, 59
    vegetable, 65
    See also Chowder
Spaghetti:
    with prawn and tomatoes, 152
    Thai noodles, 157
Spaghettini:
    with chicken and broccoli, 159
    with ham and cheese, 148
Spanish rice with coriander, 169
Spiced cider, 54
Spicy:
    chicken, 100
    popcorn, 53
    scallops, 119
Spinach, 138
    and lamb stuffing, 130, 131
    quiche, 182
    rice casserole, 166
    and turkey loaf, 107
Spreads:
    herbed cheese, 38
    lean for bread, 39
Spritzer, fruit, 55

Squares:
    fruit and fibre, 199
    lemon, 200
Steamed:
    ginger fish fillets, 110
    trout, 114
Stew:
    chicken with dumplings, 101
    potato, bean and tomato, 179
Stewed rhubarb, 225
Stir-fry:
    courgette, 139
    tofu, 184
Strawberry:
    flan, 214
    sauce, 213
Streusel topping, 203
Stuffing:
    about, 105
    mushroom and artichoke, 116
    sausage, 105
Sugar-snap peas with mushrooms,
    135
Sun-dried tomato(es):
    about, 44
    chicken burgers, 91
    and onion toasts, 44
    and pasta salad, 162
    and tortilla pizza, 47
Sunflower seeds, to toast, 144
Swede:
    about, 65
    chicken stew, 101
    Scotch broth, 70
    and vegetable soup, 65
Sweet pepper(s):
    and chick pea salad, 74
    and lentil salad, 75
    linguine with mushrooms and,
        151
    and mushrooms, 140
    Quinoa-stuffed, 176
Sweet potato:
    about, 144
    and apple purée, 144
    carrot and corn chowder, 68
    and chicken stew, 101
    oven-baked fries, 143
    tagine, 132
    vegetable curry, 180
Sweet red pepper(s):
    and basil dip, 36
    with green beans, 136

grilled, 141
roasted, 174
See also Sweet pepper
Swiss cheese, spinach rice
    casserole, 166
Szechuan beef with noodles, 158

T
Tagine, 132
Tartare sauce, 114
Teriyaki, pork, 122
Thai:
    cucumber salad, 81
    noodles, 157, 159
    pork skewers, 49
    prawn salad, 43
    sauce for noodles, 157, 159
    turkey escalopes, 108
Three-grain vegetable soup, 65
Tofu:
    about, 183, 184
    buying and storing, 183
    drink, 54
    hot and sour soup, 62
    marinade, 184
    marinated baked, 183
    miso soup, 64
    pasta Provençal, 154
    stir-fry, 184
Tomato pickle sauce, 127
Tomato(es):
    aubergine and courgette, 185
    basil dressing, 86
    canned, and pasta, 147
    couscous salad, 77
    how to store, 59
    pasta
        with cheese, 147
        with chick-peas, 146
        with prawns, 152
        Provençal, 154
    pizza, 45
    potato and bean stew, 179
    quiche, 182
    soup, 59
    Spanish rice, 169
    stuffed with bulgur, 76
    tagine, 132
    tuna salad, 72
    See also Sun-dried tomatoes
Toppings:
    berry, 214
    for chalupas, 124

dessert, 203
fat content of, 216
Tortilla(s):
    about, 46
    chalupas, 124
    cheese and tomato quesadillas,
        52
    chips, 46
    pizza, 46, 47
    salmon salad, 120
Trans fatty acids, 17
Trifle, berry, 221
Trout, 114
Tuna:
    fillets, 113
    and potato salad, 84
    salad, 72
    types, 72
Turkey:
    buying, 104, 106
    and chick pea curry, 125
    cooking times, 104
    escalopes, 108
    leftover, 102
    loaf, 107
    minced, about, 107
    roast, stuffed, 104
    skewers, 49
    smoked
        melon balls and, 42
        sandwich, 51
    thawing, 104
    vegetable casserole, 102
Turnip:
    about, 65
    oven-baked fries, 143
Tzatziki, 34

V
Vanilla cream, 231
Vegetable(s):
    cooking, 139
    couscous salad, 77
    curry with couscous, 180
    and fish chowder, 69
    food group, 11
    grilled, 141
    quiche, 182
    roasted, 143
    slaw, 83
    turkey casserole, 102
Vegetarian:
    chick pea curry, 125

food, about, 14
list of dishes, 15
meal planning, 15
Vinaigrette, 73, 162
    Asian, 85
    lemon cumin, 77
    mustard garlic, 88
    sesame, 78
Vitamin(s):
    about, 22-3, 135
    A (beta carotene), 22
    B, 22
    C, 22
    D, 14
    E, 22, 186, 194

W
Warm potato and tuna salad, 84
Water, drinking of, 12
Water chestnuts with Oriental pork,
    123
Weight control, 24
Wheat germ, muesli, 186
White bean and lentil salad, 75
Wholemeal:
    about, 194
    bran muffins, 195
    muesli soda bread, 197
    pancakes, 199
    vs white bread, 197
Wild rice, pilaf, 171

Y
Yogurt:
    about, 212, 229
    aubergine dip, 37
    chocolate cheesecake, 211
    cream, 229
    dill sauce, 117
    fruit fools, 224
    herb dressing, 87
    herbed cheese spread, 38
    honey-almond sauce, 216
    lemon
        cream, 222-3
        mousse, 213